IVOR NOVELLO

IVOR NOVELLO

James Harding

Welsh Academic Press

Published in Wales by Welsh Academic Press 1997

Welsh Academic Press is an imprint of
Ashley Drake Publishing Ltd

ISBN 1 86057 0194

© James Harding 1997

First published in hardback by W.H. Allen & Co. 1987

The right of James Harding to be identified as author of this work has been asserted
by him in accordance with the Copyright, Designs and Patents Act 1988.

A CIP record for this book is available from the British Library.

Printed and bound in Wales by WBC Book Manufacturers,
Pen-y-bont ar Ogwr.

Jacket designed by the Welsh Books Council, Aberystwyth.

For
the unknown
P.F.
and
G.C.
'In Memoriam'
6 March, 1951

CONTENTS

ACKNOWLEDGEMENTS

Miss Vanessa Lee and Mr Peter Graves offered me hospitality, information and sources in liberal measure. Mr Gordon Duttson, Ivor's personal secretary, produced invaluable documentation and generously gave me illustrative material. Miss Mary Ellis was kind enough to reminisce at length about Ivor. I am much indebted to Mr Patrick Ide O.B.E., who among his many other activities is Managing Director of Ivor Novello Charities Ltd, and to Mr J. L. Hughes, Managing Director of Samuel French Ltd, who allowed me unrestricted access to Ivor's manuscripts, press cuttings and personal papers. I must also express my gratitude to Mr Peter Noble and to Mr Sandy Wilson who both preceded me in the field. To Mr Wilson in particular I am grateful for permission to make use of the Novello list of works featured in his superbly documented biography. Among the many others who have given me their sympathetic cooperation are Mr Tom Arnold Junior, M.P.; Mr Douglas Bailey; Mrs Diana D. Bowen; Mr G. G. Boxall of Baker Rooke & Co, chartered accountants; Mrs Marie Cheyne, the daughter of Zena Dare; Mrs Helen Daniel, formerly Mrs Tom Arnold; Mr Heinrich Fraenkel; Mr Nicholas Hassall, the son of Christopher Hassall; Mr Teddy Holmes, who began his working life at Chappell's in 1917; Mr S. C. Jones of Darley Cumberland with Clayton Leach Sims and Co, Ivor's solicitors; Mr Arthur Marshall; Mrs Joan Morley, the daughter of Gladys Cooper; Mr Sheridan Morley, who knows everything about the theatre; Mr Richard O'Donoghue, Administrator and Registrar at the Royal Academy of Dramatic Art; Mr James A. Singlehurst of Hartley Laurence Marks and Co, chartered accountants; Miss Dorothea Sims, executor; Mrs Rosemary Stevens, General Secretary of The Actors' Benevolent Fund; Mr Archibald Todman, executor; and the actor Mr Thorley Walters. The secretarial skills of Miss Winifred Marshall have been, as always, indispensable.

Quotations from the works of Ivor Novello are made by permission of the Novello Estate with the exception of *The Dancing Years*, from which an extract is quoted by permission of Mr Tom Arnold Junior M.P.; quotations from the writings of James Agate are made by permission of London Management, representatives of the Agate Estate; quotations from *Ivor Novello. Man of The Theatre* (Falcon Press, 1951) are made by permission of the author, Mr Peter Noble.

FOREWORD

As Mrs Thrale observed in her anecdotes about Dr Johnson, the preface to a book should, like the portico at the front of a house, be so contrived as to catch, but not detain, the reader who desires admission within. Before the reader enters this particular building I want to make several points.

The biographer should normally keep a respectful distance between himself and his subject. When the author of a book about Evelyn Waugh referred to him constantly as 'Evelyn', his familiarity so annoyed Auberon Waugh that, in an acidulous review, he addressed the biographer throughout by his own Christian name. Yet it would be pompous to call Novello anything but Ivor. That is what he was known as, both by close friends and by a multitude of admirers who had never spoken to him, let alone met him in person. He was a man utterly without pretension.

Why another book about him? Because his career was a unique phenomenon in the history of the English theatre and because enough time has elapsed since his death in 1951 to see him in perspective. That career was largely unplanned and haphazard. His earliest talent lay in composing. By chance, despite vague theatrical ambitions, he became a leading film star with a popularity that rivalled the giants of the American box-office. Then he appeared on the London stage and won new fame as a matinée idol. A third career opened when he started writing plays. Eventually, at the suggestion of a friend, he combined all his talents in composing musical romances in which he starred as the hero. He never went to a drama school and he learned his various crafts by watching, listening, and heeding the advice of experts. Even in music, the only art for which he had any formal instruction, his training was sketchy and he relied on others to orchestrate his work. As he said, people don't remember orchestration, they remember tunes, and he had plenty of them. There are thousands of musicians who can orchestrate well. Only the very gifted few are able to create melodies that catch the imagination and endure for so long that they become a part of folklore. It is an amusing though somewhat left-handed tribute to Ivor that people often do not identify him as composer of the everlasting 'Keep The Home Fires Burning'.

He had everything: immaculate good looks, untiring vitality and a warmth that made those around him feel they were the most important people in the world. An aura of charm lit up everything he did and said. In the theatre world, a hive of bitchery unbounding, he remained free of malice and strangely innocent to the end. 'You'd have *loved* him!' say his most intimate friends.

Vast success came to him but he was not spoiled by it. Much wealth and adulation were his, and with them those riotous demonstrations of public affection which today are accorded to pop music idols. Such a man, you might think, had reason to be supremely happy. So he was, although he knew moments of despair. His good looks became an irritation to him, especially when critics suggested that he depended on them for his success as an actor, although on at least two occasions he was able to prove the critics wrong. Other disappointments ran deeper, as I will show, and there was also the unpleasant wartime incident which, aggravated by judicial spite, helped to undermine his health and shorten his life.

If it is doubtful whether his straight plays would stand up to revival, he is by no means a back number. During the thirty-odd years since he died his estate has earned well over half a million pounds, and the latest financial year's income amounts to more than eighteen thousand. These royalties derive from performances of his music and from amateur revivals of *Glamorous Night*, *Careless Rapture*, *The Dancing Years*, *Perchance To Dream* and *King's Rhapsody*. He wrote music because it flowed spontaneously from long sessions at his beloved piano – as with George Gershwin, the piano was a natural extension of himself – and the sort of tunes he liked also happened to please the general public. His instinctive gift of knowing what that public wanted, like his unerring sense of theatre, is inborn and cannot be taught. As the royalties prove, despite changes in fashion his music has not lost its appeal and continues to delight many listeners. Such is his lasting achievement, and it springs from his creation of a theatrical form, the 'musical romance devised, written and composed by Ivor Novello', which is unique and which died with him.

J.H.

Part One

DAVID IVOR DAVIES

'. . . my greatest ambition for him . . . was, and still is, that he should be a composer and conductor of English or Welsh operas.'

Madam Clara Novello Davies ('Mam')

1

THE HOME OF THE NIGHTINGALE

The Theatre was born of the Church. The Church will never forgive this. Professional jealousy!

Sacha Guitry

THE Reverend William Evans of Tonyrefail was renowned the length and breadth of Glamorganshire for the passionate sermons he delivered in a voice of gold. It was a supple voice that could whisper as gently as any sucking dove and then, at a climax, burst into the roar of a lion. Whether speaking in a chapel or addressing a Revivalist meeting of thousands on some misty hillside, the voice was crystal clear, exquisitely pitched and able to reach the farthest listener with perfect articulation. The Reverend Evans was a slight figure with a bush of white hair that aureoled his head and showed off his black burning eyes. He played upon his audience as if it were an instrument, charming it with a sweet smile, creating laughter with a pert witticism, as suddenly reducing it to tears and then, pointing a stern finger, rebuking it in words of fire. Often he enacted a dialogue between good and evil, playing both parts himself with conviction until, after a desperate struggle, he would burst out triumphantly: 'Moliant iddo yn Dragwydd!' or 'Glory to God for ever and ever!'

Throughout the first half of the nineteenth century and well into the second the minister's eloquence moved and edified the people of the valleys. He wooed them in tender tones as soft as a harp, stormed at them in a voice like a bugle, and always they heard him with submissive respect. The patriarch, small as he was, commanded his audience utterly and dominated them like a figure out of the Old Testament. Why, asked someone, should not women be allowed to speak from the pulpit too? Because, he replied with a flourish of his blanched locks, it was given to the cock to do the crowing – the hen makes a very poor attempt at it. No one dared point out that it was the hen which produced the eggs.

So he went on for years travelling the county and acting out the duel that confronted God and the Devil, although, however many times his audience beheld it, such was his artistry that they trembled anew over the outcome and only when they heard his exultant shout of 'Moliant iddo yn Dragwydd!' did they feel relief. A smile of infinite benevolence, a finger that, when raised, could still a multitude, and a voice capable of expressing every human emotion gave him a magnetism that was remembered for generations. One day the famous actor Samuel Phelps, then on a tour of Wales, came to hear him address a meeting in the open air. 'What would I not give,' said Phelps at the end, 'to show my soul in my voice as that man does!'

The Reverend Evans had a son, also named William, who farmed at Parc-Coed-Machen overlooking the Vale of Glamorgan. This son in turn produced a male child who carried on the farm, became a rich man and a leading deacon of the chapel. The deacon had a daughter, Margaret Evans, who at the age of sixteen heard a local boy called Jacob Davies sing in the chapel choir and lost her heart to him. But he was only a miner, and just a few months older than Margaret. A marriage between this penniless lad and the daughter of the community's wealthiest member was unthinkable. Arguments were heard and tears were shed. A friendly aunt gave shelter to the romantic couple, and in 1855, despite implacable objections, they were secretly married and began their new life on Jacob's weekly wage of five shillings and ninepence.

In 1861 a child was born to them, a girl whose arrival brought reconciliation with the Evans family. Jacob, who loved music, had once heard the soprano Clara Novello sing in Cardiff and had resolved that any daughter of his should bear the name as a tribute to the famous singer. The child's great-grandfather, the Reverend William Evans of Tonyrefail, was invited to conduct the christening, and a large crowd attracted by his repute filled the Bethania Chapel in Cardiff. They heard Jacob pronounce the names the child was to be given.

'Clara Novello.'

'Beth ywr enw?' ('What is the name?') enquired, twice, the Reverend William Evans in puzzled tones.

'Clara Novello,' repeated Jacob.

The golden voice pealed out sternly. 'Never will I christen a child with such a *heathen* name!'

He paused. 'What about naming her Elizabeth or Jane?'

'The name,' replied Jacob with equal firmness, 'is Clara Novello.'

His white mane a-quiver, the Reverend William Evans said: 'If you persist in this folly, you must name her yourself!' and bundled the child into Jacob's arms again. So Jacob did, very coolly.

As the child Clara grew up she proved to be not over-keen on school. Arithmetic was what she loathed most, and despite the efforts of a well-meaning aunt to instruct her she found it simpler to copy the work of a cousin who sat beside her in class. Her greatest joy was music. A harmonium was installed at the local chapel and Jacob gave her lessons in playing it. This was the first time such an instrument had ever profaned that holy spot, and people were shocked. 'What is the world coming to?' they asked. 'It is a sin: the young people of today are without shame!'

From childhood onwards Clara admired a youth called David Davies, a personable young man of indolent charm who left school to work as a clerk in a solicitor's office. For years they had an 'understanding', and the time came when Dave felt that something should be done. He was, after all, nine years older than her and he thereupon took one of the few decisive actions of his life. In a Cardiff street he hailed a cab, handed Clara in and bade the owner drive anywhere until he was told to stop. 'Now, Clara,' said David, turning to his companion, 'we're going to have it out and done with for once and all. Either you are going to marry me four weeks from now or not at all.'

The cab rumbled on. 'Make your mind up,' he added as a prudent afterthought, 'and don't forget this cab costs money.'

The meter had not ticked away many threepences before Clara decided to marry him. They announced the news to her parents, and her father, spurred by the month's deadline, immediately started rehearsing the choir in suitable anthems.

Clara Davies became Mrs David Davies at the age of twenty-two on 31 October, 1883, in Salem Chapel, Cardiff. More than fifty years later she could still remember every detail of what she wore. Her dress was of cream brocade satin buttoned down the front, her long lace veil had orange blossoms on it, and she carried a bouquet of lilies of the valley. Two little girls held her train and others strewed petals before her. Of her five bridesmaids three wore pink and two were in sky-blue. As she walked down the aisle beside her father she suddenly thought how odd it was that someone else should be playing the Wedding March at the harmonium, she who had played it so many times for other people. They joined the bridegroom who stood waiting at the front of the chapel and she looked at him with an appraising eye: was not the shade of his trousers rather too lavender a grey?

Mr and Mrs Davies honeymooned in London where they were thrilled at concerts given by those noted sopranos Adelina Patti and Christine Nilsson – or at least Clara was, for music remained the dominant force in her life and she had resolved not to let marriage end a singing career already begun. The honeymoon, though, was interrupted by news of her mother falling seriously ill, and soon after their return she died at the early age of forty-three. Clara reflected on her parents' marriage: it was, she concluded, her mother who had been the stronger character of the two, the one who made all the plans and saw them through, and to her mother was owed whatever her father had achieved. The pattern was significant and due to be repeated.

The widower moved in with the newly-married couple at No. 11, Cowbridge Road, Cardiff, a house bought with their joint savings and christened 'Llwyn yr Eos', or 'Home of the Nightingale'. Here the newly-established Nightingale, her mind filled with Patti and Nilsson, attacked the unfamiliar routine of housekeeping and cooking. She did not enjoy it, and a fine frenzy of grease spots on the carpet testified to her lack of skill.

She missed the singing engagements and music-making of her life before marriage. Cooking chops for Dave was no substitute for the thrill of charming an audience with her voice and personality, and dusting furniture was as nothing compared with the fun of milking applause and hurling encores at enthusiastic admirers. More important still, Dave's salary was too small to keep them both in comfort. As a first task she must find him a better job.

A good post with the local Government Board was due to fall vacant and she made him send his own application along with hundreds of other candidates. 'What chance have I among so many?' he protested mildly. 'You have a better chance than any,' was the firm reply, 'because *I* am going to see you get it.'

Some years previously she had canvassed for the local M.P. and seen him elected. Now was the time for her to use her experience in an even better cause. With pony and trap she whirled through the outlying districts visiting every councillor who had a vote in the matter. On each one she expended her formidable charm and, in the case of a distant relative, beguiled him into exercising his right to vote for the first time in many years. Few could resist her, and many, for the sake of peace, agreed to do what she asked of them. She even took Dave along whenever he was free to show what a handsome, well set-up candidate she had in hand.

After months of tireless badgering she got what she wanted. On the day of the vote her husband waggled a small red flag from a window at Cardiff town hall to let her know he had been chosen. For the rest of his working life he was to vegetate cosily in the rent-collecting department.

Within a year of their marriage Clara become pregnant. A girl was born whom they christened Myfanwy Margaret, black-haired, plump, and, said the new grandfather, the image of Clara's mother. A few weeks later the child died.

In her despair Clara took up with renewed energy the choral activities of her youth. She organised the Welsh Ladies' Choir and gave charity concerts in Cardiff. Their reputation spread beyond the city, and a Bristol composer, Joseph L. Roeckel, wrote a cantata for them. It was given under Clara's baton with, a novel touch this, eight pianos played by sixteen executants instead of an orchestra.

By 1890 Clara and her Welsh Ladies' Choir had set their sights on London. They would show the capital what Welsh singers could do! At a quarter to six one morning they entrained from Cardiff station to give one of Mr Roeckel's compositions at the St James's Hall. The platform was banked with tier upon tier of heavily scented flowers, and white sprays decked the white gowns of Clara's girls. They looked, she thought, 'as pretty as their posies'. This time the instrumental accompaniment was even more dramatic, for instead of eight grand pianos there were ten, with a Mendelssohn concerto thrown in as a *bonne bouche*. What an excitement it was, Clara remembered, to watch twenty hands 'scampering over the keyboards'.

Her life was full. There were singing lessons to be given, rehearsals and concerts to be directed, London engagements to be organised. She evolved a system of 'tonal physicals' for breath control with which she indoctrinated all her pupils. To aid resonance and forward production she made them do vocal exercises that began with a hum, changed into a consonant, then a vowel, and finally ended with a consonant or a vowel. 'Mawm, meem, marm, mairm,' they would squawk enthusiastically. So impressed were the pupils that sometimes, in the street, they would find themselves intoning 'Roar, ree, rah, ray' at startled passers-by.

These were, however, ideal exercises to prevent vowel sounds slipping back into the throat, a blemish that always threatens the English singer. Clara was also stern about another prevalent fault: that of singing with the larynx only rather than with the whole body. Diaphragmatic breathing was, too, something she taught well. Thus, having started her pupils 'mawming' and 'rahing' to their hearts' content, she would vanish for a while to a cupboard. The gentle clink of glass and syphon was heard. A moment later she came back, refreshed, and the trills began anew.

In the latter half of 1892 Clara was being measured for a new gown when her dressmaker noted with surprise a rapidly increasing *embonpoint*. She was expecting a child again, and this time, she swore, it would be a boy, a handsome boy with every gift and with music in his soul. During the night of 14 January, 1893, she felt so ill that she roused Dave. 'You'll be all right after a hot cup of tea,' he mumbled. But tea did not help and he had to call the doctor.

Just before two o'clock in the afternoon of Sunday, 15 January, she gave birth to a boy. The child was wrapped in a blanket and laid on the floor while the medical man tended Clara. The maid, upset by such commotion on the Lord's Day, bustled in and trod unheedingly on the precious bundle. It was picked up and offered for inspection to the exhausted mother. 'Good heavens!' she gasped. 'It's *Uncle Ebenezer* come back!'

It was indeed Uncle Ebenezer to the life, with an elfin face, wisps of black hair, tiny eyes, and, worst of all, a large nose which entirely dominated the small features. Uncle Ebenezer had been notorious for possessing the largest nose in Glamorganshire. He had, though, done many good works and been a distinguished elder of Salem Chapel. Perhaps little funny face would grow up to atone for his nose by emulating Uncle Ebenezer's godly works? She wept the rest of that day and all night.

Dave wasn't much help, either. 'Just see what God has sent you!' he chuckled. 'Looks like a wizened goblin. I knew you were asking for too much, and the trouble is you can't send it back!'

2

UGLY AS EBENEZER

'My singing voice finished at the age of sixteen and a half. Now it's like the croak of a tired bullfrog, and I would not dream of asking an audience to pay to hear me. How much more pleasant it is, in any case, always to be asked: "Why don't you sing in your shows?" than "Why *do* you?"'

Ivor Novello

HE WAS christened David Ivor, though it was by the second name that he became known, almost as if to emphasise the relative unimportance of his father Dave. Happily he seemed, as it were, to grow into his nose, the cheeks filled out, the black hair sprouted, and he lost his resemblance to plain Uncle Ebenezer. When he was a few months old Clara and her Welsh Ladies' Choir had an out-of-town engagement, and so, to ensure his regular feed, he was taken along as well. During the interval of the concert she fed him and then left him, contentedly sleeping in a nurse's arms, while she returned to the platform and dragooned her girls with a flailing baton. Music surrounded him. Did he not, she proudly noted, cry in perfect thirds?

Six months after Ivor's birth Clara was invited to bring her Welsh ladies to the Chicago World's Fair and to take part in an international competition. Where was the money to come from? What should be done about Ivor? The first problem was quickly solved by the generosity of a local newspaper anxious to sustain the honour of Wales. Ivor was left in the worshipping care of his great-grandparents and Clara swept off to the USA with her girls. In Chicago they won prizes and glory for their native country, not to mention offers of concert tours. Dave had taken time off to come on the trip, and he worked out an itinerary which led them down the East Coast before coming back to England. At Southampton where they docked a civic reception greeted them, and at Cardiff railway station a crowd of thousands hailed the conquering heroines. Clara rushed home to see baby Ivor. He clung obstinately to his nurse's arms and refused to let go. He howled, he shrieked, he roared. The more she tried to grab him the more he kicked and pushed her away. At last, worn out by crying, the little wretch fell asleep in her arms and she was able to face the newspaper reporters crowding in downstairs, a happy mother fulfilled and reunited with her beloved child slumbering contentedly in her embrace.

On Ivor's first birthday the Welsh Ladies Choir was summoned to appear before Queen Victoria who had heard the news of their Chicago triumph. They put on their traditional witch hats and aprons and sang their hearts out before the Sovereign. The reward was permission to call themselves henceforward the Royal Welsh Ladies' Choir, and, for Clara, a brooch in the form of the Queen's monogram V.R.I. in gold and diamonds. She wore it every day of her life, and, at concerts, the imposing trinket stood out among the panoply of jewels, knick-knacks and medallions which she strung across her ample bosom to flash and dazzle as with haughty gestures she guided her ranks of ladies through the tripping measures of folk-song and Handel and Mr Joseph L. Roeckel.

In the early summer of 1894 the Royal Welsh Ladies' Choir was engaged to sing at the Albert Hall on the same programme as Adelina Patti. This happened on several occasions, for the initial concert was successful and won good notices. The famous prima donna was not overjoyed by the acclaim which greeted her fellow singers, although in Madam Clara Novello Davies she recognised a dangerous opponent. She therefore adopted a subtle tactic. Awaiting her entrance one evening as the audience gave a final ovation to the Royal Welsh Ladies' Choir, she turned to her accompanist and said, loud enough to be heard by Clara: 'Listen how they are applauding *my girls*.' It was the same with the bouquets of flowers which were showered on the platform at the end. Through force of habit she regarded them as her own. Clara, however, insisted on a fair share and reclaimed her due with the vigour of an Indian brave insisting on his scalps. Throughout this battle of the flowers, Clara recalled, both ladies 'wore a gay smile'.

Even more delectable was an incident which occurred at an Eisteddfod in a Welsh town. Patti had a house in Wales and, as a local celebrity, was invited to present the prizes. Some of Clara's pupils were in the running and since they nearly always carried off most of the honours, Clara herself decided to go. At that time she was not known in the town. Word had gone round that Patti would be dressed in a red floral toque and would be carrying a red parasol. Madam Clara Novello Davies, by chance, arrived early in a red floral toque with a red parasol on her arm. The mayor and a band of dignitaries rushed to welcome the lady they took for Patti. Clara revelled in their tribute and, only when it was too late, innocently remarked that she had assumed it to be a result of the increasing lustre which her professional activities were bringing to her name. We do not know what Patti thought.

It is true, nonetheless, that Clara had won a certain fame. By 1900 she was teaching regularly in London at the Salle Erard in Great Marlborough Street, as well as in Cardiff and Bristol. She rarely spent an evening at 'The Home of the Nightingale' but managed to snatch whatever sleep her strong constitution needed in railway trains that shuttled her back and forth between the three outposts of her empire. While Dave pottered thankfully in the rent-collecting department of Cardiff Council she took her first London home, a roomy house in Maida Vale where twenty of her students joined her. The telegraphic address was 'Semibreve' and the furniture included eight grand pianos. 'What fun we all had!' she sighed when she looked back on those jolly days. The girls awaited her at breakfast, alert for the noise of the keys which jangled from her waist and signalled her approach. When they heard it they seized their teaspoons and banged out an accompaniment on cups and saucers, roaring lustily, to the tune of 'For he's a jolly good fellow,' their own special chorus of 'We want to be like Madam, we want to be like Madam, we want to be like Madam, and so say all of us.' Or so, according to Madam, they all said.

Her connection grew and flourished. George Edwardes sent his Gaiety Girls to her for singing lessons, actresses studied diction with her and leading ladies imbibed her system of breath control. In 1906 she rented another studio next to Edouard de Reszke in George Street off Hanover Square. The weekends were saved for Cardiff and rehearsals of the Royal Welsh Ladies' Choir who often sang at the famous Boosey ballad concerts and, with the long-suffering Patti, at the Albert Hall. Most of all she enjoyed the recitals she organised in the George Street rooms where the accompaniments were played on a harpsichord with keys in mother-of-pearl and black tortoiseshell which Napoleon was said to have bought for Josephine. The Reverend William Evans of Tonyrefail would not have approved.

Ivor watched and listened to all this music-making with close interest. At the age of four, says Clara, he was able to show one of her mature pupils exactly how a difficult exercise should be negotiated. He played happily in her Maida Vale studio and in the large garden outside, and she thoughtfully kept a large reserve stock of white

buckskin shoes for him so that muddied ones could be replaced
without trouble. His imagination was vivid, he attributed to inani-
mate objects the faculty of joy and suffering, and on cold winter
nights he would take to bed with him, to keep them warm, everything
from the poker to the vases on the mantelpiece. He made up a
charming story of how he was born which had been inspired by the
Choir's performance for Queen Victoria. A gentleman in a red uniform and blue hat with a white feather came to the front door, he said,
carrying a huge box from Queen Victoria. An accompanying letter
written by the royal hand in gold ink told Clara that as a tribute to the
Choir's lovely singing she was sending her 'this nice present'. Inside,
on a bed of red, white and blue cotton wool, reposed the infant Ivor.

When he was old enough Ivor started school at a private estab-
lishment not far away from 'The Home of the Nightingale'. His best
subject was French and he soon won a prize for this. Other studies he
disliked and there were days when he violently rebelled. Once he cut
all the buttons off his clothes and was saved from going to school
because by then it was too late to repair the damage. On another
occasion he plunged fully dressed into the bath. Clara stormed at his
nurse: 'How dare you let Master Ivor go out in wet clothes? Do you
want the child to *die*?' Only years later did the loyal nurse tell her that
Ivor had done it deliberately. Already, though, he had discovered
that flattery was a powerful weapon. 'Doesn't Mam look *beautiful*,'
he would murmur to her embarrassed delight. 'Isn't her face lovely
today?'

What he most enjoyed was the school pantomime *Aladdin* at
Christmas. In this he had a rôle as a page at the Emperor's court with
his own song to sing. Mam, as she must be known hereafter, sat with
beating heart in the audience waiting for him to appear. At last he
came on, trim and elegant in his pretty tabard and stockings. Instead
of the song prepared at rehearsal he piped a rather saucy ditty then all
the rage and made famous by the musical comedy star Gertie Millar.
It was called 'Keep Off The Grass!' and once everyone recovered
from the shock they all agreed he had done it delightfully.

He loved dressing up and, after posing in front of the mirror wearing in turn each one of Mam's lavish creations, would drop them on
the floor and leave them in a crumpled heap to the despair of the
maids. One of the servants had a baby which Ivor used to steal and
carry away to the music room. There he dressed it in a wig and,
holding the child in his arms, acted out little dramas. It was a very
good-natured baby.

The piano was another natural medium of expression. Ivor sat for hours at the keyboard tinkling out popular songs of the day and sometimes creating his own little tunes. He liked everything about the instrument, even the drudgery of practising scales. His touch was sure and light, and he sight-read with speed. Yet he would, he realised early, never be a pianist of the front rank: there was a weakness in the little finger of his left hand which held him back. Still, he dominated Mam's soirées, accompanying himself in the number 'Poor Wandering One' from *The Pirates Of Penzance* which he gave with noisy enjoyment, and offering, as an encore, the Handelian gravity of 'Hear Ye, Israel'.

Distinguished persons came and went through the Novello studios. At the age of four Ivor met Landon Ronald, well-known conductor and composer of that favourite Edwardian ballad 'Down in the Forest'. He climbed up on to Ronald's knee and observed: 'What a nice long nose you have.' 'You have a fairly long nose yourself, young man!' replied the musician. One day Adelina Patti called in. Despite her frequent jousts with Mam she remained on good terms, perhaps appreciating, if nothing else, her rival's gift for publicity. She heard Ivor singing and exclaimed: 'Why, that is *my* voice.' They sang duets together, their favourite number being 'If You Were Just the Sort of Fellow' from the Gaiety hit *Our Miss Gibbs*. Patti loathed autographing the books and programmes which her admirers pressed on her. 'I am so tired of signing!' she would complain. Ivor suggested he forge her signature. After a few attempts he produced a very fair version of her autograph, and over the next half-hour he worked diligently through the pile of papers awaiting signing. Thus the bold signature of 'Adelina Patti' which, in fading ink, now sprawls over many a photograph and many a title page, turns out frequently to be the artful work of Ivor Novello.

Another prima donna, the redoubtable Clara Butt, stood the six-year-old Ivor on a chair and taught him to sing one of her most popular numbers, 'Abide With Me'. Two years later she was married at a splendid ceremony in Bristol Cathedral and Ivor was chosen as one of the two pageboys. The other, he discovered with chagrin, sported a mass of beautiful golden curls, and he insisted, with an eye to effect, that he too should have some. Mam and a deft hairdresser worked hard to fake up a bunch of ringlets for him, and on the day of the ceremony he was not outshone.

Music was not his only passion. While Mam was away on one of her numerous expeditions the maids found the easiest way to keep him quiet was to take him to the theatre. Mam came back very late one evening to find him agonising in a horrible nightmare caused by a matinée visit to some chilling melodrama. She arranged for one of her pupils, then playing the Fairy Queen in pantomime, to tell him that acting was the art of make-believe, that the theatre was all about pretence. This, of course, did nothing to put him off, and soon he had his own little model theatre from Hamley's for which all other toys were quickly jettisoned. Members of the household were appointed as scene-shifters, wardrobe mistress and dressers. Friends and neighbours and Mam's pupils made up an audience which paid threepence for orchestra stalls and a penny for the pit. Ivor gave particular attention to the box-office and, at the end of the show, carried off a bag heavy with coppers and treated all his friends to unlimited ice-cream.

When he was staying with Mam at her London headquarters he often, unknown to her, borrowed half a crown from one of the maids and crept off to his favourite Theatre Royal in Drury Lane. There, up in the gallery, he entered a world of illusion that seemed to him more real than life itself. Mam was amused and touched by his absorption. Before each of his visits to her in London he would spread out the newspapers and study the theatre advertisements in order to work out a methodical programme which took into account that he was limited to Wednesdays and Saturdays when matinées were available. At a performance of Seymour Hicks's *The Gay Gordons*, one of the most successful Edwardian musicals, Ivor, wearing Eton suit and stiff white collar, sat in the front row of the stalls. The conductor tapped his baton, the music began, and Ivor moved up to the rail separating orchestra from audience. He watched, and then, eyes shining, face aglow, started to 'conduct' them himself.

The theatre, for Mam, was only a diversion. Music, she resolved, was to be Ivor's destiny, and in any case the time had come for serious schooling away from the excitements of her studio and the London stage. She sent him to stay with friends and continue his education in Gloucester, a town conveniently placed on the line she regularly travelled between Cardiff and London, so that she might see him once a week. Their brief meetings were painful. He clung to her and wept, and she felt the cruelty of their separation, though she persisted in it; the arrangement, she thought, was good for them both. Gloucester he loathed, and the placid charms of a county town were no substitute for the feverish delights of London. He was never to be cured of his love for the theatre. On holiday one year from school he took down a family heirloom, a rather valuable calf-bound set of Shakespeare, and pawned it for the cost of a subscription ticket to a complete Gilbert and Sullivan season then being played in Cardiff.

Even in Gloucester, however, he was able to taste forbidden fruit. Some grand neighbours had a private theatre in their house and they mounted a production of *The School for Scandal* for which he was cast as Sir Peter Teazle. In this, his first speaking part on any stage, he wore an eighteenth-century costume as picturesque as he could make it. On the night things did not go well. The little girl playing Lady Teazle forgot her lines and dried up completely. Her dilemma struck Ivor as so very funny that he roared with laughter and the audience joined in. He would never have allowed himself such grossly unprofessional conduct in later life.

It was Adelina Patti who, impressed by Ivor's voice, had first put into Mam's head the idea of his entering for a choral scholarship to Oxford. Enquiries were made and forms were requested. Dave was not at all keen on the project. He saw the boy in a regular business career, perhaps to do with shipping, as he and Mam knew important Cardiff owners whose influence they could rely on. It would be much better for Ivor to settle down in a comfortable job like his father and to enjoy a secure income and the prospect of a pension. Dave's recreations were smoking a pipe, playing cricket and sometimes indulging in a mild game of bowls. These he reserved for his leisure hours, and Ivor, he argued, could do the same with music. When the entry forms for Magdalen College Choir School arrived at No. 11, Cowbridge Road, he quickly put them away in an obscure corner where he hoped Mam would not notice them.

But Mam did, for she never missed anything, and on the eve of the very day the scholarship was due to be awarded she came upon the vital envelope in a kitchen drawer where her husband had secreted it. A dramatic telegram flew to Oxford. The reply told Mam to bring Ivor and the forms with her. She set off next day, stimulated as she always was by challenge and confident that the ten-year-old Ivor would succeed. Dave, who now saw that the game was up, insisted on accompanying them and they all three arrived in Oxford to deliver the entry forms. Mam had other engagements and pupils to look after in London, and unless Ivor were to be heard early and out of turn she would not have the time to wait. She stated her case to the examining board and they, a trifle bemused, conceded the point. Ivor had not prepared the test solo, 'How Beautiful Are The Feet' from the *Messiah*, but she knew he would be equal to its difficult tempi since he had often heard her pupils sing it. So he proved to be, and although there were forty contestants she had the satisfaction of knowing that he had made a good impression. Without loitering to hear the result she bustled off to London where her pupils awaited her. At the end of the day an announcement went up on the notice board: 'Soprano Scholarship won by David Ivor Davies.' Mam was not at all surprised. 'I do not know what his father thought,' she drily observed.

For the next five years Ivor studied at Magdalen College Choir School. He loved it there, and as one of the sixteen boys in England's then most famous church choir he distinguished himself for the purity of his tone and his musicianship. As early as his first term all the solo parts came his way since the boy who usually sang them had met the inevitable fate: his voice broke. It was a piece of luck for Ivor, but also an unwelcome reminder that his free schooling would only last as long as his voice did. In the meantime he widened his range enormously. His repertoire included the oratorios of Mendelssohn, whose popularity still survived from Victorian days, and the austerer reaches of Bach, with – for we are only at the beginning of the century – small doses of Mozart. He also often sang the church music of Sir Charles Stanford, Sir Frederick Cowen and Sir John Stainer, those melodious knights whose uplifting works, now mostly forgotten, pleased congregations of the time. For relaxation and, one suspects, with much greater enjoyment, he would trill the flamboyant Jewel Song in *Faust* and the showy Polonaise from *Mignon*. Old ladies, overcome by his angelic face and lovely singing, would discreetly press ten-shilling tips into his ready hand. At celebration dinners he sang grace and was allowed to eat rare delicacies, some of which he stowed away for future use. On such evenings he would return to the dormitory with his mortar-board full of raspberries and redcurrants, and legs of chicken peeping out of his trouser pockets.

As often as she could Mam came to visit him on Sundays, frequently arriving just in time for Evensong. She waited in a corner by the old chapel door and watched the bobbing mortar-boards as the boys filed out. 'Davies, there's your Mater!' said a voice, and Ivor came running up with his quick glad 'Darling!' to be crushed to her enveloping bosom. Time flew, there was a last-minute scurry for the train, and as it drew away she looked out and saw his mortar-board waving frantically in the distance. He wrote her long letters during the week, none of them dated, a habit he preserved in adulthood since he was always in a hurry. They gave news of his 'ripping' new suit, of his white waistcoat, of how he'd added 'As Pants the Hart' to his repertoire, of a three-bob tip for a cabby after a late night out. Millions of kisses were sent but no punctuation, which he ignored as he did dates.

Often he would end with a *cri de coeur*: 'I want some grub badly –
will you send me a big hamper with plenty of fruit and sweets, choco-
late, cakes, shortbread biscuits, potted meat and jams.

> Goodbye
> Beauty
> Popsy
> Darling
> Love
> Ivor'

There is no doubt that people liked the eager impulsive boy whose
natural charm captivated men and women both young and old.
When Ivor had completed three years at school the organist of Magdalen College wrote to Mam: 'Your darling boy is quite well and very
happy. We are all *proud* of him.' An elderly don took him under his
wing and, during the vacation, escorted him around the London
theatres. One evening at dinner, as the time of curtain-rise drew
perilously near, Ivor burst out impatiently: 'Oh, sir, do come on, or
we'll be late.' His venerable mentor obediently pushed away his plate
and rose to accompany him.

There had been many sweethearts in his childhood. Winnie of the
brown eyes and brown hair monopolised his early days in Cardiff.
Then it was the turn of Dilys and after that of Dorothy who had forgotten her lines as Lady Teazle. His taste, indeed, was catholic, for he
liked boys as well, and while still in his early teens he was conducting
romantic liaisons with his fellow choristers, some of them quite as
handsome in their fresh-faced youth as he was, and all of them desperately attractive in their pretty gowns. Eighty years later one of his
choirboy lovers could still remember Ivor's irresistible methods of
seduction. No one that he knew of, he recalled, had ever said no.

3

KEEP THE HOME FIRES BURNING

'Cigarette-smoking among women has increased during the war.
It is the way they Keep The Home Fires Burning.'

The Star newspaper

OXFORD WAS heaven for Ivor: the atmosphere, the beauty of the place
and above all the music. Music compensated for the dull routine of
mathematics, geography, history and the rest of the boring stuff that
had to be gone through in dusty classrooms. In later life he could
remember none of this although he could recall every detail of every
solo he sang during his musical training: Spohr's 'Lord God Of
Heaven and Earth', 'Angels Ever Bright And Fair', and the standard
numbers prized by admiring old ladies in the congregation. 'I think,'
he once said, 'I must have been a dreadfully conceited little boy.'

Alas, Mendelssohn's famous 'O For The Wings Of A Dove' was to
have unpleasant memories for him. In 1909, when he was sixteen and
a half years old, he sang it on the last night of term. The Mendelssohn
piece was a favourite of his and, despite its taxing difficulties, he performed it with his usual brilliant ease. 'Eh, boy,' said the organist,
'you'll be singing for me like that when you are twenty.' Next morning
he woke up feeling a slight soreness in his throat. He had trouble
speaking and thought he must have caught a bad cold last night in the
draughty chapel. The matron took him to the doctor who glanced
briefly down his throat. 'That's all right, my boy,' said the medical
man casually. 'Your voice has broken.'

'But, doctor,' Ivor stammered, 'it can't be. I sang last night. I was
good. They all said so.'

'Sorry, Davies, your voice has broken. There is simply nothing to
be done about it.'

Ivor ran out of the room and over to the playing fields where he
threw himself down in the long grass and wept. He had always
known this would happen, but now it had taken place he was filled
with a sense of tragedy and injustice. No matter how many times he
told himself that his last performance had been the finest in his career

as a star boy soprano, it was quite a while before he recovered from his anguish.

Oxford no longer knew him for his parents could not afford to send him to the University. Dave once more suggested a nice quiet job in a Cardiff shipping office. A friend of his could arrange it, he went on, and Ivor would be established in a comfortable niche for life. His son protested hotly at the idea and Mam supported him. Dave shrugged his shoulders and returned to his pipe.

Ivor still did not quite know what he wanted to do except that his ambitions were vaguely musical: he saw himself as a conductor, as a composer perhaps, with, maybe, the theatre in the background. Mam sent him to Gloucester once again to stay with her friends. There were no theatres there to distract him and he would be able to study the organ and harmony with Dr Herbert Brewer, later Sir Herbert, who was organist at the cathedral. A well-known teacher, a leading personality in the Gloucester Festival and himself an assiduous composer of oratorios which posterity has chosen to ignore, Dr Brewer found Ivor an exasperating pupil. In all his years of teaching, the learned doctor complained, he had never come across a lazier student. Mam wrote later that Dr Brewer gave Ivor 'little encouragement in his youthful efforts at composing'. This remark may be interpreted as meaning that Brewer detected talent but warned that it would never develop properly until Ivor settled down to the discipline of learning and succeeded in training his wayward gifts. Nevertheless, even Dr Brewer could not resist Ivor's charm and there were occasions when, traduced by his friendly smile, he actually worked out the exercises he had set for him.

The stay in Gloucester was blessedly short. Back in London, on the advice of Henry Wood, Mam sent Ivor for lessons with Lewis Prout, another distinguished pedagogue who may or may not have been a relative of his namesake the famous Ebenezer, author of textbooks which have laid a chill on generations of music students. Mr Prout was no more successful than Dr Brewer at inculcating the rudiments in Ivor. Why, after all, should he be interested in the arid business of fugues and 'passing notes' and diminished thirds when all the time his mind was bubbling over with natural melodies?

He helped out at Mam's concerts by accompanying soloists and, in her studio, gave lessons when, as often happened, she was away elsewhere. Gradually he built up his own little clientèle of pupils to whom he taught the piano. They were all of them, significantly, girls. The business side confused him and he asked the help of Mam's financial adviser, an accountant by the name of Frederick W. Allen. Mam had come across Fred Allen in the office of a concert agent who handled her tours and since, in her extravagance, she did not know one side of a balance sheet from the other, he proved to be a valuable associate. Discreet, level-headed, he was the only person ever to grapple successfully with her chaotic business affairs and to keep her reasonably solvent. He gave the same assistance to her light-hearted son. 'Dear Mr Allen,' Ivor wrote to him on 10 April, 1909, 'Mother has told me you are going to be kind enough to look after my lucrative business! Will you be satisfied with five per cent (whatever that may mean)? I can see you increasing your income by at least three-half-pence a year! I am enclosing a list of pupils, number of lessons and the times they come. Yours, Ivor Novello Davies.' In the end Fred Allen went on to administer all Ivor's business affairs and, over forty years later, he was to be an executor of his will.

Whether, in the meantime, his five per cent commission amounted to much more than Ivor's facetious 'three-half-pence a year' he could never remember. The income from piano lessons turned out to be small and in any case Ivor was far busier with composing. He wrote song after song in the ballad style then popular, and modelled his compositions on the type of light and sentimental piece which earned encores at matinée concerts and which, not too difficult, could be sung by amateurs in the drawing-room. 'You have no future in music,' Dr Brewer had declared. Ivor proved him wrong, although at first the going was difficult. He took one of his songs to Mam's friend Clara Butt at whose wedding he had been a pageboy. She disliked it and told him so in brutal terms. Another of Mam's colleagues, the singer Evangeline Florence, agreed to perform a waltz-song he had written called 'Spring of the Year'. Mam thought it 'florid' and was a little annoyed when he insisted on altering the ending against her advice. He also decided to accompany Miss Florence himself at the concert which was being given in the Albert Hall, though Mam tried to dissuade him by pointing out that while he was a fine pianist his touch at that time was too light for such a big place. He persisted, the song was heard, a modest scattering of applause rippled through the audience, and Miss Florence stalked off the platform hissing to Ivor: 'I couldn't hear a note you played!'

Yet 'Spring Of The Year', described as a 'vocal waltz' to his own words and music, was accepted by Arthur Boosey, head of the publishing firm which sponsored the famous Boosey Ballad Concerts, and brought out by him in 1910 when Ivor was seventeen years old. Another song, 'The Little Damosel', was taken up that same year by no less a star than Galli-Curci whose records Ivor had worn out through incessant playing on his Edison phonograph. Here was success, with his first song now in print and another one adopted by a leading prima donna. 'Ivor Novello' is the name given on the title page of 'Spring Of The Year' and the surname Davies was lost once and for all. At about this time Mam was looking for a new flat and sent one of her protégés on the rounds of estate agents. An 'unusual and artistic' property was stipulated. 'It is for Ivor Novello and his mother,' said the protégé. Mam began to realise, in her wry words, 'that there was a second fiddle awaiting me, an instrument I hadn't been called upon to play in all my life before!'

An 'unusual and artistic' flat was discovered on the top floor of the Strand Theatre in the Aldwych. A small, terrifying lift, which in the early days could only be operated by tugging vigorously on a cable passing through holes in the roof and floor of the cage, jolted you up to the eyrie. On completing an ascent which often could be hazardous and nerve-racking you found yourself before a quaint convent-like door in which a small square window gave a peep through into mysterious depths beyond. Mam's bedroom was decorated in white and pink with a dado picked out in enormous pink roses. Ivor found himself allotted a small bed-sitting-room next to the kitchen, whence a smell of kippers gave the place a distinctive character enduring from breakfast until late afternoon unless he remembered to open each window wide. A top stair outside the flat led to the roof where there was a little hut. Here settled a pupil of Mam's, a young South African with lung trouble who decided that the air at this altitude would be good for him. The view, too, was superb and extended for miles over London's rooftops. The eccentric lift being inadequate to cope with Mam's three grand pianos, those massive instruments were hoisted up on cranes outside and slung through a window. A series of prissy little jars containing electric lights ran round the walls of the drawing-room and showed up the stains on the ceiling. Ivor detested them and at a party encouraged his guests to shy apples at the hideous objects. The whole lot were shattered and all the lights in the building fused.

One of Ivor's earliest friends was Alec Robertson the musician and, later, a very successful broadcaster. Like Alistair Cooke, another star of the medium, Robertson was to develop such mastery that he could sit in front of a microphone and, without a note to guide him, deliver a talk that was admirably fluent and graceful. Inevitably

Ivor's good looks conquered and they enjoyed a romance which mellowed into lifelong friendship. Alec would go to breakfast with him and spend the day in his company until suppertime. Occasionally Mam surged into the room, an ebony black wig on her head, her moon-like face elaborately made up to represent at once a pouting baby and a shrewd woman of the world. 'Little Alec!' she boomed, advancing towards him and wrapping him in a voluptuous and richly scented embrace.

Alec was then studying music with an earnestness which Ivor had not been able to summon up for such dry details as counterpoint and fugue. Robertson also wanted to be a composer and had written songs, although his critical spirit told him that, technically correct as they might be, they were otherwise not much good. Ivor's music, he could see, showed talent but, as Dr Brewer had said, lacked a solid technical basis. Among the plans they discussed was one to study orchestration together. This was something Ivor had never done, and his interest had been stimulated by a recent experience at the Crystal Palace. There, one Sunday afternoon, he heard his setting of 'O God Our Help In Ages Past' played with a full orchestral accompaniment. All morning he sat listening to the rehearsal and marvelling at the way in which the monochrome piano version was transformed into a tissue of sound luxurious and glittering with colour. It gave him, he said, one of the greatest emotions he knew in life. For some time his enthusiasm flourished and he debated endlessly with Alec the merits of various instruments and their combinations. Then other things came to distract him, other new ventures and ideas which put orchestral studies into the background. In later years all his music was to be orchestrated by very efficient craftsmen and he was content to accept their expert assistance. Alec argued that violins in octaves were not the only resources to be drawn on, that harp and celesta soon cloyed through over-use, and that wind instruments could be very effective in enhancing his melodies. Ivor merely laughed. He replied, very shrewdly, that tunes are what people want. They remember tunes, he said, they do not remember orchestration. In a way he was right.

Now that he had left Cardiff behind him and was living permanently in London he could go to theatres as much and as often as he liked. He enjoyed everything, from Wagner and Puccini to music-hall and farces, although two theatres in particular were his favourite haunts: Daly's and the Gaiety. Here Edwardian musical comedy had reached its apogee with luxurious and immaculately staged spectacles like *The Shop Girl, The Beauty Of Bath* and *The Duchess Of Dantzic*. The haunting but exquisitely simple tunes of Lionel Monckton embellished *The Quaker Girl* and *The Arcadians*, and the deft touch of Paul Rubens raised *Miss Hook Of Holland* to the level of a minor art. The scenery in these productions was lavish, the costumes were opulent and the large chorus teemed with beautiful girls. George Edwardes, the emperor of this domain, made sure that the eye, if not the brain, was dazzled by a constant succession of enchanting scenes and restless colour. His theatre, the Gaiety, became a synonym for extravagant romance purveyed by handsome men and lovely women. After his productions had finished their London run he sent them on a tour of the provinces where, in those days, over two hundred prosperous theatres stood ready to welcome them. The whole country admired Lily Elsie whose appealing charm decorated *The Merry Widow*, perhaps the greatest of all these musical plays with one of the loveliest waltzes ever written. Ivor certainly thought so, for, even as a schoolboy, he had managed to see it twenty-seven times.

The theatre was romance. In this place dreams could be brought to life, glamour sparkled and problems were always resolved in the last act with a melting waltz and a brisk reprise of the hit number. Ivor longed to be a part of it. One morning he slipped off to an audition at Daly's for a chorus part in a touring production of *The Count Of Luxemburg*. He sang one of his own songs at the piano and was taken on. Full of excitement he went home and told Mam. The calmness with which she took the news rather surprised him, but any forebodings he may have experienced were overcome by delight. The days passed. No word came from the theatre. Had Mam been up to something? At the end of four weeks he wrote enquiring when the first rehearsal was to be held. In the morning, before the household awoke, he crept down to the letter-box while his mother still slept and found a letter from the theatre. Since he had not attended rehearsals, it told him, his place had been taken by someone else.

He flew into Mam's room and shook her angrily awake. She heard his reproaches in benevolent silence and, lolling majestically on her pillow, waited until he had quietened down. Did he really think, she smiled, that being a chorus boy was of more value to him than his career as a composer? Did he believe that she would stand by and watch him ruin his life as a musician?

Damn his music! he replied. He wanted to go on the stage.

Probably he would one day, she beamed, but this wasn't the way to start, and eventually he would see that she was right. She turned over and went to sleep again.

His resentment took months to die down. He had been forced to miss experience that would have been useful to him and a wonderful chance had been thrown away. Sadly, and not for the first time, he gave in to Mam's dominant will, although he always thought afterwards that it was mistaken to do so. He took up again the score of a musical comedy he had written, both words and music, which had recently won second place in a nationwide competition run by the music publishers Chappells. It was called *The Fickle Jade* and drew heavily on all the musical comedies he had ever seen. Now he revised it and sent it to every theatre manager he could find. Each one turned it down. But nothing is ever wasted, and many years later he used one of the themes from it for the Skating Waltz in *Glamorous Night*, his first big success.

There were other compensations. In 1911, at the age of eighteen, he went to Canada. In the previous year he had written music for a Festival of Empire, one of those jamborees high-minded patriots were always holding at the Crystal Palace. It included a pageant, a scenic railway and thousands of extras wandering the grounds dressed as Ancient Britons and Red Indians. Someone proposed to take the Festival to Canada, and Ivor, all expenses paid, was included in the deal as resident composer. While the organising committee wooed mayors and financiers for support he composed sheet upon sheet of new music. In between he inspected Toronto, Montreal and Winnipeg before passing on to the electric atmosphere of New York where the ever-optimistic pedlars of the Festival hoped to arrange an opening as well. Nothing, either in Canada or the USA, came of their efforts, but meanwhile Ivor was able to spend a stimulating three months in New York.

It thrilled him with its vivacity. He heard *Tristan Und Isolde* for the first time at the Metropolitan Opera House and concerts by Toscanini. At one of many parties he met Nellie Melba and Mary Garden. At another he danced a tango with that flawless beauty the soprano Lina Cavalieri. The most important acquaintance he made there was the actress Constance Collier. She was then in her thirties, a statuesque woman whose Portuguese descent gave her velvet eyes a touch of exoticism. Her acting experience was formidable since she had played her first part at the age of three as the Fairy Pease-Blossom in *A Midsummer Night's Dream*. After a brief stay in the ranks of Gaiety Girls she went on to the more intellectual company of Sir

Herbert Beerbohm Tree whose putative mistress and leading lady she was in a number of his famous productions. After this she divided her time between America and England. For a while she was engaged to Max Beerbohm, though she, perhaps wisely, ended it and, after a provincial tour, suddenly married an obscure young actor. Did she do so, people asked, to protect Tree's reputation? She herself explained nonchalantly: 'You know how it is – on tour. Something more exciting turns up.' Ivor impressed her as 'very good-looking and with charming manners' and she moved on to chat with someone else. Years later they were to meet again and she was to have a decisive influence on his career.

The high life of New York did not blind Ivor to his interests at home in England. Just before he departed from London he had launched a new song, 'In The Clouds', and was anxious for it to be played and heard as much as possible. The big hit of the moment was Hermann Finck's 'In The Shadows', one of those Edwardian pop tunes that survives today thanks to an insidious melody which, once it hooks itself into the brain, tends to obsess and eventually madden until it has been dislodged. The faithful Alec Robertson was instructed in a letter from New York 'to ask the orchestra at tea-places and restaurants' for 'In The Clouds' and to badger all their friends to do the same. 'I would love to come home and find "In The Clouds" almost as popular as "In The Shadows" was. I feel sure it can be done,' Ivor added.

He nearly, however, did not come home at all. Towards the end of his stay in New York he acquired a dog of mongrel appearance but affectionate personality and baptised her 'Wudge', she having refused to answer to the name 'Little Damosel' which he originally gave her in memory of his early song success. She was to come back with him and he reserved tickets for the *Empress Of Ireland* from Ontario to Southampton. A few hours before sailing-time Wudge vanished and could nowhere be found. Ivor refused to leave without his beloved dog so he postponed his journey until the next boat. On the following day Wudge reappeared. Meanwhile the *Empress Of Ireland* was rammed in a thick fog as she nosed her way along the St Lawrence River and sank with the loss of nearly a thousand lives.

Soon after his return Mam discovered the charms of the country-side. While on holiday near Biggin Hill she looked at the open expanse which surrounded her rented bungalow and suddenly thought: 'Why not establish a colony of pupils here?' She burst into action and, within a few weeks, buildings, tents and several caravans dotted the empty space. Her pupils, wearing loose garments to encourage healthy breathing, clambered to the top of a hill, did exercises and rehearsed operatic numbers so that Mam, perched on another eminence nearby, could check that their enunciation was perfect. *Hansel And Gretel*, she believed, was more realistic when played out of doors.

Everything Mam did was good 'copy', and the *Tatler* obliged with a page of photographs headed: 'An open-air colony which is putting the beaks of Kentish nightingales out of joint'. Here was Mam in flowing robes teaching eager damsels to strike artistic poses and to speed over the grass with elegant motions. Another picture showed her, arm raised, expression nobly resigned, in the attitude of a Brünnhilde contemplating Valhalla rising out of the Kentish woods. In a much smaller photograph her gifted son was to be seen crouched on the turf and poring over his music paper. On warm summer nights they all dragged out cots and slept in the open. The girls, thought Mam, blossomed forth 'like flowers', and under her ever-present eye their limbs grew in suppleness, their voices rounded out and, yes, even their souls gained in freedom.

Each member of this artistic community had a job to do, whether it was cleaning, cooking, making the beds or singing in the chorus. They feasted on new-laid eggs and cream fresh from the dairy. Wholesome food and country air, decided Mam, were the ideal method of improving voice production. Often, when they had completed a scene from *Madame Butterfly* before what they thought was an audience of appreciative cows, a row of human heads would arise from behind the hedge. Village shopkeepers and farmers were grateful to her for the extra trade she brought and they were curious to watch the antics of this unlikely gynaeceum.

Ivor, like some bohemian king, inhabited a garish caravan borrowed from a local gypsy. Although essentially metropolitan by nature he enjoyed the picturesqueness of Mam's rustic idyll and cherished the illusion of pastoral contentment. Seated on the steps of his caravan in the bright sunshine he threw off song after song. Each week he sent them to London publishers, and, each week, most of them came back to him with polite regrets. Those that did at last appear in print had titles like 'Why Hurry, Little River?' and 'The Haven Of Memory'. There was even a 'Bravo Bristol' to verses perpetrated in an off-moment by the celebrated Fred E. Weatherly who is better known for the words of 'Danny Boy' and 'Roses Of Picardy'.

Were his ballads, Ivor wondered to himself, too highbrow for the popular market or too popular for the highbrows? He continued to write: songs, ballads, dance numbers, whole scenes for projected musical comedies. Mam looked over his shoulder and told him to work harder. He was lazy, she stated, and had yet to achieve anything big. 'Darling,' she said helpfully, 'do you realise that if you died tomorrow it would not make the slightest difference to the human race?'

Ivor's problems seemed even less important in the summer of 1914 when war began and a way of life ended. At first Mam thought it safer to stay at Biggin Hill. She changed her mind on glimpsing, in the blue Kentish sky, the vague but unmistakable shape of a Zeppelin floating overhead. 'As well be killed comfortably at home as in this out-of-the-way place,' she reflected, and the bungalow was vacated, the tents struck, the caravans returned to their gypsy owners.

Back they went to 'The Flat', as Ivor's friends called it, where, from the window, he could see the Gaiety Theatre, home of his inspiration and ambition. Mam and Ivor were soon joined by Dave. Now that he had retired from his rent-collecting job with Cardiff Council there seemed no point in keeping on the 'Home of the Nightingale' in Cowbridge Road where Ivor was born. Dave settled in happily at The Flat. He was a born idler who did not ask much of life: a comfortable berth, three good meals a day, a well-filled pipe and an occasional game of bowls or golf were enough to keep him content. Even as he grew older and his moustache whitened he preserved the good looks which captivated Mam all those years ago. It had been a perfect marriage of opposites. While Mam tore about arranging monster concerts, dragooning her pupils and bullying Ivor into making greater efforts with his music, Dave sat placidly in the wings, an incredulous observer. How was it that he should have found himself bound up with two such improbable creatures as his wife and his son? He, the personification of lazy charm, was to remain until his death 'a darling old peasant' as one of Ivor's friends called him.

Stirred by the mood of feverish patriotism that swept the country, Mam decided it was time for Ivor to write what she called a 'war song'. Nonsense, he replied, everyone was writing one.

'Well, look at "Tipperary",' she argued.

'Exactly, *look* at "Tipperary". It's a *great* song.'

'All right, dear,' she sighed. 'One of us two is going to write a successor to it, and if you won't I will.'

Whereupon she concocted a jingoistic air called 'Keep the Flag A'Flying' and showed it to Ivor.

'Do you like it, Ivor?'

'*Like* it? Why, it's *awful*.'

'Well, in any case it's going to the publishers straight away.'

'Over my dead body!' said Ivor, appalled. 'Oh, Mam dear, can't you realise how terrible it is?'

He thought about what was needed: a tune for the boys going off to war, something emotional and sentimental, a message of hope not at all like the usual patriotic songs. Three weeks later he wrote 'quite a beautiful song' that might have done – but no, it wasn't what he wanted and he put it aside for other purposes. Then one day at The Flat he looked out of the window at black clouds storming by and got an idea. Without hesitation he sat at the keyboard and played verse and chorus straight off. He felt immediately that this was the music he sought: a sturdy march rhythm that led to an eight-bar melody once repeated. A friend was summoned, an American woman called Lena Guilbert Ford who had written lyrics for some of his earlier songs. She enthused about the music and he explained that he wanted words that were easy to learn and remember. They should speak of the homes the boys had left, the homes to which they wanted to return, where their families awaited them. As he spoke to Lena Ford the maid came in and put wood on the fire.

'That's it!' he exclaimed. 'That is just what I want! The fireside and the logs burning brightly.'

He turned to the piano and played the tune again as words came together in his mind. 'Keep the home fires burning, while your hearts are yearning.' He paused. 'You take it from there,' he told Lena.

Within half an hour she completed the lyric and he jotted down the words on the score of what he originally called 'Till The Boys Come Home'. As he asked, she had preserved the line 'Keep the home fires burning' which opens the refrain.

Now, convinced that the song was absolutely right, he arranged for it to be included in a Sunday concert given at the old Alhambra Theatre by one of Mam's pupils, Sybil Vane. That afternoon the audience was in a quiet mood. They heard the first half with restrained enthusiasm, and when, at the end, Sybil and her pianist Ivor came on the platform to launch 'The first performance of a new song accompanied by the composer' their interest was polite but no more. Ivor played the introduction, his hands at first trembling a little with nervousness, and Sybil launched into the opening verse. She came to the chorus, that splendid tune, one of the best he ever wrote, with its optimistic rising figure and yet, for all its robustness, with a tinge of the poignance to be found in other songs of the period like 'There's a Long, Long Trail Awinding'. As she repeated the chorus he had an odd sensation of hearing an echo. The sound grew in volume and he realised that the audience had begun to sing it with her. Suddenly everyone stood up and chanted the entire chorus. The Band of the Grenadier Guards at the side of the stage joined in with an improvised accompaniment and the audience stamped their feet vigorously. In all they played and sang the piece half a dozen times. Mam wasn't there to see this noisy triumph, having been kept in bed at home with a cold, but Dave was, and, shaken out of his usual tranquillity, he kissed Ivor and said: 'You've done it, my son.' Ivor threw his arms round Sybil and Sybil threw her arms round the conductor of the band. The audience went on singing. 'Next day the music shops were besieged with people who wanted to buy copies of it,' said Ivor, 'and I knew that I had the first great success in my career as a composer.'

The song, quickly to be known as 'Keep The Home Fires Burning', was published by Ascherberg Hopwood and Crewe, for Boosey's, who up to then had taken Ivor's work, made the mistake of turning it down. The contract was drawn up by their director Harold Booth, a florid and dandified charmer. A clever businessman as well, he also ran a company which relayed plays on the telephone and held the concession for supplying opera glasses in London theatres. He offered twenty-five pounds a year as retainer and a royalty of threepence on each copy of the sheet music. Furthermore, he agreed to spend a hundred pounds on advertising 'Keep The Home Fires Burning'. For once, perhaps, he was not quite so shrewd as usual, since there was no need of extra publicity – the song sold itself without any prompting at all. It was heard everywhere: in music-halls, at concerts, in the street, in the Palm Courts of hotels, in tea lounges and in family parlours. Mam was so thrilled to hear it played for the first time on a barrel organ that she sent the startled owner a pound note to grind it out over and over again for the rest of the day.

The British Army took it up and spread the familiar tune around France. Even French soldiers began to sing it – there were in the end translations into five foreign languages – and in some countries the melody was thought to be that of the British National Anthem. At America's entry into the war the song gained renewed life and became more popular than 'Tipperary' since words like 'Piccadilly' were unfamiliar to Americans who also, many of them, did not know how to pronounce 'Leicester Square'. In all, Ivor reckoned, he made some £15,000 out of that song alone, or £18,000 as he once told Beverley Nichols. When, after the war, he saw impoverished ex-soldiers in the gutters playing the tune on old mouth organs to beg a living he remarked: 'If I hadn't spent the lot, I'd give it to those poor devils.' He was, by then, thoroughly sick of the ubiquitous melody from which there was no escape.

'Keep The Home Fires Burning' went on and on until it entered the realm of folklore and people were no longer able to remember the name of the composer, so entrenched was it in popular legend. Its simple and direct appeal stood up to countless parodies and adaptations. Wartime propagandists sang it to new words expressing anti-German sentiments. Politicians adapted it for their campaigns. Even Mam, who in the nineteen-thirties became entangled with Pacifist movements, took the liberty at mass rallies of changing the hallowed line to 'Keep The Peace Fires Burning'.

The triumphant progress of Ivor's first hit was marred only by the plight of Lena Guilbert Ford. She had little business sense and failed to insist on royalties for the words she contributed. In 1918 a Zeppelin cruised over Maida Vale where she lived with her small son. A bomb fell and scored a direct hit on her home. Both she and the boy were killed outright.

Part Two

COMPOSER AND FILM STAR

'I am not a highbrow. I am an entertainer. Empty seats and good opinions mean nothing to me.'

Ivor Novello

1

EDDIE

'He [Ivor] had a genius for happiness, and for spreading happiness around him, and it was remarkable that neither the greater nor the lesser pleasures of his life ever palled on him, as on so many others they do; to him his success, his popularity, his possessions, never grew stale or flat or unprofitable – he turned naturally to the light like a flower.'

Sir Edward Marsh

HE WAS to write other topical songs. In 1915 Ascherberg Hopwood and Crewe published his 'Laddie In Khaki', sub-titled 'The girl who waits at home', and 'When The Great Day Comes' and 'Just A Jack Or Tommy'. They did reasonably well, though not much better, despite instant publicity, than his more usual style of ballad such as 'Radiance Of Your Eyes' or 'The King Of Love'. Nothing could rival 'Keep The Home Fires Burning', and on his visit to France that year this was the song audiences demanded at troop concerts which invariably ended with everyone present bellowing the celebrated refrain and insisting on encore after encore.

He had gone to the Front as member of a concert party organised by the actress Lena Ashwell who gave up her career in wartime to entertain troops stationed abroad. She was only one of the many friends he was gathering around himself. Another one to join what soon became known as his 'Gang' was Viola Tree, daughter of Sir Herbert Beerbohm Tree the actor-manager. Ivor met her in 1914 and was enchanted by her tremendous entertainment value. She was Sir Herbert's first and probably best-loved child. At the age of two, when W. S. Gilbert came to the family home, she was exhorted to kiss the tetchy librettist of the Savoy operas. She refused. 'Oh, kiss Gillie,' said her father, 'Daddy loves Gillie.' 'Then Daddy kiss Gillie!' she snapped. A few years later she asked for a pony, to which he replied he could not afford one. Well, she said, if he could afford to put on *Hamlet* he could afford to buy her a pony – and perhaps, if he acted *Hamlet better*, he would have the money for an especially good breed of animal.

Herbert liked her wit, although, given her upbringing, it is no surprise that she had a quick tongue. Lady Tree, her horse-faced mother, commanded a pretty turn of phrase. One evening Sir Herbert sat up very late after dinner enjoying a close tête-à-tête with an extremely handsome young actor. His wife decided to go to bed, and, at the door, wishing them goodnight, murmured: 'Remember, Herbert, it's adultery all the same.' On her deathbed she was visited by her solicitor to put her affairs in order. Her daughter asked if the interview had tried her. 'Not at all,' she replied, 'he was just teaching me my death duties.'

At the age of seventeen Viola was nearly six feet tall, though she moved with grace and played an exquisite Ariel to her father's Caliban in *The Tempest*. She also acted Portia and Trilby with him before deciding to concentrate on song and dance. After studying in Italy she asked the composer Richard Strauss for his opinion of her vocal talents. She decided to give up her ambition to be a prima donna when he answered that she sang like an actress. So she went back to the legitimate stage, and, although never in the front rank, showed occasional flashes of genius and relied on her striking personality to make up for technical flaws. Offstage she was equally lively and resourceful. While on holiday once she was stopped at the frontier between Italy and France and ordered to pay duty on some bananas the Customs discovered in her baggage. Her solution was simple: she went back over the border, gobbled up the forbidden fruit, and crossed the frontier again free of tax.

She married, very happily, a civil servant in the Home Office called Alan Parsons who loved the theatre. After much thought he decided to leave his safe job and become a drama critic. For months, however, his official duties had been overshadowed by a Minute whose purport he could not for the life of him understand. Someone, somewhere, in the big grey Home Office was waiting for an answer to this ominous thing, and he could not give it. On the day of his resignation he threw the document in the fire. The Minute was no longer a problem. As a drama critic he found it very difficult to grasp plots, with the result that his eleven o'clock deadline to make the early editions threatened recurrent nightmares. He solved the matter by persuading friendly theatre managers to supply him with an advance résumé. Neither he nor his wife cared for convention. They had a beautiful house in Regent's Park, and, going home one evening when Viola was out, he found, scrawled across the imposing Nash front door, the legend: 'Out. Don't worry. Have fed the cat.'

On an evening in 1916 Viola took Ivor to see his adored Lily Elsie in a new play. He had already seen it once, and this time he was to sit in Viola's box. She warned him that she had 'an awfully nice man' called Edward Marsh coming too. When Ivor heard this he was alarmed; perhaps the unknown guest might not approve of Lily, in which case he, Ivor, would be forced to argue with him. Viola tactfully arranged for Marsh to sit in the stalls. At the end of the first act a tall, square-shouldered man entered Ivor's box. He had fair thin hair and a strong nose. His eyebrows, defiantly thick and brushed up into points at each side, gave him a severe and patrician air emphasised by the eye-glass dangling at the end of a black cord which swung to and fro as he spoke. He seized Ivor's hand, and, as he did at every new meeting, held it tightly until he had delivered his first remark. The voice was gentle, a little fluttering even, and you had to strain your ears to hear what he said.

'Edward Marsh!' said Viola, adding that Ivor was the composer of a new song very popular at the moment. He did not quite catch the title.

'Keep the what?' he enquired.

'Home fires burning,' supplied Viola, and she hummed the tune.

'Oh, *that*!' exclaimed Marsh. 'Isn't Lily Elsie superb?' he went on. Having thus entered Ivor's good books he spent the rest of the evening with him in the box.

Eddie Marsh was to play an unusually large part in Ivor's life, although both men came from wholly different backgrounds. A product of Westminster School and Cambridge, where he took the highest honours in Classics, he was already, at the age of forty-four, an important figure in the Civil Service. His discretion and his perfect knowledge of all the arts of administration had won him the intimacy of Winston Churchill whose private secretary he was for years. He knew everyone of influence and power. At the same time he was a very cultured man. His ancestor was Spencer Perceval, the one-time prime minister assassinated in 1812, and his family for generations benefited from the sum of fifty thousand pounds which an outraged government voted to be held in trust for Perceval's twelve surviving children and descendants. Nearly a century later Eddie became heir to one-sixth of this generous grant. The 'murder money', as he jokingly called it, he used for the encouragement of promising young artists and writers.

The walls of his little Gray's Inn flat were plastered with modern canvases which he had bought or commissioned from deserving painters. Here, cosseted by a deaf housekeeper who devoted her life to ensuring the comfort of her master, he entertained his protégés with tea and advice. At the time of his meeting with Ivor he was still shocked by the death of Rupert Brooke, a close friend whose gifts and personal beauty he cherished. With Brooke he had planned the first volume of *Georgian Poetry*, and in the years that followed he issued other collections featuring the verse of Drinkwater, Masefield, Robert Graves and Flecker. Quite a few of the poets he supported have faded from sight, but his sincerity and his generous urge deserve recognition, although D. H. Lawrence, in a malicious tilt at his organising activities, described him as 'a policeman of poetry'. He himself translated Horace and La Fontaine into elegant but conventional measures. One of his favourite pursuits was what he called 'diabolising' the work of his friends Somerset Maugham and Churchill. This consisted of scrutinising their proofs and correcting the grammar, amending stylistic lapses and adjusting faulty cadences. Proof-reading is a tiresome occupation, and his delight in assuming this unpleasant chore never ceased to surprise grateful colleagues. Eddie was what the French call *serviable*, always keen to help those whom he liked, and in particular young men of intellectual gifts and attractive appearance. He knew everyone in fashionable London society and attended all the important private views. A confirmed bachelor is what people would have termed him then. In more brutal modern parlance, he was a closet queen.

Still mourning the death of Rupert Brooke, he could not but he affected by Ivor's dreamy charm and ravishing looks. Here was the poet's successor in his life, another creative talent that needed affectionate guidance and instruction. Ivor appeared at Gray's Inn and said all the right things about the pictures, the china, the antique furniture. On the wardrobe stood a huge Greek lexicon. Nearby were row upon row of shoes, Eddie being inordinately proud of the small feet which occasioned one of his few extravagances. Yes, Ivor was a very promising subject and fit for improvement, Eddie decided. This young artist had still not found his place, and his education had been sadly neglected. He was given books to read and poetry to study. More to the point, Ivor wanted to join up and fight for his country. The branch he preferred was the Royal Naval Air Service – the uniform, he thought, was so smart and romantic. Eddie promised to do what he could. Letters were written to the appropriate government departments and telephone calls were made to high officials.

Ivor invited him back to The Flat. He met the redoubtable Mam and the self-effacing Dave, 'the laziest man I've ever known', he thought. Ivor by now had turned his own room there into what he described as 'Arabian Nights-cum-Wembley Exhibition-cum-Oriental Tea Rooms' dominated by a profusion of photographs showing Lily Elsie in scenes from *The Merry Widow*. Eddie raised his beetling eyebrows. This young man needed him badly. He set up a reading programme for him and began a commonplace book into which he copied out from time to time verse and prose intended to edify his new ward. At Gray's Inn he installed an upright piano so that Ivor could work in peace away from the hubbub of Mam's pupils. The Flat became a second home to him, and there, after dinner in Soho, with Viola Tree and Ivor, he would revel in what they termed a 'jolly', forerunner of those hectic nineteen-twenties parties when people sang songs round the piano and performed the latest crazy American dance. The three of them, until Ivor joined up, were inseparable. For the next twenty years or so Eddie looked in every morning at The Flat as he walked from Gray's Inn to his Whitehall office. The fun and laughter he discovered there helped to dull the pain of Rupert Brooke's death, and, by an amusing return of circumstances, he learned from his pupil as well as teaching him: under Ivor's influence he developed into an enthusiastic first-nighter with a growing love of the theatre and, in particular, of musical comedy which up to then his intellectual tastes had forbidden him.

Eddie summed up Ivor's case. 'He has a dangerous facility of turning out catchy tunes which are very pretty and great fun, but not so good as he ought to do,' he noted. He presented Ivor with some poems by Robert Graves to set, for Eddie visualised him as a composer of English lieder. Ivor was, perhaps, wiser than Eddie, and while he politely did what he was told, he knew his own limitations and did not waste much time over the job. For a matinée of *King Lear's Wife* by Gordon Bottomley, another of Eddie's forgotten Georgian poets, Ivor produced two settings which Viola Tree was to sing at the performance. There were squabbles between them when Ivor criticised her technique and she responded with acrimony. They appealed to Eddie as referee and only succeeded in annoying him into the bargain. 'Curious man Eddie Marsh,' wrote Ivor when he made up the quarrel, 'must I with great ceremony *ask* you to join us at our frugal meal of macaroni-cheese and strawberries?' He sat with Eddie in a box at the matinée, all differences forgotten and harmony restored.

Eddie could not for long be on bad terms with those he loved. His nature was too open and too sunny. Why waste time brooding? His insatiable capacity for enjoyment of books, people, theatre and art sometimes disturbed his friends. 'Eddie's a miserable fellow,' grumbled Arnold Bennett, 'he likes everything.' His eagerness to help was, too, something quite unusual. There is a story that a girl once came up to him at a ball. 'I want you to do something for me,' she said. 'Yes?' 'I want you to marry me.' 'When?' replied Eddie without hesitating. Withal he had a delicate sense of humour. He went on a picnic in the French countryside and, as the cold meats were passed round, a lady guest complained of the light in her eyes. Eddie swung his monocle and quavered: 'It may be the *glare* from the veal, my dear.'

Ivor was soon introduced to the distinguished society Eddie frequented. At dinner with Lady Randolph Churchill he met her son Winston, and over the port music-hall songs were sung to Ivor's accompaniment. Some of them were before his time, but he managed to keep up as Winston carolled ditties that went back to the eighteen-eighties. Suddenly Winston barked: 'Do you know you'd be far better off in a home?' The two guests looked at each other anxiously. Had Ivor given the impression of incipient madness? It took a little time for him to realise that 'You'd Be Far Better Off in a Home' was a music-hall song he'd never heard of before.

On another occasion Eddie took him to tea in Downing Street – Asquith was then prime minister and Eddie worked for him as private secretary – where a meeting with the adored Lily Elsie had been arranged by the prime minister's daughter Elizabeth. Lily had married and retired from the stage when only twenty-four. It was intimated, however, that she might agree to appear for charity in an operetta Ivor had written. 'Mrs Ian Bullough', announced a footman, and the goddess entered the room. Overcome with excitement at beholding in the flesh the beauty of his dreams, the star whom he had waited hours to glimpse at stage doors, Ivor had a sudden attack of nervous hiccups. Everyone politely ignored his anguish and sipped tea. He sat down to play some music from his operetta, at which point a regimental band struck up nearby and drowned the piano. When he came to the big waltz tune the prime minister's wife herself appeared in the room and danced with energy but little finesse around the tables and chairs. Lily sat and giggled. All was lost – or so he thought until a few months later she invited him to accompany her at charity concerts and even, highest mark of favour, to sing duets with the star of *The Merry Widow*.

At last, thanks to Eddie's work behind the scenes, Ivor was able to report at the Crystal Palace Training Depot as Probationary Flight Sub-lieutenant D. Davies, R.N. It was a June day in 1916 and he wore a dashing uniform beautifully cut by his own civilian tailor. The badges were all wrong, of course, but he thought the effect was rather striking. Much to his surprise he found he could understand the lectures he had to sit through, although Service discipline grated on him and rising at unthinkable hours in the morning imposed severe tests on his good humour. Fortunately there was always the piano at which, in off-duty hours, he entertained his mess-mates. Next month the authorities posted him to the airport at Chingford and, as a reward for making a senior officer's wife laugh with a ragtime version of 'Onward Christian Soldiers', he was taken up into the air for a spin.

After training at Chingford and more lessons on navigation, engineering and control drills, none of which Ivor really grasped, the time came for his first solo flight. The wind blew hard and the aeroplane, a contraption of wood and linen, spat flames from the engine as it quaked uncertainly on the runway. Ivor climbed in and managed to get it off the ground to an altitude of five hundred feet. Word spread that he was in the air and everyone ran out to see what would happen next. They crossed their fingers as he banked steeply and swooped over the roofs. For a quarter of an hour he zoomed and floated with the engine cut off, which was all very well had it not been for the fact that he had completely forgotten how to come down again. Once more he swished dangerously low over the roofs, seemed to hover for an eternity and then flopped to the ground like some ungainly animal sinking to its rest. Wheels flew off to right and left, the undercarriage smashed into pieces, fuselage crumpled. Nevertheless, unharmed, Ivor stepped out and calmly walked away.

Among his colleagues at Chingford was the actor Henry Kendall. Another was Ben Travers who, then an instructor, had the ungrateful task of initiating Ivor into the art of flying, and who, later on, was to find more congenial work in writing the classic Aldwych farces. Henry Kendall witnessed Ivor's second solo flight which was even more dramatic than the first. Ivor reversed the usual procedure by getting the nose into the air before the tail and then shot off upwards at a rate that chilled the blood. The machine dipped and hurtled down to crash on the ground. An ambulance clattered up, and Ivor, this time stunned and with a damaged ankle, was borne off to the sick bay. After his ankle had been dressed he suddenly remembered that he and Kendall had tickets for an important first night that evening in

London. They could not miss it, he insisted, and although Kendall argued that he should rest his ankle which was causing him great pain, they ended up as Ivor always intended at the theatre.

These two mishaps clearly proved that Ivor had to be found something else to do. Eddie had him transferred to an Air Ministry office in the Hotel Cecil. Although this meant learning how to operate a typewriter, of which Ivor's mastery was as capricious as his command of flying techniques, he was at least back in London and conveniently near theatres again. Eddie contemplated his young friend, mercurial, disorganised, a creature of whims and impulse. He thought of Mam and noted: 'She accounts for a good deal of Ivor but he's still a freak of heredity.' Dave, he reckoned, was a 'dear pathetic old thing, but not much of an asset to the vortex.' Often Ivor became fevered with over-excitement and had to have medical treatment for his heart. 'It's times like these,' wrote a friend, 'when one wishes he had a family life in the usual sense of the word – to be properly taken care of.' Eddie resolved that Ivor should benefit from all the care he could give him. Under his tuition the playboy began to acquire a sense of balance, to learn the meaning of proportion, to appreciate the need for self-discipline. Where the gruff exhortations of Dr Herbert Brewer had failed to move him, the subtler methods Eddie employed began slowly to train his wayward nature and give it a sense of direction.

2

FROM MUSIC TO FILMS

'I can't tell you what fun I'm having – the best for ages – to start with there's a cinema strike which entirely prevents me from working . . . We're all going to *The Merry Widow* tonight . . .'

Ivor, in Rome, to Edward Marsh

THE YEARS of the 1914–18 war were prosperous ones for the London theatre. The Edwardian actor-managers who reigned elegantly over what one among them described as 'our little parish of St James's' were fading fast and their place was taken by dashing young men like Gerald du Maurier. The most successful area was the musical stage. Soldiers home on leave from the trenches did not care to spend their precious evenings in the company of Ibsen or Shakespeare. What they sought after was the nostalgic charm of *The Maid Of The Mountains*, the jingling idiocy of *Chu Chin Chow*, and the high spirits of a youthful Jack Hulbert in *The Light Blues*. They crowded into the Alhambra month after month for *The Bing Boys Are Here*, an adaptation of a French revue in which George Robey and Violet Loraine sang 'If You Were the Only Girl in the World'. Ivor wrote a song for this show and called it 'The Garden of England', although, in an attempt to profit from his biggest hit so far, it was listed on the Alhambra programme as 'Keep The Home Flowers Blooming'.

A much more important commission reached him in 1916 from George Grossmith, son of the famous Gilbert and Sullivan player and himself a versatile actor, singer and entertainer. After his great success with *Tonight's The Night* Grossmith hoped to follow on with a musical comedy entitled *Theodore And Co*. Three of the numbers had already been written by Philip Braham, an experienced theatre composer of the time, and four by the American Jerome Kern. Ivor provided twelve which he started to write fitfully in between turns of duty as an R.N.A.S. officer. Grossmith became restless and pressed him for the songs. They were finished in a determined burst of concentration, whereupon Ivor lost the manuscript in a taxi. The work of three months never appeared again, and he had to rewrite everything from memory in three days and nights.

The dozen items he contributed have a notably Edwardian ring, especially 'Saracenne' and its wispy melody in the style of the famous *Destiny* waltz that every drawing-room pianist played in those days. 'What a Duke Should Be' is a rollicking piece of hey-nonny-no-ery after Edward German, and 'Every Little Girl Can Teach Me Something New' is a perky number which develops into a little dance according to the formula Ivor was to use many years later in his big musical plays. Sometimes, when he takes the trouble, he works out quite an elaborate harmonic structure, and the opening chorus has a strong middle section with a nonchalant ambling tune that appeals instantly. The numbers he composed are more effective than those by Jerome Kern, who does not seem to have been at his best on this occasion.

The discovery of *Tonight's The Night* had been a comedian named Leslie Henson. 'That's the boy we have to look after in the next show,' Ivor was told. In *Theodore And Co* Henson amply justified his promise and from then on was a star. No one has caught the particular genius of this gifted droll more exactly than James Agate, who wrote of him: 'He will, in moments of ecstasy, look at you out of eyes bulging like those of a moth which has eaten too much tapestry. Or, in the matter of indignant denial, shoot his head with the scowl of a tortoise accused of being born yesterday. Or, thrown by the passions, expire like Mrs Leo Hunter's frog. Or, when the mood is abstract, crumple up his visage like a monkey contemplating the folly and ugliness of his keeper.' It is as well that Henson, then as later in his career, had an acting skill which transcended the mediocre lines he was called on to deliver. The dialogue in *Theodore And Co* is as awful as anything else in musical comedy. 'Tell my chauffeur to bring the Rolls round to the stage door at 11.20,' commands one of the ladies. 'The Rolls shall come round, the butter shall follow,' replies Henson. At one point he carries in a bust of Beethoven. 'Who is your anaemic friend?' enquires Davy Burnaby as a portly duke. 'Herr von Beethoven,' replies Henson. 'Naturalised?' says the duke. 'Oh yes, and on the Stock Exchange – changed his name to Beetroot.' Henson had dire need of his bulging eyes and tortoise scowl to carry him through exchanges like this – though it must be admitted that the soldiers on leave who comprised most of the audience were not over-troubled by the mediocre dialogue.

The public's taste for this sort of thing is shown by the run of *Theodore And Co* which extended to over five hundred performances. Henson's clowning and Ivor's music inspired the verdict of 'capital entertainment' from one newspaper critic who did but echo general opinion. As for Ivor himself, he was now established as a young theatre composer who could be relied on to deliver the goods. What is more, *Theodore And Co* was played at the Gaiety Theatre where, from the gallery, he had as a boy watched Gertie Millar and other heroines. Now, he stood behind the footlights taking his bow, an intimate of backstage life, a fully qualified member of the glamorous community he had always longed to enter.

Commissions began to flow in. Later that year he wrote several numbers for a new André Charlot revue called *See-Saw* with Jack Hulbert and Phyllis Monkman, both of whom were to become his friends. Next year he had a hand in *Arlette*, a musical comedy with a Ruritanian setting which, at the height of his celebrity, he was to make his own. And in 1918, when the war was coming to an end, Ivor composed several numbers for Beatrice Lillie to sing during a revue called *Tabs*. A few days before *Tabs* opened the Ascherberg publishing firm revised his contract. They now offered him a yearly retainer fee of £200 instead of the original twenty-five, the new figure demonstrating that his value to them had risen eight times in three years. He made a habit of passing on this retainer to Dad as a means of eking out the modest pension which a grateful Cardiff Council allowed to superannuated rent collectors.

Despite Ivor's continuing success in the theatre, Eddie Marsh was still not convinced that his protégé's gifts were essentially musical. He thought he detected a talent for writing and tried to encourage self-expression by asking Ivor to describe on paper his feelings as he sat in his office. The young man even wrote a short story which Eddie managed to place in a newspaper. Surely, too, Eddie argued, he was capable of better things than revue numbers and ragtime songs? Once more he gave Ivor poems of Robert Graves and Siegfried Sassoon to work on. One evening, as Ivor was extemporising at the piano in The Flat, he struck on a rather good melody to which Eddie wrote some words. The song was published as 'The Land Of Might Have Been' with a lyric by 'Edward Moore'. Maggie Teyte recorded it and, later on, Clara Butt sang it in the Albert Hall, having first asked 'Mr Moore' to rewrite the second verse 'on a note of optimism'.

Eddie persisted with his civilising attempts. The commonplace book he put together for Ivor was filling up, and so were the volumes of autograph letters he compiled from famous writers of his acquaintance. One of these volumes included a fragment in the hand of Michelangelo whom even the gregarious Eddie did not claim to have known. It must be said that, although the aim was to excite Ivor's imagination and broaden his horizon, Eddie got quite as much enjoyment from pursuing it as did anyone else. He worried, though, about Ivor's irregular ways. He would come upon him asleep at strange hours, or, when not asleep, playing the piano for ages at a time, locked into a distant world all of his own and oblivious of everything save the keyboard. Ivor would invite him to lunch, and, having risen from bed for the soup, would dress in stages, course by course. Once, as Eddie sat primly at the table, his monocle popped from his eye in disbelief at the sight of Ivor peeping round the door, a purple cushion on his head, announcing that he was a sultan.

What was to be done about this wild youth and his mad caprices, his eccentric ways, and, above all, that heart of his which he constantly threatened to overstrain? Eddie took him to the soirées of such well-known hostesses as Lady Ribblesdale, had him presented to the Prince of Wales and tried generally, with quite a bit of success, to perfect his social graces. But Ivor's personal magic was insidious, and while Eddie strove to change his willing pupil he changed himself in the process. Before he met Ivor he had always spent Christmas and the New Year at one of the great country houses. Now he passed them at The Flat, where Heifetz played piano duets with Ivor and Violet Loraine sang items from *The Bing Boys Are Here*.

Eddie, unwittingly, was the cause of Ivor meeting the man who became one of his closest friends. They went to a first night at the Strand Theatre in 1917 and there Eddie saw a handsome young actor whom he already knew and whose looks had pleased his discerning eye. He introduced him to Ivor as Robert Andrews, known to everyone as 'Bobbie'. The new acquaintance had dark hair and neat features. He had been on the stage since he was five, and, having survived struggles and hardship, he had acquired a steely realism which contrasted with Ivor's feckless outlook. Ivor took to him instantly. Mutual infatuation gave way in time to steady companionship, and Bobbie stayed at Ivor's side for the rest of his life. He was a competent but not outstanding *jeune premier* who had a disconcerting habit on stage of looking past his fellow actors when they gave him his cue. As Ivor grew in fame and celebrity Bobbie's main contribution was to shield him from bores and to keep him as far as possible anchored in reality whenever a fantastic whim threatened to carry him away. He also had a not undeserved reputation as a wit. His stories were well rehearsed and delivered with greater skill than he showed on stage. When you heard them for the first time they were amusing. Performed at the sixth repetition without a single change of gesture or intonation they became wearisome, and Ivor's entourage groaned quietly when one of Bobbie's familiar stories threatened. Even Ivor, the kindest of men, would shut his eyes and murmur: 'Oh Bobbie! Not again!'

Yet most of them were worth hearing once. When the flamboyant critic James Agate published the second volume of his *Ego* autobiography, it was Bobbie who, at the Ivy restaurant, coached Ivor to tell Agate that he was entranced by it but that he thought the Grossmiths' *Diary of a Nobody* was better. At the wedding of the actress Dorothy Dickson the officiating clergyman summoned bride and bridegroom to the altar and spoke to them in earnest undertones at great length. 'I think he's trying to sell them a play,' hissed Bobbie.

Another close ally was Lloyd Williams, a childhood friend of Ivor, who at about this time met him again and stayed to work as his secretary and personal assistant. 'Lloydie' had musical training and his vocal judgement was impeccable. He helped with scoring and arranging music, he ran errands, he kept engagement books, he wrote letters, he administered medicines, he sacrificed himself with passion to ensuring in every way the greater happiness of Ivor Novello. In time he learned to forge with perfection the autograph signatures which thousands of fans demanded. The one tribulation in his life was the size of his nose. Often he lamented the shape of this unsightly thing, and, some years later, Ivor made an appointment for a plastic surgeon to operate. 'But I don't want to have it changed,' Lloydie said pathetically. 'I've had it with me so long that I've got used to it.' 'Nonsense!' replied Ivor, and he bundled him off to the operation next morning. For a week everyone fearfully awaited the result. When the bandages came off Lloydie was ecstatic with delight. His new profile was everything he had always wanted. In fact, an objective observer would have said that little had been changed. But Lloydie was pleased, and Ivor and his friends pretended to be so too.

Of all the people Ivor met during the war the most famous was Noël Coward. In 1917 *Arlette* had come to Manchester on its pre-London run and Ivor was there to carry out the necessary rewriting involved. As he stepped out of the Midland Hotel with Bobbie Andrews one morning they saw the friend whom Bobbie had known when both were child actors. Introductions were made and Noël tried to adjust himself to the shock of seeing Ivor in the flesh. For the romantic composer of 'Keep The Home Fires Burning', the handsome naval officer, the Galahad of innumerable photographs, was in person a rank disappointment. 'His face was yellow, and he had omitted to shave owing to a morning rehearsal. He was wearing an old overcoat with an astrakhan collar and a degraded brown hat,' Coward remembered, 'and if he had suddenly produced a violin from somewhere and played the 'Barcarolle' from *The Tales of Hoffmann* I should have given him threepence from sheer pity.'

Coward was then acting in a play at the Gaiety Theatre, and when he finished that day there was time for him to see the last act of *Arlette*. The score, he thought, was charming. Afterwards he had tea with Ivor at the Midland Hotel as his host, now trim and shaven, changed into a dinner jacket for a supper party the *Arlette* company was to hold. 'I envied thoroughly everything about him,' Coward wrote. 'His looks, his personality, his assured position, his dinner clothes, his bedroom and bath, and above all, the supper party. I pictured him sipping champagne and laughing gaily, warm in the conviction that he was adored by everybody at the table. . . . I don't think honestly that there was any meanness in my envy. I didn't begrudge him his glamorous life. Nobody who knew Ivor for five minutes could ever begrudge him anything. I just felt suddenly conscious of the long way I had to go before I could break into the magic atmosphere in which he moved and breathed with such nonchalance.' Later, in his drab bed-sitting-room, he devoured minced haddock on toast with distaste and frustration.

This was the beginning of a friendship which Coward described as 'hilarious'. Often he took the lift up to The Flat, that jolting conveyance which started, stopped, hung poised for an eternity and then complainingly started again before, with reluctance, yielding up its passengers at the top. Eddie Marsh, it was said, had once been trapped in it for five hours when it suddenly decided to stop between floors. Yet the journey was worth it, for at the end there were the fun and laughter of Viola Tree, of Gertrude Lawrence, of Bea Lillie, of Leslie Henson, of Seymour Hicks, of Jack Buchanan. Maggie Teyte would sing round about midnight, and at one o'clock in the morning Mrs Patrick Campbell, who was still a dramatic power to be respected, would recite a poem or a speech from one of her plays. Much tea was drunk and supper was brought in from the Savoy. Coward doted on the theatrical gossip which, he recalled, was 'occasionally enhanced but never interrupted by peculiar noises from the next room, in which Madame Novello Davies gave interminable singing lessons to small Welsh women in grey clothes.'

He was anxious for advice about a play he had written, probably

The Rat Trap, and Ivor passed on the manuscript to Eddie. The latter went through it with his usual care and prepared a detailed critique. The dramatist was grateful for Eddie's '*brilliant* criticism of my play, you've pointed out a lot of very important faults which I hadn't noticed – I *know* I'm too deliberately epigrammatical.' Some years later Eddie went to a Coward first night and was very disappointed. 'Not *this* time, Noël,' he said disapprovingly. For once Eddie had made a mistake. The play was *Hay Fever*.

In August, 1918, Ivor temporarily deserted The Flat for a goodwill mission to Sweden. German entertainers were very popular in Stockholm and the British Intelligence authorities were anxious to combat their growing influence. Eddie having persuaded Winston Churchill to give Ivor leave of absence from the R.N.A.S. for three months, the latter was put in charge of a small troupe of representative artistes who had been chosen for the trip. Eddie's friends in the diplomatic service organised an audience for him with the Crown Princess to whom he sang 'Keep The Home Fires Burning' and, more ambitiously, a setting of a poem by Walt Whitman. His notion of Ruritania was stimulated by the atmosphere of the Swedish royal palace, and his romantic impulse aroused by a young ballerina whose exquisite movements entranced him. Absolute beauty, whether feminine or masculine, always found him responsive.

With the end of the war in November, 1918, and, at last, demobilisation, he was soon packing his bags again for another journey, this time to New York. Mam was already there teaching a band of faithful pupils and, due to Prohibition, was obliged to rely for her supply of whisky on a bootlegger who solemnly assured her that his product was the finest liquor available since it came to him through 'Government' sources. Ivor turned up at her studio, accompanied by Bobbie Andrews, in time for his twenty-sixth birthday on 15 January, 1919. She announced that she would give a party in his honour, ignoring the fact that he already had a weekend engagement on Long Island.

'Well, Ivor,' she trumpeted on the morning of the event, 'everybody is coming to the party.' 'What party?' 'Now, Ivor, you know perfectly well I'm giving a party for you this afternoon.' He refused to give up his weekend and they stormed angrily at each other. If, she declared, he did not appear she would be hopelessly humiliated. The only thing she could do would be to go back to England that very day. Mam paused, her bosom heaving pathetically, her hand grasping the door-knob ready to make a dramatic exit. He looked at her with amusement, and soon she knew why. She crashed open the door and vanished majestically into a clothes cupboard. 'That's done your exit in, Mam!' he giggled.

Once again the vitality of New York invigorated him. By April, he wrote to Eddie, he had seen '26 plays, 6 operas, and been to 18 parties.' The drabness of wartime England was forgotten in the ceaseless absorbing bustle of the American city. He had taken five hundred pounds with him but it was not enough, and four times Lloydie back home received urgent demands to cable out more. His stay there extended to five months with a grand total of a hundred and sixty plays witnessed, countless films glimpsed and many, many celebrities encountered. New York left him at once dissatisfied and encouraged. He saw that his life up to then had lacked consistency. He decided that now he must concentrate his energies and channel them into more worthwhile directions.

No sooner had he made this resolution than his career flew off at yet another unexpected tangent. While he was sailing back to England a cable arrived from a London theatrical agent asking if he would like to act in a silent film. Apart from amateur dramatics in his schooldays he had done little on stage, let alone a film set. Elated, but also a trifle anxious, he showed the cable to Mam and Bobbie. They, as surprised as he was, advised him to agree. What had happened was that the French film director Louis Mercanton had seen a photograph of Ivor and decided that he would be the ideal romantic lead in his next film. 'But he's a composer!' argued the agent. 'I don't care what he is,' replied Mercanton. 'If he's at all receptive we'll soon knock that out of him!'

Louis Mercanton is little known these days, although he lingers on as a historical footnote since he directed, in 1911, a film which starred Sarah Bernhardt. It lasted an hour, a very long time in that era, and was an ambitious attempt to make movies 'respectable' launched by Adolphe Zukor, fur salesman turned Hollywood magnate. The film, entitled *Queen Elizabeth*, also made a lot of money. Mercanton now wanted Ivor for a version of Robert Hichens's novel *The Call of The Blood*. The best-seller Hichens, remembered today, if at all, for an amusing satire on Oscar Wilde called *The Green Carnation*, specialised in romantic nonsense of which *The Garden of Allah*, often filmed, is a lurid example. *The Call of The Blood* was a typical melodrama which occurred in Sicily and involved passionate love, a dishonoured daughter and a grieving father who kills her seducer.

On a quick visit to Paris, and after lunch near the Champs Elysées,

Ivor was adjudged to have lived up to his photograph and Mercanton gave him a contract. Much of the film was shot in and around the novelist's own home on the island of Sicily, and then there was a stay in Rome to complete the interior shots. Ivor proved, as Mercanton hoped, extremely receptive: he did what he was told, looked to the right if required, or straight ahead when instructed, and displayed enough emotion to convince. In short, he turned out a worthy partner to his co-star Phyllis Neilson-Terry, the bearer of a famous name in the theatre and by no means one to suffer fools gladly. Without training of any kind, without any proper experience, and basing himself only on what he had observed of other actors' techniques, Ivor blossomed as a natural performer in front of the camera. The film revealed to him that he had a profile and a physical presence which, though unassertive, was an invaluable asset. To Eddie he wrote exultantly: 'Apparently I'm thought to have a marvellous flair, and a great future and fortune, and really, Eddie, it does seem to come so easy.'

In Rome he was entertained at the British Embassy where Eddie had alerted the staff to receive him. When a strike held up filming for several days he took the opportunity to work on a new operetta he was composing. Then came a sightseeing trip to Venice with Neilson-Terry – it was, he said, 'one long holiday'. Months later *The Call of The Blood* had a very successful première. Ivor was praised for his sympathetic playing and his subtle use of gesture and facial expression. Madame Sarah Bernhardt attended a private showing and was reported to have spoken well of him. A newspaper critic wrote that Mercanton 'can even make the rocks act'. 'That's nothing,' remarked Bobbie Andrews. 'He can even make Ivor act!'

Mercanton thereupon engaged Ivor for his next film, a version of *Miarka*, a novel by Jean Richepin, the Algerian-born writer and member of the Académie Française. Before reaching the immortality of the Académie Richepin had been a dock-hand, a stevedore, a sailor and even member of a gypsy band which he left abruptly when, on a point of honour, he was invited to marry one of the girls. A great deal of this colourful experience is utilised in *Miarka*, where the heroine is a gypsy fostered by a performing she-bear. Ivor falls in love with her (the heroine, not the bear), and at the end is revealed to be a gypsy prince. Richepin himself, a wonderful ham, played the part of Ivor's father, and the famous Réjane took the rôle of the heroine's grandmother. A true-born Parisian, the incarnation of *chic*, she was then at the end of a lengthy and triumphant career. Parisians esteemed Bernhardt: they loved Réjane. No longer able to play beautiful women, in *Miarka* she contented herself with a stately presentation of old age. It is dangerous, as W. C. Fields knew well, to appear with animals or babies. Both Réjane and Ivor were able to give a good account of themselves despite the presence of a live bear which, in its fight with the villain, threatened to outshine them.

'It is thought by Parisian experts that the handsome young composer–screen star will cause quite a flutter among fair film-goers in England,' observed a magazine. They were soon able to admire the black hair, the pale complexion, the finely-cut profile and the graceful movements in his first English film, an adaptation by the actor-manager Matheson Lang of the play *Carnival*. Ivor impersonated an actor who plays Othello and is so overwhelmed by the part that jealousy impels him to live it in real life. Some of the critics were disturbed by the excessive ardour he showed in his embraces of the leading lady, and these vivid scenes were later edited out. Ivor did not worry. He was, after all, being paid the then substantial sum of two hundred pounds a week.

Ivor's next film rôle was in *The Bohemian Girl*, the one work among the twenty-five or so operas by the Irish composer William Balfe to have survived in our time. The opera was a favourite with Sir Thomas Beecham, who used to lavish great tenderness on the famous aria 'I dreamt that I dwelt in marble halls'. In a silent film, of course, all that remained was the absurd plot, an imbroglio involving a heroine brought up among gypsies and a hero who is a Polish count in disguise. The cast included C. Aubrey Smith, in later years to be Hollywood's stock Englishman. *The Bohemian Girl* obliged him to wear an enormous black moustache as an entirely improbable gyspy elder. Another character part, that of the nurse who with a carelessness that would have been deplored by Lady Bracknell manages to lose the heroine as a child, was taken by Ellen Terry. The consort of Henry Irving and member of a partnership which had been among the stage's greatest glories, she fascinated Ivor who watched her every move with reverence. At the same time as she was making *The Bohemian Girl* she was also working on another film at the Elstree studios. So exquisite was her playing of a particular scene that Ivor and his colleagues who saw her do it were themselves moved to tears. When it was over, the tears still fresh on her own cheeks, she brightly enquired: 'Can you tell me, my dears? Which picture am I playing in now?'

The new film also brought together Ivor and Gladys Cooper. He had often seen her on the stage and admired the peerless beauty which, reproduced in hundreds of picture postcards, made her the most famous woman in England. After they finished *The Bohemian Girl* he often spent weekends at Charlwood, her country home in Surrey. There she kept a small menagerie of wallabies, a snake, parrots, ducks, geese, cows, and a monkey which acquired the habit of biting him. It was, however, an impartial creature, for it would bite Gerald du Maurier with just as much relish. Miss Cooper, as she was always called in those more polite days – she even, on many of the picture postcards, posed in the company of her small children, perhaps as a guarantee of respectability – prized above all good looks in her friends. She could not bear ugly people, and neither could she stand those who tired easily or were stupid enough to fall ill. On every count Ivor satisfied her strict criteria: he was handsome, full of energy, and always an exuberant companion. His music, too, she liked and would often whistle it to herself. Her grandson, Sheridan Morley, reports a widespread view that she was actually in love with Ivor to the extent of contemplating marriage. It would, she thought, sharing an illusion which many women often cherish, cure him of his bisexuality.

After making *The Man Without Desire*, an extravaganza set in modern times and in eighteenth-century Venice which evoked the paintings of Guardi and Longhi, Ivor returned to America. On his visit in 1919 he had been an unknown composer. Now, in 1923, he was a famous film star and, what is more, to appear in a new production by D. W. Griffith. The creator of *Intolerance* and *The Birth of a Nation* happened to be dining at the Savoy one evening with the peppery old journalist Hannen Swaffer. He caught a glimpse of Ivor at a nearby table and exclaimed: 'What a fine face!' 'That's Ivor Novello,' explained Swaffer. 'I'd like to see him,' added Griffith. The tart and often venomous Swaffer was no friend of Ivor, but he mentioned Griffith's interest and advised him to get in touch. Next day Ivor saw the film director who told him how he had reminded him of the then famous actor Richard Barthelmess, star of his *Broken Blossoms*. Not long afterwards Ivor was summoned to America and the leading role opposite Mae Marsh in *The White Rose*.

'Please, please don't write me up as the Handsomest Man in England,' Ivor begged reporters when he arrived in New York. 'I was never more embarrassed in my life. Promise me you'll cut out all that rot.' They did not. They went even further. Gladys Cooper, whom they described as the most beautiful woman on the English stage, happened to sail for New York on business, and huge headlines announced that her purpose was to marry Ivor, who, they said, was hopelessly in love with her. 'Will love find a way?' they asked anxiously. It never did, but in the meantime a great deal of useful publicity was generated for *The Bohemian Girl*, then being premièred in New York, and that was one of the reasons why Miss Cooper had decided to cross the Atlantic.

The White Rose was not, alas, to be in the same category as *Broken Blossoms* or *Intolerance*. The plot told of a young ordinand who falls shamelessly in love with a waitress and, under the stress of guilty passion, forgets his religious vows. Ivor, all in black, agonised soulfully among the trees while Mae Marsh as 'Bessie' tormented him with immortal longings. The synopsis lamented: 'And the youth plucked a white rose and pinned it to her bosom. And their lips met. . . . And on such a night. . . . As the stars faded before the dawn Bessie hurried home – to her honour. And Joseph arose – a MAN OF SIN!' Even in 1923 such a high tone was thought a little overdone, and despite the thousand waxed-paper roses drenched in scent which were given away to ladies at the London première, the film made no great impression. Griffith himself was by then well into decline and unable to raise finance for subsequent productions in which he had hoped to feature his new British discovery. Ivor's ambition of becoming a star in the USA trickled away into the quicksands of legal action against Griffith claiming the eleven thousand dollars he would have earned had the director taken up the options promised.

He came back to England and made a film, again with Gladys Cooper, of *Bonnie Prince Charlie*. Miss Cooper played Flora MacDonald to his Prince Charles in a melodrama of battle and exciting escape untainted by any relationship with history. For displaying his profile and, it must be added, a genuine loyalty to the tosh he was putting over, he received a fee of three hundred and fifty pounds a week, a high figure which reflected his value at the box-office. An English popularity contest put him sixth in a list headed by Rudolph Valentino and including Ramon Novarro, Jackie Coogan and Harold Lloyd. He was the only British-born star to be mentioned in it. His fans were even prepared to overlook a scene in *Bonnie Prince Charlie* where he put on a dress and an apron as a rather fetching maid in order to make his escape with Flora MacDonald. On location in the Highlands he became so attached to the kilt he wore in front of the camera that he continued to flaunt if off-set – until Miss Cooper discreetly warned him that true-born Scotsmen thereabouts were getting a little restless over his Sassenach impertinence, if nothing else.

3

THE RAT

'Nobody ever threw his heart at the feet of every audience as Ivor did, and they always picked it up.'

Constance Collier

WHILE IVOR was busy turning himself into one of the most popular film stars of the nineteen-twenties he did not give up composing. For *Bonnie Prince Charlie* he wrote 'Prince Charles' and 'Flora MacDonald' themes which were rattled off by those excellent and versatile musicians, the pianists who accompanied silent films from a dim-lit corner beside the flickering screen. For André Charlot's revue *A To Z* in 1921 he composed a song which, though it owes a great deal to a witty lyric by Dion Titheradge, is musically apt and deliciously pointed:

> We lunch at Maxim's
> And her mother comes too!
> How large a snack seems
> When her mother comes too! . . .
> To golf we started
> And her mother came too!
> *Three* bags I carted
> When her mother came too!
> She fainted just off the tee,
> My darling whisper'd to me –
> 'Jack, dear, at last we are free!'
> But her mother came too!

'And Her Mother Came Too!' with a swinging melody as robust in its way as 'Keep The Home Fires Burning', was sung by Jack Buchanan, who gave to it all the suave charm for which he was famous. Even without Buchanan's skill, however, the song has originality enough to stand on its own and is virtually singer-proof.

Ivor made other small contributions to current shows: ballads and a jazz number for *Who's Hooper?* based on an old Pinero farce; romantic songs for José Collins in *A Southern Maid* and *Our Nell*; and a ditty for Binnie Hale to sing in *The Dippers* by his wartime friend Ben Travers. His first opportunity to write a complete score arrived in 1921 with *The Golden Moth*, a musical play set in and around Paris. The title is the name of a gangsters' rendezvous frequented, inevitably, by an apache, and, for reasons of the plot, by an ex-opera singer and a crook masquerading as a marquis. The flavour is, nonetheless, inescapably British, as is shown in the lyrics which were written by that experienced practitioner in the art, P. G. Wodehouse. One of them, a duet entitled 'If ever I lost you', reflects on how sad lovers would be without a moon, or flowers without sunshine, and continues:

> Think how sad a carrot would be
> If no boil'd beef was near.
> Think how sad an egg would be
> If ham should disappear.
> Think how a sausage's hopes would be dash'd
> If one day it awoke and missed its mash'd;
> And what grief a steak would feel
> If it found
> There wasn't an onion around.

Ivor set these whimsical lines to a pretty little waltz tune which, though not at all facetious like the words, matched them very neatly. 'Dartmoor Days' was another comic item to benefit from a ripe and wholly serious melody. 'Dear Eyes That Shine', the big romantic number, he treated with Puccinian boldness. A 'one-step' no worse for being reminiscent of 'Who Were You With Last Night?' and some adroit key changes led irresistibly to a finale conceived in the vein of Lehár. The mixture pleased audiences for many months and ensured a run of two hundred and eighty-one performances. As a fully-fledged theatre composer Ivor showed that he knew how to give the public what it wanted.

Would it, though, want him as a stage actor? Despite success in films his heart really lay in the theatre. Acting on the screen was no substitute for the warmth of the theatre, the excitement of contact with a living audience, the feeling that each performance was something to be created and experienced anew. The theatre had influenced him since his earliest days, and it was to the theatre that most of his friends belonged. Why should he not now go ahead and win another reputation on the stage, just as he had on the screen?

People tried to discourage him. Noël Coward warned him to stay in films where he could rely for success on his profile and a sympathetic cameraman. Others pointed out that, at the age of twenty-eight, he was, might they say?, a little mature for a stage debut without the slightest professional training or experience of any sort. He ignored them all.

In the autumn of 1921, a month or so after *The Golden Moth* opened, he appeared at the Ambassadors Theatre in Harley Granville-Barker's adaptation of Sacha Guitry's play *Deburau*. Bobbie Andrews also had a small part in a strong cast which included Robert Loraine and Leslie Banks. Instead of the large film fees he had grown used to receiving, Ivor gladly took a weekly pay packet of fifteen pounds for his playing of 'A Young Man'. He looked good, he wore nineteenth-century costume with an air, he remembered not to bump into the furniture, and he spoke his lines so that they could easily be heard. There was a clause in his contract allowing for an extra five pounds whenever box-office receipts went above a thousand. They never did because *Deburau* soon closed. Despite being one of Sacha's most sensitive plays, despite Granville-Barker's thoughtful production, this moving evocation of the great French mime, later to be impersonated in the film *Les Enfants du Paradis*, failed, like good wine, to travel well.

But Ivor was not displeased. He had seen the footlights from what, for him, was the right side, and his initiation had been an easy one. Next year, at thirty-five pounds a week, he emerged as juvenile lead in a new play called *The Yellow Jacket*. One does not care to linger over this since the name of the character he played was Wu Hoo Git. He did not, thankfully, do so for long because within three months or so he was acting a lad of handsome Iberian looks in *Spanish Lovers*. The critics were kind and so were younger members of the audience. For the first time, on coming out through a stage door, he found himself caught up in a mob of admirers offering him presents and grubby autograph books to be signed.

His next venture on the stage was a partnership with Gladys Cooper at the Playhouse where she had gone for a season into management. Their popularity as co-stars in the films of *The Bohemian Girl* and *Bonnie Prince Charlie* seemed an admirable reason for giving London audiences the chance of seeing them in the flesh. Unfortunately the play chosen, an adaptation from the French called

Enter Kiki, was not at all propitious. The plot involved a chorus girl who pretends a cataleptic fit in order to retain her lover, a man-of-the-world theatrical manager. On Broadway, featuring an actress of flaming melodramatic power, it had been successful. Miss Cooper, whose gift lay in quieter directions, was not the woman for the part, but she was determined to play it, and with Ivor as her leading man. She even rejected Noël Coward's offer of a leading rôle in *Fallen Angels* to do so. When, in rehearsal, *Enter Kiki* proved in need of rewriting, she asked Coward to lend a hand. He, with extreme good nature, obliged and did what he could.

Coward's expert help did not prevent *Enter Kiki* from being a flop. Even before the première Ivor had begun to feel he was miscast. After the first night on 2 August, 1923, he knew he was right. He had neither the technique nor the assurance to carry him through three acts in the part of a sophisticated Frenchman. His 'French' accent was entirely unconvincing – although, like Noël Coward, he had a fatal habit of adopting it in later rôles – and he acted, said one critic, 'as in a trance'. Others described him as 'amateurish' and 'self-conscious'. The incident, he later recalled, 'succeeded in giving me an inferiority complex which it took years to overcome.' Yet there was always the pleasure of acting opposite Gladys Cooper.

Although the experience had been a daunting one it led him finally to go into management on his own account. While making *The Man Without Desire* he had offered to its director Adrian Brunel, the well-known British film pioneer, an original screenplay called *The Rat*. In order to help Brunel he suggested a percentage and his own services at far below his current market value. Brunel tried very hard but none of the major film companies was interested. *The Rat* languished in Ivor's bottom drawer until a day when, *Enter Kiki* having started its run, he took the manuscript out once more. Constance Collier had now come back into his life and had appeared with him as a flamboyant Queen of the Gypsies in *The Bohemian Girl*. She was not then feeling either flamboyant or particularly gypsyish, for her husband had just died and life was bleak. Ivor, sought after by the whole world, made a point of spending as much time as he could with the depressed widow, entertained her, sang and played to her, and worked hard to make her laugh. He told her about *The Rat* and how difficult it was to find backing for it. Her advice was unexpected: he must turn it into a stage play.

The idea startled Ivor. It was one thing to act in a play and to speak words put into your mouth by somebody else. It was quite another to write one with all the technical expertise of a very special sort which is demanded. He did not feel he could do it. Constance persisted. She saw in the script the makings of a very effective melodrama and was sure that it would do well in the theatre. Why not, she suggested, work together on it? Ivor's flair would be supported by her own forty years' practical experience in every type of play from musical comedy to Shakespeare, from farce to Ibsen. She quickly convinced him, and, while filming by day and acting in *Enter Kiki* by night, he devoted every spare moment to *The Rat*. A first sketch was completed and Ivor jubilantly booked a nine-week provincial tour for the new play. By the time the second act reached its final draft he was optimistic enough to draw up a possible cast.

The two collaborators argued, quarrelled and sat up until four in the morning working on their play. The toil of rewriting dialogue and adjusting climaxes was lubricated by cups of tea and stimulated by innumerable cigarettes. At the end of it all, amid piles of unwashed crockery and overflowing ashtrays, they wrote a triumphant final curtain. Exhilaration faded into anxiety when they thought of the money that would be needed. Ivor had put a lot of his own high earnings into a film distribution company, Novello-Atlas Renters, and could not expect a return from it for some time. Ready cash was scarce. Somehow he contrived to raise two hundred pounds, thanks to the help of Eddie Marsh who dipped into the famous 'murder money'. As some sort of insurance against failure, Eddie started translating a French play which might come in handy if *The Rat* did not please.

The Rat had a provincial opening at Brighton in January, 1924, with Ivor in the leading rôle. His two hundred pounds had long since been spent, and rehearsals, in the best tradition of the theatre, were chaotic. Relations between Ivor and Constance Collier grew reserved. A mutual acquaintance took Constance aside and advised her, for the love she bore Ivor, to stop him going on with the disastrous venture. In her embarrassment she tried to avoid Ivor. Then it struck her that he, too, was giving her the slip whenever he caught sight of her. Later they learned that the acquaintance had said the same thing to them both. Misunderstandings flourished. People got drunk. In a flurry of bad-tempered cutting and rewriting the dress rehearsal agonised throughout a wintry Sunday and on into the early hours of Monday.

The curtain rose on the first performance with Ivor crouched apprehensively in the prompt corner. The audience appeared to be attentive and he realised that the opening scene was holding well. He went on and met with enthusiastic applause. The first act ended in an ovation. For the rest of the evening the audience was wholeheartedly with him, and at the final curtain they demanded thirty-nine calls. Constance Collier was not there since she was playing in *Our Betters* at a London theatre. She arrived at Brighton station on the midnight train to be met by Ivor's chauffeur.

'Well, Morgan, how did it go?' she asked anxiously.

'I'm afraid, Miss Constance . . .'

'Oh, don't, Morgan.'

'I'm afraid, Miss Constance, we have a hit on our hands!'

As Sacha Guitry used to say, plays that read well usually act badly, whereas those which seem tedious in the study often do brilliantly on the stage. *The Rat* belongs to the second category. The hero is a murderous apache with whom a glamorous kept woman falls in love on one of her trips to the Paris underworld. Her protector, a rich banker, attempts to seduce the Rat's own humble mistress and is half strangled for his pains. Undeterred, he tries it again and, this time, is killed by the Rat. The mistress bravely shields the Rat by taking responsibility for the crime, whereupon he reforms his ways, gives up his passing infatuation with the kept woman, and settles for life in the company of his humble and self-sacrificing adorer.

As the Rat Ivor wore a black jacket, a rumpled foulard, and, dark locks a-tumble, suggested all manner of devilry. With the heroine Dorothy Batley he danced a fox-trot, 'The Rat' step, which he had written for the occasion. Isabel Jeans, who played the kept woman, dazzled her admirers with an imposing chinchilla cloak over a gown embroidered in silver and diamonds. You hardly knew which way to look: at Ivor's lovely profile or at the kept woman's flashing pearls. 'As a work of art the value of *The Rat* is about ninepence, at a liberal estimate,' commented one newspaper, 'but as a box-office attraction I should think it ranks at about £1,500 a week.'

The reckoning was correct. Brighton sold out completely and Ivor extended the tour from nine weeks to fourteen during which every house was full. The next obvious step was a London production. Many people advised against it, the most eloquent being Noël Coward. Over a lunch of extended 'finger wagging', and driving afterwards round the park, he begged his friend not to go ahead. *The Rat*, he argued, was a mediocre play unsuitable for London. Besides, Ivor was not yet ready for the capital, and, surely, another flop after *Enter Kiki* would end his acting career for good. Ivor heard him out with grave attention and politely agreed to all that had been said. Then he carried out his plan exactly as he had always intended.

The Rat had its London première at the Prince of Wales on 9 June, 1924. Billed as the work of 'David L'Estrange', the nom de plume being Ivor's first and Constance's married name, it earned even more curtain calls than at Brighton. Having writhed with embarrassment during the play, Noël Coward went backstage and prepared himself to confront Ivor. Before he could say a word Ivor beamed from his make-up mirror, jumped up, and, hugging him warmly, exclaimed: 'A-a-a-a-a-ah, ducky. I *knew* you'd like it!' This little comedy was to be repeated at all of Ivor's subsequent first nights. 'He always defeated me,' Coward recalled affectionately. 'All along the line.'

It is true that Ivor was inexperienced as an actor. It is true also that he made many elementary mistakes which a first-year drama school student would have known how to avoid, but he never made the same ones twice. He learned very quickly. The veteran Constance Collier, who taught him a lot, once remarked: 'Well, you know, he had such power over audiences, especially the women in them, that when he really made mistakes which were clear even to them, they would just smile and say, "Poor dear, he's only young – he doesn't know. He'll soon learn –" and forgive him his gaucheness and inexperience entirely and probably love him all the more.' A fan who waited for him at the stage door said much the same thing, though in a different way.

'Did you enjoy the play?' he asked pleasantly, as he scribbled in her autograph book.

'Oh, Mr Novello,' she breathed adoringly, 'you were marvellous. You looked so lovely when you spat!'

James Agate summed up *The Rat* with professional briskness: 'This play should have a long run. It is a collector's piece, complete in every detail. No cliché in the way of phrase has been omitted and no tag of sentiment neglected. David L'Estrange may possess his soul in peace: the home fires will keep burning throughout the summer.'

And so they did, for two-hundred and eighty-three performances which continued well beyond the summer of 1924. A collector's piece, too, was the film hastily made out of it a few months after the opening. Ivor, heavily laden with make-up, repeated his original part, and Isabel Jeans in a bubble cut and elaborate dresses was again the kept woman. Scenes in the 'White Coffin' nightclub, haunt of the Rat and his underworld friends, were even more spectacular than on the stage and turned Ivor's apache dance into an exotic highlight. Better still, there was a location sequence mounted at the Folies-Bergère itself which introduced a genuine Parisian tang – or Parisian, that is, as understood by foreigners.

The heroine on this occasion was Mae Marsh whom Ivor had partnered in Griffith's *The White Rose*. In America their friendship off-screen had been so warm that Miss Marsh's husband suspected an affair between them, although it did not take long for him to see that Ivor, while thoroughly enjoying the company of women, was by no means anxious for passionate involvement with married ones. When Mae Marsh arrived in London to make the film she discovered that she was pregnant with her second child. It was too late for a replacement, so shooting began with a nurse at hand and a retiring-room specially built where the expectant mother might rest between times. She was ill throughout most of the shooting, and Ivor, gallant as ever, helped to keep her going with unending kindness and patience. In the middle of a scene she often felt faint, and Ivor would pick her up and carry her swiftly to the dressing-room where he ministered to her with all the devotion of a lover. Despite these awkward conditions the film proved to be the most successful of 1926. It had cost eighteen thousand pounds to make and took eighty thousand pounds at the box-office.

With *The Rat* Ivor established himself as the leading British film star of the time. The swagger he adopted in the main rôle compensated for the slightly effeminate look critics had up to then remarked on, and his air of cynical raffishness carried off the part with bravura. The producer, Michael Balcon, just then inaugurating what was to be a heroic age in British films, congratulated himself on his choice of subject and actor. 'When Griffith took him for *The White Rose*,' said Balcon, 'it was just for his lovely profile. But to me a box-office name means only one thing: does it draw money at the box-office? And until *The Rat* I don't think he did.'

The Rat was too good a thing not to follow up, and in the same year another film, *The Triumph of The Rat*, pressed hard in its wake. Here the Rat has left his humble lover behind – dead? vanished? – and, wearing fashionably tailored clothes and silken socks, moves in with the kept woman who is, again, Isabel Jeans, even more beringed and begowned than previously. Despite a lavish fancy dress ball intended to impress the audience, *The Triumph of The Rat* soon dwindles into bathos and incredibility. Two years afterwards another sequel, *The Return of The Rat*, showed the hero married to the kept woman. Disgusted by her affairs with other men, he returns to the underworld and finds a new mistress played by the waif-like Mabel Poulton. His rival is a villain acted by Gordon Harker who had just begun to familiarise spectators in theatre and cinema with that bulbous under-lip, that sneering pointed nose, that air of dogged shiftiness which made him the embodiment of crookdom. By now, though, the seam of invention was completely worked out, and *The Return of The Rat*, made as a silent film and then partially dubbed with a sound track, did not prosper. In 1937 a sound version of *The Rat* was made. Ivor had many other things to do by then and rejected an offer to appear in it. The underworld hero took on the features of Anton Walbrook, whose foreign accent, albeit Austrian, was more convincing than Ivor's, although it never raised the film above the status of a second feature.

At one time in the late nineteen-twenties Ivor thought of deserting the stage and concentrating on films. Apart from *The Rat* his ventures in the theatre had not been unqualified successes. As the romantic lead in *Old Heidelberg*, a play of German origin and later the basis of Romberg's *The Student Prince*, he just managed to survive what Agate called 'a uniform reminiscent of a municipal bandsman from Southend' and a run that lasted only a few weeks. He escaped from this to take over a part opposite Gladys Cooper in *Iris*, a Pinero revival which he helped keep afloat thanks to much increased takings stimulated by his film reputation. In *The Firebrand*, the only occasion of his acting on stage with Constance Collier, he had the part of Benvenuto Cellini. 'Of course,' wrote James Agate, 'no artist could ever have talked the unmitigated bosh that falls from this hero's lips, and it is largely to Mr Novello's credit that he makes it sound like mitigated bosh.' The bosh survived ten weeks and confirmed Miss Collier's verdict as she took off her make-up after the first night: 'It's a flop!'

Another doomed foreign import was the Hungarian Ferenc Molnar's *Liliom*, which, although produced by the illustrious Komisarjevsky and featuring Charles Laughton and Fay Compton as well as Ivor, met failure at its second appearance on the West End stage. Ivor, said James Agate, was miscast in this 'pure highbrow gammon'. He should have blustered gracelessly and shown himself as a hulking brute. Instead: 'His body was a river of grace, his thighs were cascades of loveliness, and his soul shone with a glow like that of a fountain lit up by coloured electric lights.' Anglo-Saxon audiences were able to accept *Liliom* only as the foundation, decades later, of Rodgers and Hammerstein's musical *Carousel*.

The most disastrous of his theatrical appearances was in a play by Noël Coward entitled *Sirocco*. The first night on 24 November, 1927, is recorded in stage annals as among the worst of its kind, and, for some time afterwards, the title was used as a synonym for an appalling flop. 'How was it last night?' an actor would enquire of another. 'Sirocco, old boy.'

Coward was already the successful author of *Fallen Angels*, *Hay Fever* and *Easy Virtue*, and a dramatist who, if much admired, was also much envied. He had written *Sirocco* in his early youth and, one day, took it out again from among his papers. Ivor, when shown *Sirocco* with a view to production, judged it below 'Coward standard' and frankly said so. *Sirocco* went back on the shelf. A year or so later the producer Basil Dean became interested in it, Coward rewrote the play extensively, and an embarrassed Ivor was offered the leading rôle. Finally, Dean and Coward persuaded him, against his better judgement, to agree. Perhaps, he thought reluctantly to himself, Dean as one of the best producers of the time and Coward as one of the most famous younger dramatists would combine to spark off a success. He was very relieved when he heard that, after all, Coward had decided to play the part himself. But soon afterwards Dean ruled that it must be Ivor: the rôle of Sirio, who was supposed to be dark and Italian, could not possibly be taken by Coward.

Rehearsals went agreeably and those concerned thought that the play would do quite well. At the first night Ivor had a hysterically warm welcome from the gallery, though other parts of the house became restive. During a second act love scene with Frances Doble rude noises were heard, and the interval brought scuffles between those who were for the play and those who were against. The evening ended with Ivor, as Sirio, throwing a tremendous fit of temperament and declaring; 'I go to my mother', an exit line which inspired a storm of unfriendly laughter and a curtain-fall greeted with boos and derision. The smell of failure hung heavy in the air. Unfortunately Basil Dean mistook the noise from the auditorium for applause and ordered the curtain to be rung up and down so that the cast might take their bow. He walked on stage into a hurricane of protest. Coward escorted Frances Doble to the centre. It had been her first major rôle, and she, in tearful hysteria, involuntarily delivered the speech she had carefully prepared. 'Ladies and gentlemen, this is the happiest night of my life,' she stammered, and the audience erupted into more cruel laughter.

Ivor had surveyed the proceedings up to then with calm and dignity. Now he saw the funny side of a terrible evening and could not help giggling. Noël caught the infection and laughed outright. So furious were the galleryites at this that when he eventually left by the stage door they spat on him.

After such a debacle, Coward reflected, should he leave the country? He took some friends to the Ivy and there saw his leading man and entourage full of laughter and high spirits. If Ivor could meet failure with the same grace as he met success, Coward decided, then so should he. Maybe, after all, he would stay on in the land of his birth.

Part Three

ACTOR-MANAGER

'Acting is the knowledge that every word and every line has its proper value – and when that knowledge is there, discard it – it will always be there, solid – a background – found everything on *reality*. Would the character behave like that if she were real? Make an ugly gesture if it's the *right* gesture – and although you may seem sublimely unconscious of the people out there in the dark, never lose them for one moment. If you can convince them they don't exist they'll never take their eyes off you – and you must respect them. Or your career will be in the dust – broken – wasted.'

Party, Act III

1

A CUTE SHOT A DAY

'I have always had an immense respect for Novello's talents, and an intense personal admiration for him. He was a professional actor in the very best meaning of that phrase – sensible, conscientious, patient, and a really brilliant artist. Friendly and unassuming, he made filming with him a pleasure.'

Sir Michael Balcon

ON 15 January, 1927, which was his thirty-fourth birthday, David Ivor Davies changed his name officially to that of Ivor Novello. The deed poll he took out marked the final stage in a process which had been going on since his early twenties.

Ivor had great charm. Now charm is the stock-in-trade of actors. They listen to you with flattering attentiveness. They react with pleasing interest since they are trained to be on the alert for cues. Their gestures are neat and controlled, their voices elegantly pitched to convey warmth. They are immediately distinguishable from ordinary people who live in the real world of missed trains, burst pipes and ugly faces. Around actors hovers the glamour of floodlit illusion. It does not matter that they have no idea of where next week's rent is coming from or that they have been out of work for months. Their job is to keep the customers happy, and they do so with an attractive and faintly cynical air of amusement which helps them through the bad patches of their career and makes them good company. They need, above all, an audience, and in private life, wherever two or three are gathered together, they find it and they cannot help but please.

Ivor's charm was genuine despite being nurtured by conscious discipline. While still a very young man he decided that he should be nice to everyone. He schooled himself to create, deliberately, an atmosphere of pleasantness and welcome. By stressing and cultivating his natural charm he turned it into one of his most attractive characteristics. Whomever he met was entitled to courtesy and consideration. When, to these qualities, were added the dark Italian eyes, the clear skin, the black hair, the dazzling smile, it is easy to see why men and women could not resist his famous charm. 'He had

merely to appear on the stage or walk into a room for that stage or
that room to glow with what seemed to be the light of many lamps,'
wrote the actor Micheál Mac Liammóir. 'One felt happier merely by
looking at him or listening to him, whatever sense or nonsense he
talked, and he talked plenty of both. He also listened with apparently
concentrated delight to what other people were talking about.'

His humour was not, like Coward's, formal and epigrammatic, but
dependent on time and circumstance. The point of a remark would
spring from an actual incident, and outside the context of that incident it would not seem very funny. In a world where malice
flourishes he was noticeably unmalicious. 'Yes, you're perfectly
right,' he once observed about a popular actress whom the profession detested. 'What a cow. What a cow. What a *cow*. But what a
dear . . .'

He was notoriously benevolent. An actress recovering from a
heavy operation was sent off, all expenses paid, to recuperate for a
fortnight in an expensive luxury hotel. Actors who were ill or down
on their luck received large cheques under oath of anonymity. People
whose sole claim was friendship were sent presents which were not
only expensive but also gave proof of careful thought in selecting the
right object, the only object that would do.

The severest trial of his kindness was provided by Mam. Round
about the time he became, officially, 'Ivor Novello', she decided to
retire at the age of sixty-five. Since the end of the war she had lived in
the USA where she taught, sang and gave birth to a variety of wild
schemes quite as moonstruck as those which she was in the habit of
unleashing upon her compatriots. They also called for a lot of money
she did not possess, and, as Ivor's earning capacity grew, he often
received urgent appeals for funds to rescue her from her latest imbroglio. He always provided them, quickly and without reproach.
Mam's ship docked at Liverpool where Dave, 'looking handsomer
and younger than ever, in spite of his seventy-four years', came to
meet her, Ivor having a matinée to play that afternoon. Lloydie
attended in his place and shepherded her through the Customs shed.
On the way she gaily wondered to herself how she was going to find
room in The Flat for her seventeen trunks and pieces of luggage, not
to mention a steel filing cabinet nearly as big as a wardrobe.

Ivor greeted her at the railway station in London, 'crying and
laughing, while he held me as though he could never let me go, this
son who was so much a part of my very self.' The party arrived at the
Strand Theatre and jerked and bumped in the tiny lift up to The Flat

which, for the past few years, had been Ivor's bachelor home. Early next morning, very early, a truck full of her luggage arrived. The huge filing cabinet was somehow squeezed into the bedroom, and the hall piled high with a barricade of suitcases which nearly reached to the ceiling. Mam and Dave slept in twin beds, and her secretary spent the night on a bed set up in the small 'office'.

Over the next five days Mam enjoyed playing at Darby and Joan with Dave, sitting over the fire and entertaining visitors to tea. She quickly tired of it and, at three o'clock one morning, awoke her secretary and announced that they must be going back to New York. The life of inaction was killing her and she found it impossible to sleep in a room filled with Dave's pipe smoke, especially as he never opened a window. Her secretary argued that she could not possibly 'unretire' herself in less than a week, and that, if she really wanted to get back into action, she must first prepare some plans.

In the short term Mam solved the problem of tobacco smoke: she kept the lights on all night and marched back and forth until a sleepless Dave could stand it no more. He gratefully accepted her suggestion that he pass his nights in the 'office' and smoke his pipe there to his heart's content. Mam's secretary took over his twin bed, and the two women chattered away into the early hours discussing projects and thinking up new opportunities to channel Mam's restless energies. One of these was to write a book entitled *You Can Sing*, which was surely appropriate enough work for a retired singing teacher. She could not, however, work on it in the noisy surroundings of The Flat. A midnight telephone call secured her the rental of a seaside cottage in Pembrokeshire, and nine hours later she and her baggage train set off for that thankfully remote spot. The Flat was Ivor's again, and Dave's as well to smoke himself silly to his heart's content without the nagging of a wife obsessed by the need for pure air.

She was always swooping in and out of Ivor's life like this, and, always, his well-trained equanimity stayed unruffled. He loved her, was amused by her, and would smile even at her most outrageous demands. Although she cost him a great deal of money he did not grudge it. Perhaps he realised that his own success had put her in the background, and that this egocentric woman, torn between maternal feeling and professional rivalry, could never resolve the conflict within her as she grew older and saw, one after another, her most cherished projects wilt and crumble into disappointment.

His attitude towards failure was compassionate. If somebody he employed, actor or actress, technician or servant, did not measure up to what was required, he spoke discreetly to Lloydie. The matter was attended to, the offending person vanished, Lloydie reported 'It's all arranged', and Bobbie Andrews would gravely comment: 'So our dear Miss X will be seen no more. Ivor is feeling much happier now about the opening night.' Ivor's wish to avoid confrontation may be seen as a weakness on his part. It may also be construed as a distaste for unpleasantness, a fear of anything likely to shadow the genial atmosphere he preferred to sustain around himself. Was it not, furthermore, an example of the kindness he practised to himself as well as others?

He could, on the other hand, show anger. There are people who can be angry with a smile on their lips. Ivor was one of these, and during such moments the expression in his eyes would narrow to pinpoints of icebound fury while his mouth continued its fixed warm smile and uttered a stream of profanity. Such occasions were rare and were inspired by faults Ivor hated: inefficiency, sloppiness, unprofessionalism. He loathed drunkenness. Robert Newton once appeared in a play of his and was drunk on stage. After the run they met at a party and Newton stepped forward, hand outstretched. 'Don't *ever* expect me to shake hands with you,' said Ivor, and he turned away.

Ivor could not understand people who squandered their talent as the result of some vice or flaw. Such waste made him angry. His own career was built on hard work and a touching eagerness to learn. Although he knew little about the technicalities of screen acting when he first entered a studio, he impressed everyone by his humility and his readiness to be taught. Directors and photographers were carefully heeded and their advice was followed. As he was to say later on, there is no school in existence which can teach you how to write films or plays. You do it by watching, by observing as much as you can and then by harnessing what you have absorbed to your own intuition. Until the end of his life he would, every day when not otherwise committed, see a couple of films and a play.

Dedication of this sort brought him rewards such as the contract he signed in 1927 with Michael Balcon's Gainsborough film company. Three films were to be made in the following year and he was to receive ten per cent of the gross with three thousand pounds on account in weekly instalments of six hundred. By 1928 the guaranteed receipt had increased to twelve thousand pounds. The contract for this was handled by Ivor Novello Productions Ltd., one of the many companies he set up to look after his interests. His total income during the financial year from 1928 to 1929 amounted to fifteen thousand four hundred and sixty pounds, a figure which should be multiplied by ten to give an idea of present-day values. On the screen and on the stage he might be a dealer in dreams, an artist in romance, but where money was concerned he had a shrewd and realistic outlook. This down-to-earth trait also preserved him from vanity. The huge success he had won did not go to his head and he accepted it as a matter of simple fact. There was nothing, he felt, to wonder at. The actress Jean Webster Brough once asked if he did not feel at all conceited about his achievements. 'Conceit, ducky?' he asked her, a little puzzled at the question. 'No, indeed. Why? You see, it's always been like this, hasn't it?'

The films he made under the contracts described above did as well at the box-office as his annual rise in fees suggested. One of them had its origins in a play called *Downhill* which, inspired by the success of their collaboration on *The Rat*, Ivor and Constance Collier had written as, once more, 'David L'Estrange'. In this melodrama a public schoolboy is accused of having made pregnant a girl at the local tuckshop. The real father is, in fact, his best friend, but Roddy, as our hero is called, manfully takes the blame and is expelled. He goes on the stage, has an affair with an actress, and, after this ends badly, becomes a dock worker in Marseilles. Back in London he is about to commit suicide by jumping into the Thames when the friend for whom he sacrificed himself comes to the rescue. Noble Roddy's name is cleared at last. As a West End play *Downhill* just managed to achieve some eighty performances and did better in the provinces where Ivor's film fans were thrilled by a scene in which he washed his legs. 'The scent of good honest soap crosses the footlights as Roddy Berwick, footballer, washes his feet after the scrum,' wrote James Agate, '. . . and a crowded house delightedly watched Mr Novello as he laved and frictioned each little ivory pig on its way to market.'

Alfred Hitchcock directed the film of *Downhill* and made it into something rather better than the plot would suggest. Sudden juxtapositions and cleverly interlinked images gave it an impetus which carried the melodrama through and helped, almost, to suspend disbelief. Even he, however, could do nothing about a subtitle which, brought over from the play, enshrined Ivor's despairing cry when told that he was to be expelled: 'Does that mean, sir, that I shall not be able to play for the Old Boys?' For years afterwards this was a favourite catch-phrase with studio crews. Ivor himself, commenting on the overflowing incident of a story which among many other things called for the hero to become a gigolo and to win the Calcutta sweep, blandly observed: 'As you will see, the film was not without incident!'

A better-known film he made with Hitchcock, and one that occasionally turns up in art-houses, was *The Lodger*. It stems from a very workmanlike novel by, unexpectedly, Mrs Marie Belloc Lowndes, and has Jack the Ripper as its subject. In those days Hitchcock was only at the beginning of his career and had to accept Ivor as the star whom Michael Balcon insisted on. It would never have done for Ivor's many fans to think him capable of villainy, and so he was in the end shown to be innocent – an alteration which detracts from the power of the film and introduces a nonsensical element. Ivor was decidedly not up to the demands which the part made and was hampered into the bargain by a poor script. On completion *The Lodger* was deemed unpresentable. Scenes were re-edited and others were shot again. When it eventually appeared it was hailed by the trade as 'the finest British picture ever made' and indeed emerged as the box-office success of 1926. A few years later Ivor again played the part in a sound re-make. Although his acting ability had improved by then, the new version lacked the magic of Hitchcock: the London streets wreathed in creepy fog, the sequence where an enraged mob nearly lynches Ivor on suspicion of being Jack the Ripper, and, everywhere, the suggestion of hidden menace. *The Lodger* certainly justifies Michael Balcon's faith in Hitchcock, of whom he said: 'Although I was his boss, he knew a damn sight more than I did. His mind was a camera.'

A film of *The Vortex*, Noël Coward's play, presented other difficulties. The least of them were the topics of drug-taking and promiscuity which had contributed to the play's *succès de scandale* in the theatre. The one intractable problem was the absence, in a silent film, of the dialogue which is essential to Noël Coward. Robbed of the all-important words, unable to suggest the warring emotions of the young neurotic he played, Ivor nevertheless did his best and was damned with faint praise as 'quite good'. Adrian Brunel directed the film and tried to make up for the handicaps imposed on him by incorporating visual devices and unexpected camera angles to distract attention from the bowdlerised story. The final editing, not unexpectedly in the mad world of the cinema, was entrusted to someone else, but enough of Brunel's ideas survived to make *The Vortex* a peculiarly interesting film. Ivor encouraged him by composing the music for a little jingle:

A cute shot a day
Keeps the critics at bay.

Much more suitable for the mass public was *The Gallant Hussar*, described in publicity as 'A Charming Love Story with a background of Hungarian Military Life'. One of the reasons that induced Ivor to sign his Gainsborough contract was Balcon's arrangement with foreign companies to make films abroad. Since *The Gallant Hussar* was shot on location in Hungary Ivor combined the pleasures of filming with the fun of travelling, something he enjoyed very much indeed. One critic declared that his acting as the young hero, sympathetic and appealing in hussar's uniform, carried a hint of Ramon Novarro. Others were made slightly uneasy by the appearance of a disgusting little moustache in the style of Ronald Colman. He wore it again in *South Sea Bubble*, his last silent film, and topped it with a peaked sailing cap, for the story concerns a hunt after buried treasure on an island in the South Seas. Benita Hume played the heroine, and, later the wife of Ronald Colman, may have been reassured by the presence of a familiar moustache. There was little else to distinguish *South Sea Bubble*. 'It was really a load of nonsense . . .' remarked Michael Balcon grimly. 'In fact it was a failure.'

South Sea Bubble was preceded by *The Constant Nymph*, a film which, artistically, is perhaps the most satisfying Ivor made. Margaret Kennedy's best-selling novel features a childlike heroine who worships a rough and unmannerly composer. He marries someone else, but, tiring of his wife's bourgeois ambitions for his career, returns to the girl whose adoration of him is entirely disinterested. Their reunion does not last long for she dies, tragically. As a stage play *The Constant Nymph* equalled its success in novel form. Ivor had hoped at one time to play Lewis Dodd, the hero, but the part went to Noël Coward who soon afterwards had a nervous breakdown and was succeeded by John Gielgud. The book had obvious film potential and Michael Balcon secured the rights for his Gainsborough company. Who should play Lewis Dodd? Basil Dean, who had produced the play and was to oversee the film jointly with Adrian Brunel, approached Ivor. He, still a trifle piqued at not having been asked to take part in the stage version, refused. Dean tested a dozen or so other actors but could not find an alternative. Again he asked Ivor. In the meantime Ivor had seen a country house near Reading which he dearly wanted to buy. The price was four thousand pounds. He told Dean that he would do the part at that figure. The producer agreed, and both *The Constant Nymph* and the house became Ivor's.

The film was made chiefly on the shores of Lake Achensee in the Austrian Tyrol. The part of the heroine Tessa fell to Mabel Poulton, a protégée of the French director Abel Gance who had been impressed by the sweetness and purity both of her looks and her acting. She proved to be an ideal Tessa, and one whose 'Method' style, though it had not yet been formally recognised as such, inspired her to immerse herself so thoroughly in the rôle that she ended up by consciously living it. The Bohemian Sanger family of which she was a member included the West End actress Mary Clare in a highly amusing performance and Benita Hume as Tessa's kindly sister. Tony de Lungo, an Italian-born actor, gave a delightfully comic account of the Sangers' long-suffering domestic, and Elsa Lanchester provided a neat cameo of a singer at a musical soirée organised by Lewis Dodd's ambitious wife. Lewis Dodd is supposed to be an abrupt and unconventional artist who lives only for his work, and to this extent Ivor was miscast: he seemed unconvincing as he grappled with the spectacles and the pipe which were essential props in the stage play, and he looked much happier later in the film when he was allowed to smoke cigarettes. Yet his interpretation was a valid one, and Tessa's infatuation with his boyish charm was seen as entirely understandable.

Romance is the essence of *The Constant Nymph*. The photography of the picturesque Tyrolese backgrounds is beautiful, the subtitles are discreet, and clever editing helps the scenes to follow each other in a perfectly judged rhythm. This was largely the work of Adrian Brunel. He had many arguments during the shooting with his colleague Basil Dean, an excellent man of the theatre but not as yet fully aware of the limitations or, conversely, the possibilities of film, and often Ivor had to intervene and smooth down ruffled feelings with his usual good humour and light touch. In particular Dean exasperated Brunel's American cameraman with his imperious ways. Once all three of them were crossing Lake Achensee in the little steamer that served as ferry. Someone pointed out a fellow passenger, Anton Lang, the man who played Christ in the Oberammergau Passion Play. 'Gee,' said the cameraman, 'to think that I've travelled six thousand miles to be on the same boat as Christ – *and God*!' Dean laughed as much as anyone.

For the cast, however, the weeks spent in Austria were as idyllic as the mountain scenery. The company was enlivened by acid quips from Bobbie Andrews whom Ivor had brought along with him. One evening at dinner Brunel was looking forward to a chat with Ivor. He suddenly noticed that Ivor had retired quite early on. 'Strange, I never noticed him going,' said Bobbie, '*no personality!*'

The Constant Nymph, enhanced by Mabel Poulton's youthful idealism and Ivor's romantic nonchalance, made as great an appeal to the public as had the novel and the play. As soon as the four thousand pounds were in the bank he spent them on the house of his dreams, a property called Munro Lodge at Littlewick Green just outside Maidenhead. On 11 November, 1927, he became the legal owner and immediately started renovating the place which included two staff cottages, later joined by four others he bought and used for housing various pensioners of his. Even before he moved in Ivor had been to Eddie Marsh's flat and chosen fourteen pictures to hang on the walls of his new house. Eddie also let him select a hundred and ten volumes from his library to stand on the shelves of the drawing-room. They drove down there one evening with Bobbie Andrews and stayed up until three in the morning arranging furniture. On the journey they discussed what name to give the house. Ivor was in favour of 'The Constant Nymph', though he soon dropped it in the face of Bobbie's tart comments. Finally, the roof being covered in red tiles, they decided on 'Redroofs'.

The new home, white-washed and two-storeyed, looked out on spacious gardens planted with trees and flower-filled borders. Beyond the swimming pool, the tennis courts and the lilac bushes was a kitchen garden. Redroofs had five bedrooms. One, known as 'Married Quarters', was reserved for married guests and another was Bobbie's. The third was slept in by Lloydie, and the fourth, 'Constance's room', stood ready for Constance Collier whenever she wanted to stay. Ivor's bedroom, large and sunny, contained a massive double bed in grey and silver with flecks of blue, his favourite colour. He could stand on a balcony and see over the wide lawn in front. Down a flight of steps into the garden was a glass-enclosed room with a piano where he worked undisturbed. You entered the house through a little hall. On the right was the drawing-room, its chimney piece surmounted by a painting of Arab horses by Neville Lytton which Eddie had given him. French windows led into the garden and at the other side of the room was a grand piano. A pair of wrought-iron gates from David Garrick's house filled one of the doorways. Much of the décor was in white or off-white, a fashion launched and popularised by Sybil Colefax and Somerset Maugham's ex-wife Syrie. Mirrors proliferated and everywhere there was light. Roses grew on the outer walls around the door and windows. 'Here we are at last!' Ivor would exclaim as he arrived for the weekend. 'Isn't it the most beautiful place you've ever seen?'

A staff of six ran the house. They included a butler, a housekeeper, Morgan the chauffeur and two maids. The one who perhaps had the easiest task was the cook. Ivor's tastes were simple. For breakfast he preferred toast and coffee. He liked cereals, fried chicken and lobster *à l'Américaine*. Cold rice pudding was his favourite, and for chips he had a consuming passion, often entering the kitchen and helping himself straight out of the pan.

In London, now that he was earning large sums of money, he had The Flat redecorated. Although he could do nothing about the decrepit lift – it remained, to the end of his life, the most terrifying means of locomotion his guests ever encountered – he turned 11, Aldwych into a place of luxury. The austerely panelled hall had doors opening off into the various quarters: a drawing-room with two pianos standing on a raised platform, a library entered through a neatly contrived archway, a bedroom with a double bed even more huge than at Redroofs and a wall covered entirely by a mirror which created the illusion of size, for The Flat was in reality extremely small.

Thus, when he wanted to give a really big party, he would take a suite at the Savoy as The Flat could not accommodate all his friends. Somerset Maugham was a guest at one of these occasions and so was the young and pretty ballet dancer Anton Dolin. Maugham cast a predatory eye on Dolin and said, in his famous stutter, 'L-let me t-take you home.' The dancer, unimpressed by Maugham's withered charms, politely declined, although Ivor jokingly whispered in his ear: 'Don't be a fool. It'll mean a gold Cartier cigarette case tomorrow.' Dolin went home unaccompanied to bed and was suddenly aroused by a violent hammering at his front door. He looked down into the street below and recognised Maugham, a little drunk, rapping the knocker with impatient lust. He picked up a chamber pot from under his bed and emptied it on the unwanted suitor.

Ivor was not often a guest in other people's homes and felt much happier entertaining crowds of people on his own ground. In later years Mary Ellis was one of the very few friends who managed to coax him into staying with her at her country house. Otherwise he was perfectly content to divide his life between The Flat and Littlewick Green. Redroofs suited him ideally, being far away enough from London to be 'country' and yet near enough for a quick journey at the weekend or for driving down after an evening performance. In the existence he had so far created for himself every prospect seemed to please – except that of the irrepressible, the pertinacious Mam.

He had been wrong to assume that the mere writing of a book would be enough to keep her out of mischief. She soon tired of her distant Pembrokeshire village and decided to launch herself on Hollywood, not in films but as the sponsor of a new, brilliantly promising and infinitely talented pupil, or so she described her. The pupil enhanced the good impression made on Mam by advancing funds for the trip, but money was still needed. Ivor sighed, and, through his accountant Fred Allen, increased her weekly allowance to twenty pounds each Friday: seven pounds for rent and rates, thirteen for everything else. He wrote off all the other debts she owed him.

Mam replied with a long lament. Nobody wanted her, not even her own wonderful darling son. She would gladly have stayed in England, but she was broke and could see no chance whatsoever of making money at home. It was heartbreaking, especially as 'here I am with so much to give, in myself I have never been better, and beautiful singers, all ready, I am working hard for nothing – *no money – nobody wants me or my choirs if they have to pay for it!*'

The grand design of her Hollywood trip was to make money so that Ivor could save it up for her and avoid having to subsidise his old Mam. Could he not grasp the businesslike logic of her idea? The flaw in the argument, which of course she did not see, was that all past experience showed that she would lose money rather than make it. A triumphant postscript declared: 'I tell you not to worry about me – I shall be all right when I get to Hollywood!!! N.B. I paid a ten pound account out of the thirteen you sent me yesterday.'

The mirage of Hollywood faded in time but other crackbrained projects came to take its place. America held a dangerous lure for her, and she dreamed of finding there the fortune which, in the event, always eluded her. A cablegram from America usually meant that she was entangled in another of her escapades. One such reported that her landlord intended to evict her from her flat and that only five hundred pounds would save her and Ivor from unwelcome publicity. He paid up and agreed to settle her other debts of fifteen thousand dollars on condition that she returned immediately. He went to meet her off the boat and saw a stretcher being carried towards a nearby ambulance. A steward told him that Madame Clara Novello Davies had fallen unconscious on the voyage and was being sent to a London hospital.

Ivor, conscience-stricken, sat beside her in the ambulance and tried to bring her out of her coma. Tears ran down his face as he implored her to look at him, to give a sign of recognition. The plenteous form lay inert, eyes closed, bosom jellied. For a week she remained unconscious and he kept vigil at her bedside. Then he said: 'Mam darling, if you will only get well I'll never mention your troubles in New York, and I'll give you everything you want for the rest of your life.' Instantly her eyes opened and a pudgy hand sought his to grasp it with surprising firmness. A beam lit up her raddled features.

He kept his word and bought her a little house at Marble Arch where, with three of her Welshwomen for company, she busily started hatching out new and still more wonderful ideas. Oh Ivor, dear Ivor, darling Ivor!

2

THE BATSMAN AND THE BAT

'Even today [1950], with all my years of experience in the theatre, I have not lost the capacity of being frightened or moved by a plot on the stage. I have been in love with the theatre since the age of five, and I know I always shall be.'

Ivor Novello

HE STILL went on writing music, lots of it. For hours he would extemporise at the piano trying out chords and harmonic progressions from which, sometimes, a worthwhile melody would emerge. Then, as he tried to develop it, the shadowy idea might vanish into a smudge of faltered notes, to be succeeded, perhaps, by another and better tune capable this time of being shaped and polished. At moments like these he was oblivious to everything else and lost in a cloud of music. The piano became an extension of himself.

Ivor was often asked to provide individual songs for revues or to help out a performer with a number tailored to specific talents, as he did, for example, with Cicely Courtneidge in *The House That Jack Built*, an entertainment presented by her husband Jack Hulbert at the Adelphi Theatre. Among the five songs he gave her was 'The Dowager Fairy Queen', an item which, knees akimbo, zany smile on her lips, she sang with unstoppable vitality.

On his passport he could have described himself as one of a number of things: composer, or film star, or actor. He was not yet a fully-fledged dramatist or actor-manager. In 1928, at the age of thirty-five, he decided to try both these activities. His work on *The Rat* with Constance Collier had given him training in the construction of a play, and for the rest, he said: 'The only way to learn more and more about drama and dramatic technique is to keep going to the theatre and studying new plays and new productions. All I know about writing plays and music and acting has been taught to me from watching other people's successes and failures in the theatre.'

An idea for a play came to him and he wrote a three-act comedy first entitled *Taken by Storm* and then *The Truth Game*. He had four thousand pounds to spare from his film earnings and used it on launching the production. The part of the hero he had written for himself and that of the leading lady, he dared to hope, for Lily Elsie. She, still in 'retirement', could not decide. Neither could his old friend Viola Tree whom he approached with the offer of a rôle. Viola counselled him to see Gerald du Maurier about producing it. Ivor did so, sketched out the plot and read a brief scene to him. The great man said yes, he would produce, and he even persuaded Lily Elsie to join them. Viola Tree succumbed to the lure of the character part Ivor wrote for her, and he felt he had assembled the perfect cast when the name of Constance Collier was added to it.

A theatre was taken at a high figure – even then everyone was complaining about the rents of London theatres – and seven Hartnell dresses were ordered for Miss Elsie, as beautiful as when she first charmed the town in *The Merry Widow*. All the players turned up at a first rehearsal on a cold Monday morning and waited for Gerald du Maurier. There was a delay. Mr du Maurier's stage manager arrived with the message that his employer had sent him along to get things under way. The rehearsal began, uneasily. Constance Collier, playing her part like an automaton, disappointed Ivor by expressly ignoring all the opportunities he had written into it for her particular brand of drawling comedy. Ten days passed, du Maurier remained invisible, and Ivor struggled to give the play a sense of direction.

The next blow fell when Constance withdrew. Using Noël Coward as her intermediary she told Ivor that she did not like the part. Long afterwards she confessed she gave up because she thought that the play was doomed to failure and that, if she left, Ivor would cancel the whole thing and save himself both humiliation and money. Another actress, Ellis Jeffreys, was offered the rôle and, after reading the play, turned it down. A fortnight had by now been spent in rehearsal and du Maurier still shone by his absence. Weekends at Redroofs became tense and anxious.

Finally, du Maurier came out of his shell. Ivor asked him to intercede with Ellis Jeffreys and to tell her what a good part she was rejecting.

'Ivor,' he blandly replied, 'I can hardly say that. You see, I haven't read it!'

Lily Elsie, remembering that du Maurier had advised her to do the play, turned on him in a fury. 'I just want you to know,' she said, 'that your advice about doing this play meant nothing to me at all. I said I would do it because I believed in it. And I still do. Please inform me when rehearsals start again.'

Unperturbed, du Maurier addressed himself to Ivor. 'Well, you're not going on with it, are you?' he enquired.

Too much money, too much effort had been put into *The Truth Game* for it to be dropped now. Ivor, swearing that he would engage the finest actress in London for the part, stormed out of the theatre.

He decided on Lilian Braithwaite. In her dressing-room she heard with sympathy his tale of woe and poured him an extra large glass of port.

'Darling,' she assured him, 'I will play that part if it is the worst in the world.'

The remark was typical of her. In her youth an Edwardian beauty, as a mature woman she still preserved something of her aquiline looks. Forty years in the theatre had given her perfect mastery of comedy technique. She also acquired a reputation which equalled that of Mrs Patrick Campbell for stinging witticisms. In her case they were known as 'Lilians'. Of an actress colleague she once remarked: 'B. told me that she is off to do a play in New York tomorrow . . . but I don't think it can be a very big part as she is going on a very small boat.' At a celebration party for a long run, she pointed to her dress and said loudly: 'Someone has given me a dear little diamond brooch . . . Can you see it?'* During the 1939–45 war she played one of the mad old sisters in *Arsenic and Old Lace*, an American comedy produced by Firth Shephard which ran for so long and gave employment to so many that she declared: 'The Firth is my shephard, I shall not want!'

These 'Lilians' were delivered with the immaculate diction and timing she had perfected on the stage. If a sentence finished with a consonant she held on to it momentarily. 'I'll see you again' she gave as 'I'll see you againnn', which ensured that it reached every member of the audience. On a weekend at Redroofs she demonstrated her virtuosity in the matter of pauses. It was very hot and all the other guests had driven to Henley for the regatta. Ivor, who worshipped the sun, was basking in the solarium he had just had constructed. Unknown to him Lilian spent the morning resting in her bedroom. She decided to take the air, and, as she opened a parasol to shield her Edwardian pallor, she beheld a naked Ivor. In silence she steadily looked him up and down. 'What a nice big surprise,' she said, and paused . . . 'to see you up and around so early in the day.'

---

* The donor was Ivor. Probably the remark got back to him, and probably, with his usual good nature, he would have dismissed it as Lilian being typically outrageous.

The Truth Game is built on classic lines. The first act unfolds a situation which, at the climax, adroitly raises expectations. In Act Two the plot warms up and ends with a *coup de théâtre* showing hero and heroine apparently at loggerheads. The concluding act picks up all the threads and arrives at a dénouement where everything is sorted out into a happy ending. It is not real life but an airy comedy written with brio and polish that passes an evening agreeably. The hero is Max (Ivor), a penniless but handsome young man, who falls in love with Rosine (Lily Elsie), a rich widow. His persistence amuses her, and when he tricks his way into her Mayfair house they exchange badinage of this order:

> *Rosine* (sarcastically). When are you thinking of moving in?
> *Max*   Almost immediately. I should say – directly we're married.
> *Rosine* And when will that 'happy occasion' be?
> *Max*   'That' is for you to say.
> *Rosine* Oh! It is for me to say – then –
> *Max*   (interrupting). But I won't be rushed, I've got a lot to do.

He invites himself along to a house party where Rosine is also a guest and takes part in the 'truth game' of the title, a parlour diversion where the player is supposed to say exactly what he or she thinks of everyone else. Max describes Rosine in such witty but penetrating terms that she capitulates to him. Unfortunately she discovers that under the terms of her late husband's will all his money on her remarriage goes to his cousin once removed . . . and that distant relative turns out to be Max. The second act curtain falls on her disillusioned rejection of the suitor whom she imagines to be a mere fortune-hunter. In the last act she has decided to marry someone else but, in the end, comes round to Max again. All this time her chequered romance has been counterpointed by a sub-plot involving Mrs Brandon (Lilian Braithwaite), a society lady who lives on the commission she makes from introducing the right person to the right deal and fixing up desirable marriages – as she does in the case of Lady Joan Turner (the gangling Viola Tree), whom she pairs off with a wealthy gentleman in return for a percentage of the marriage settlement. Both main and sub-plots are skilfully intertwined, and the dialogue, especially in the rapid exchanges between Max and Rosine, is taut and crisp.

The play, attributed to 'H.E.S. Davidson' ('he's David's son'), although everyone knew it was Ivor's, opened at the Globe on 5 October, 1928. It was eventually directed by W. Graham Browne, husband of Marie Tempest and, despite being overshadowed all his life by her greater fame, a capable man of the theatre. The programme distributed at the first night is now a historical item. It promised cake, tea and coffee specially brewed for each order and supplied by Fortnum & Mason. Liberty's offered silk blouses at £1.15s.9d. In a signed testimonial Miss Lilian Braithwaite emphatically stated that Pond's Cold Cream cleanses, soothes, softens 'and, in my opinion, it also heals.' Keith Prowse declared that YOU want the best seats, WE have them. Another advertisement, without which no inter-war theatre programme would have been complete, announced: 'No Smoking – not even Abdullahs!'

Many people, including as nearly always Noël Coward, had been horrified by the ghastly pre-production troubles of the new play and had argued that Ivor should give it up. Once again they were confounded. The first night was a thumping success and brought ovations for Lily Elsie and Ivor. *The Truth Game* had a respectable West End run, went out on tour and, as late as 1940, was the subject of a film adaptation by Christopher Isherwood, then working as a scriptwriter in Hollywood. It even, after the provincial tour, came back to the West End for another season. Although the original production lost money Ivor did not suffer: he drew a salary as leading man and royalties as author of the play.

His next play, *Symphony in Two Flats*, which he wrote in the following year, struck a darker note. He played the part of a young composer who is going blind and, unable to afford treatment, is obliged to write popular music which he regards with contempt. A big money prize offered for 'the best English symphony' inspires an entry from him. He is told by kindly friends that he has won, but when he listens to a broadcast of the winning symphony from an Albert Hall concert he realises the subterfuge and goes back, with cynical resignation, to writing the stuff that brings in money. The threat of blindness and professional failure clouds existence with his beautiful wife (Benita Hume), although finally their problems are resolved. While the composer agonises in the flat above, in the flat below a widow, Mrs Plaintiff, who is none other than Lilian Braithwaite, acts out a broad comedy involving her awkward daughter (Viola Tree) and her own subsequent marriage to a frozen-mutton millionaire. She is abetted by Maidie Andrews, Bobbie's sister, and

by Minnie Rayner, a stout, moonfaced actress whose forte was
always to play comic maids and loud-spoken vulgarians. This
accomplished team, who became something of a Novello repertory
company, appeared in many more of Ivor's plays.

Symphony in Two Flats is neatly put together – the scene where
the blind composer listens to the broadcast is a cunning piece of
stagecraft – and the two plots run in smooth conjunction. Lilian
Braithwaite had good lines to put over, and although in print they
may not seem wildly amusing, with the benefit of her impeccable timing and arched eyebrow they scored with the audience:

> *Mrs Plaintiff*   (Reads lease). Whatever's a messuage?
> *Peter*   Another name for dwelling.
> *Mrs Plaintiff*   Sounds most improper.

Like *The Truth Game, Symphony in Two Flats* lost money on its
first run but made up for this to Ivor with fees as dramatist and leading man of well over three thousand pounds. There were also film
rights. In 1930 *Symphony in Two Flats* was adapted for the cinema
by Michael Balcon. As a concession to the mass market the hero's
symphony became a jazz affair played by Jack Payne and his band
while the comic sub-plot disappeared. It was Ivor's first sound film
and as principal actor he revealed a pleasing voice, light and attrac-
tively accented with the trace of a Welsh lilt. Two versions of the film
were made: one for the English market with Benita Hume in her original part, and one for the USA with an American actress imported
for the rôle. Ivor received payment as actor and also as owner of the
film rights. In the words of the old Victorian humorist, he could
claim:

> *I* am the batsman and the bat,
> *I* am the bowler and the ball,
> The umpire, the pavilion cat,
> The roller, pitch, and stumps, and all.

It was, however, a matter of taking the cash and letting the credit go.
A friend who went to the trade show of *Symphony in Two Flats* rang
him up afterwards and said: 'It's very good, isn't it?' 'No,' replied
Ivor, very quietly.

3

HOLLYWOOD

'Cash or Kisses? It's Amusing What You Can Get Away With If You Have Technique!'

Publicity for *But The Flesh Is Weak*, a Hollywood version of *The Truth Game*

A STORY is sometimes told about the Hollywood tycoon interviewing a writer for a job. 'So you're a writer, huh?' snapped the tycoon. 'Here's a pen and paper. Prove it.'

By the nineteen-thirties the Hollywood policy of buying up all the talent available was well established. If you wrote a best-seller or a long-running play there was bound, sooner or later, to be an offer from the studios. Native authors such as Scott Fitzgerald worked there, and so, for a time, did foreign imports like Hugh Walpole, P. G. Wodehouse and Anthony Powell. Once they had been taken on the payroll novelists were classified as odd fish best kept out of the way and treated on the principle of battery-farming: each was provided with his own little cell and expected to sit there quietly blackening paper throughout office hours. The capacious Hollywood trawl netted others beside writers: artists, designers with the slightest spark of promise, and actors and actresses who were signed up and did not in some cases make a film for years, if at all. Although this wholesale purchase may have seemed extravagant, if, by the alchemy of Hollywood, an international box-office success came out of it, then massive profits made the original outlay seem trifling. Ivor, like many others, was fated to undergo the process.

He went to Hollywood by way of New York. In the summer of 1930, as *Symphony in Two Flats* neared the end of its run, he had an offer from the impresario Shubert brothers to play it on Broadway. Here was a chance to make his American debut as actor, dramatist and composer, and he quickly took it. Except for Viola Tree, who was detained in London, the cast remained the same, and the producer was Raymond Massey. There was a brief try-out in Montreal before the company opened at the Shubert Theatre in September. He did not choose a good time for his visit. The Wall Street crash of some months previously had ruined many people and shattered the economy. The theatre, regarded as a luxury, was among the first items to be cut down on and no one wanted to invest in new plays. The Shuberts owned several theatres which they had to keep open since a small amount of money coming in was better than none at all, and they put on *Symphony in Two Flats* as quickly as possible.

Unfortunately their timing coincided with an intense heat-wave and the hottest day of the year. Ten minutes after the curtain rose in an atmosphere that made it hard just to breathe a violent thunderstorm broke out with a noise that drowned the actors' voices. Outside, in the streets, heavy rain crashed down and drummed loudly on the roof of the theatre. *Symphony in Two Flats* limped on for another seven weeks, at the end of which all the company, except for Ivor, returned to London. He, however, was not disheartened and resolved to try his luck again, this time with *The Truth Game*. Viola Tree, whom he regarded as his mascot, came over to play her original role, and for the Braithwaite part he was lucky enough to have Billie Burke, the English-born actress whose red hair and exuberant grace had won her a large American following. The play succeeded and generously atoned for the disappointment of *Symphony in Two Flats*. Half a dozen Hollywood companies instantly pursued Ivor with dangerous allurements.

He had always loved New York. The volatility, the optimism and the capacity to think big thrilled his mercurial nature. At first he lived in an apartment lent him by Beatrice Lillie, another expatriate who had fallen under the American spell, while she, on a brief visit to London, stayed in The Flat. On her return he installed himself and his secretary Lloydie in a flat where he planned lavish parties. These were given in the much larger apartment belonging to his new friend Richard Rose, a young American who later went into theatrical management with him. Bea Lillie performed eccentric songs of the type with which she enlivened otherwise dreary films while the charades played by guests were done with much more skill than is usual, since everyone involved was either an actor or an actress. Among the other guests was one who became a particular friend of Ivor. He was Clifton Webb, at first a dancer and then actor on stage and in films. 'I'm not kind, I'm vicious,' he said in one of his rôles. 'It's the secret of my charm.' This was a true summing up of a character which enabled him to play many waspish parts with conviction, especially that of the evil columnist in the film *Laura*. He had, like Ivor, a mother and was devoted to her, though she often drove him mad with her tiresome behaviour. At last, well over the age of ninety, she died, and he was inconsolable. In a long telephone call to Noël Coward he related the tragic news and wept for minutes on end. 'Unless you stop crying,' said Noël, exasperated, 'I shall reverse the charges.' It must, reflected Noël, be tough to be orphaned at seventy-one.

Of the Hollywood offers that came his way Ivor chose one from Metro-Goldwyn-Mayer. As the train approached Los Angeles a fit of melancholy overtook him. Everyone had warned him about the place and told him what an awful time lay in store for him. Viewed from New York, Hollywood seemed warm and inviting. As reality dawned the film capital took on a forbidding appearance. At the station he was cheered by the sight of Joan Crawford and her then husband Douglas Fairbanks Junior who had been at his New York parties and who now came to greet him. Next day she took him round the M-G-M studios and introduced him to everyone. Then he settled in the tiny office allotted him and began to read a film treatment of *The Truth Game* which was put on his desk. He stared at it in nauseous disbelief.

The anonymous adaptor had done little to turn the play into a film and had, moreover, introduced some awful jokes to hurry it along. Why, thought Ivor, had M-G-M bothered to engage him at such expense and then allowed his work to be butchered in this way? He settled down and rewrote it. He rewrote it again. There were script conferences at which everything was changed. There were others where the changes were dropped and the play restored to its original form. In all, during his nine months' Hollywood stay, he wrote eight different versions of *The Truth Game*. After the script had been through the mangle all that remained were the title and the names of the characters. Even these were tinkered with on the first day of production and the result emerged as *But The Flesh Is Weak*. It starred Robert Montgomery and featured C. Aubrey Smith, now the professional Englishman, white-haired, bushy-browed, not at all the gypsy chieftain as Ivor first knew him in *The Bohemian Girl*.

Ivor's disappointment at not being asked to play the leading rôle in the film version of *The Truth Game* was mitigated by the sunshine of California. He took a house in Santa Monica which looked as if it had been stuck absent-mindedly on a cliff beetling over the ocean. From a distance it seemed to be no more than a tower, perhaps built by some fanciful star of the silent screen, although it proved to have three floors below ground level and was really quite big. The most inviting feature was a large patio where Ivor could sunbathe to his heart's content with nothing but the ocean around him. It was, said Lloydie who stayed with him there, 'like being on a ship'.

Despite the horrors Ivor encountered in the studios he made many new friends. Among them was Ruth Chatterton, then one of the most prominent Hollywood stars and also a woman of some culture. During a New York party she had been impressed by his piano rendering of the 'Liebestod' from *Tristan Und Isolde*, and, hearing that he was bound for Hollywood, promised to help him during his stay there. When he did arrive she gave him the freedom of her house and generally made him welcome. She liked to think of herself as mistress of a salon where famous singers and violinists were invited to perform. Ivor enjoyed these musical evenings which were held on a Saturday, the usual time for such functions, that being the only day when film people could stay up late and did not have to rise next morning at an early hour for attendance at the studios. Ruth Chatterton was also responsible for Ivor making his first and only Hollywood film as an actor. She was just about to star in a production called *Once A Lady* and suggested him as second lead. He read the script and saw that there was nothing in it for him: the part was negligible. Don't take any notice of what the script said, darling, Ruth urged him airily, it would be built up into something worthwhile. Of course it was not, and *Once A Lady*, in which Ivor could do little more than look debonair, quietly failed. No one ever again asked him to act in a Hollywood film.

Another and quite different sort of actress was the outrageous Tallulah Bankhead. Her division of time was peculiar to herself. 'Daytime is so boring,' she used to say. 'It's better to sleep through it and have all one's fun at night.' Thus she would rise for breakfast at four in the afternoon. Her guests were served lunch at eight o'clock in the evening and dinner arrived at two in the morning. How she fitted in her professional engagements was a secret she kept from everyone. Ivor had known her in London as the heroine of Michael Arlen's *The Green Hat* and Noël Coward's *Fallen Angels*. She received him at her Hollywood home merry with drink and wearing a scanty costume. The night was unruly and consisted chiefly of a monologue about herself. Ivor, who was austere in matters of alcohol, rose to leave and explained that he had an early call at the studio next day. 'Darling, I haven't shocked you, have I?' she asked. 'You haven't shocked me at all,' he replied, 'but you've bored me intensely.'

In the morning a huge box of roses was delivered to him. The card with it read: 'Ivor darling, forgive me for last night. You know that I adore you more than anyone in the world. Talu.'

The third actress, and the most impressive, whom Ivor consorted with in Hollywood was Greta Garbo. He had worked, as had a dozen or so other writers, on the script of her film *Mata Hari* but never expected to meet the deity in person. One day, wearing trousers and a sailor's reefer jacket over a striped sweater, a beret pulled tight over her hair, the famous dark blue glasses masking her eyes, she walked into his drawing-room. At first Garbo was shy, but when Ivor spoke about people he knew in Stockholm and even tried out a few words of Swedish he remembered from his propaganda trip there during the 1914–18 war her reserve melted and she chatted easily. She looked, he thought, even more beautiful than on the screen. The camera was powerless to record her honey-coloured skin, the blue-grey eyes and their golden lashes and the essential warmth of her personality. Suddenly she stopped talking, as if she regretted the intimacy of Ivor's charm had created. 'Auf Wiedersehen,' she murmured. 'Really auf Wiedersehen?' he asked. 'Really auf Wiedersehen!' she answered. But he did not see her again during that stay in Hollywood.

One day, as Ivor abandoned himself to the sun on his patio with its creeper-grown trellis-work and, below, the Pacific rollers booming onto the shore, a mongrel dog wandered in to join him. The animal showed signs of Airedale ancestry, of Alsatian and of others too vague for definition. Ivor could find no one to claim it so he adopted the dog and acquired an affectionate companion which he later took back to England with him. The dog came into his life on a Wednesday. A week afterwards came a letter from Ivor's father reporting that his pet fox-terrier had died that very day. As if on cue Dave himself passed on a short while later.

Dropsy and a subsequent heart attack finished him off and made his death as quiet and unobtrusive as his life had been. He died around six o'clock in the morning while Mam held his hand, speechless for once. She had loved him in her youth and although her flamboyant nature made a conventional marriage impossible, she loved him still, after her fashion, and was loyal to him. Easygoing, divinely happy to do nothing except play an occasional game of bowls, he floated through an existence of ease assured by his son's brilliant career. His only positive achievements were once to have played bowls with W. G. Grace when the latter took up the game in old age, and to have been the father of Ivor Novello. On the other hand, these combined distinctions may be claimed by no one else, so it must be admitted that Dave was, in his way, unique.

There was then no Concorde to whisk Ivor back in time for Dave's funeral, so he stayed on in Hollywood increasingly homesick and cast down by his bereavement. Dave was cremated at Golders Green Cemetery where the mourners were led by Mam, dignified and statuesque in black, a shade which suited her rather well and brought out the pallor of her features. A few years later she was to join him there, and so, in the course of time, did Ivor. He, meanwhile, continued without much relish to work on film scripts. One of them, *Lovers Courageous*, a romance featuring Robert Montgomery, was based on a stage work by Frederick Lonsdale, an amiable man, often wittier than his own plays, with whom Ivor enjoyed an easy collaboration. Another was *Tarzan The Ape Man*, first in a series which still delights the amateurs of cult films. It includes the classic scene where Jane, the English heroine, establishes identities by pointing at Tarzan – 'Tarzan' – and at herself – 'Jane' – whereupon Tarzan gets the idea and babbles excitedly, 'Tarzan – Jane . . . Jane – Tarzan!' The studios had a lot of spare film left over from the shooting of *Trader Horn* and, anxious to be thrifty, used it for a new production which they thought would be a routine affair. *Tarzan The Ape Man* surprised them by triumphing as one of M-G-M's greatest successes. Ivor was more familiar with the drawing-rooms of Mayfair than with the African jungle, although, since the code of conduct is often identical in both places, he may have been better fitted to the subject than anyone else. Maureen O'Sullivan, who played Jane, thought his dialogue 'so witty and charming'. This was not reflected in publicity which included the slogan: 'Girls! – Would you live like Eve – If You Found the Right Adam?'

Ivor had had enough. He went to see his employer Irving Thalberg, the very young but very powerful dictator of M-G-M later to serve as model for the hero of Scott Fitzgerald's *The Last Tycoon*. Thalberg heard him out incredulously. Why should this quaint English writer be unhappy? What did he have to complain about? Wasn't he being paid very generously? Although M-G-M did not quite know what to do with him, they were reluctant to let talent out of their grasp. Suppose he stayed on for another three months? Ivor agreed. Immediately the period was up he prepared for home. With him he took two new plays he had written during his ample spare time, one called *I Lived With You* and the other *Party*. Both were essentially English and as far removed from the exotic Californian atmosphere as anything could be.

To celebrate the end of Hollywood thraldom he gave a party and invited, among others, Edgar Wallace, who had just been involved in the making of *King Kong*. Although Edgar could not come – he had, he pleaded, a nasty cold and did not quite feel up to a celebration – the party at Ivor's beach home went off happily in a blaze of Californian sunshine. On the long train journey from Santa Monica Ivor regularly visited the guard's van to feed his new pet dog which he had christened Jim. At Chicago he changed trains and, as usual, went to give Jim his dinner. In the van he found a Negro porter sitting on a large packing-case and engaged in compiling a list of passengers. 'What an enormous case,' joked Ivor, 'I hope there's no one inside it.' 'There sure is,' grunted the porter. 'A film writer who died in Hollywood.' He showed the label to Ivor. On it was the name of Edgar Wallace.

4

SIX PLAYS IN TWO YEARS

'A rather curious fact about my stage career is that although I make no claims that my plays are in any way better than anyone else's, they are apparently right for *me*. Whenever I have been in a play by anyone else it has failed.'

Ivor Novello

OVER THE years a Novello homecoming assumed the ritualised status of a first night. A crowd would gather at the railway station – Mam, Bobbie Andrews, Eddie Marsh, Viola Tree and others – to wait expectantly for his appearance. Everyone fidgeted and looked nervously at watches as the time of arrival drew slowly near. The train rumbled in and carriage doors opened. Someone would shout: 'There he is – there's Ivor!' The excited group wavered uncertainly and then stampeded down the platform. Ivor jumped out and ran towards them, buoyant and smiling like a schoolboy released for the holidays. Arms wide open he gave that strangulated cry of delight so typical of him, 'A-a-a-a-a-ah!' and became submerged in a flood of embraces. 'Duckies' and 'darlings' flew through the air. The jubilation suggested that he had come back unscathed from some earthshaking adventure rather than a routine Atlantic crossing. Then, flashlights popping, he made his way with Mam to the Rolls-Royce where Morgan attended to drive him on to The Flat. The others piled into a taxi and completed the procession. The truth is that, unselfconscious and utterly spontaneous, Ivor really was overjoyed to see them again. And, such was the effect he had on them, they reacted with a feeling no less genuine.

I Lived With You, the first of the two plays written in Hollywood, opened at the Prince of Wales in the early spring of 1932. Among the rival West End attractions with which it had to compete was Ralph Lynn, monocled, grainy-voiced and rubber-faced, in *Dirty Work*, another famous Aldwych farce by Ben Travers. Noël Coward's *Cavalcade* went on filling the vast auditorium of Drury Lane and at Wyndham's Theatre Gerald du Maurier pleased his many fans in a new Edgar Wallace play. A. P. Herbert's comic opera *Derby Day* could be seen out at the Lyric, Hammersmith, while its namesake in Shaftesbury Avenue offered thoughtful entertainment with J. B. Priestley's experimental piece *Dangerous Corner*. Musical comedy was represented by Stanley Lupino and Jessie Matthews in *Hold My Hand*, by Delysia in *The Cat And The Fiddle* and by Heddle Nash in *The Dubarry*. The most spectacular bill was *The Miracle* in which Lady Diana Cooper exhibited her well-known beauty, and the most curious a play about Napoleon written by Mussolini and adapted by John Drinkwater. All the famous names of the inter-war London theatre were on show in various plays: Henley Ainley, Owen Nares, Gertrude Lawrence, Gladys Cooper, Ronald Squire, Bobby Howes and Seymour Hicks. Persons of an intellectual turn could have booked for Cedric Hardwicke and Edith Evans in Shaw's *Heartbreak House*, or Ernest Milton in *The Merchant of Venice*. Certainly the most stimulating original play was generally thought to be Ronald Mackenzie's *Musical Chairs* in which John Gielgud was establishing his reputation.

Ivor's new play was an amusing diversion about a mysterious and handsome young foreigner whom two sisters come across at Hampton Court. He turns out to be a Russian prince in exile – yet another opportunity for Ivor to demonstrate a 'foreign' accent – and they take him home to Fulham and tea with the family. Mum is Minnie Rayner again and Dad is Eliot Makeham, an excellent character actor who during his lifetime played innumerable middle-aged gents in slippers and shirt-sleeves. Prince Felix enjoys the atmosphere so much that he stays on, selling his ancestral diamonds to pay for his keep and to encourage his hosts in working out their fantasies. Under the influence of his persuasive talk about romance and seduction and living life to the full, Dad buys a car and sets up a mistress, Mum acquires the fur coat she had always longed for, the son is despatched to an expensive boarding-school, and one of the daughters, with an eye to the future, allows her employer to become her lover. The other falls in love with Felix. The humour of the play comes from the clash between the exotic hero and the lower middle-class family whom he dazzles with his aristocratic nonchalance. The best scene is a tea party where Felix is introduced to the neighbours. It begins stiffly, but vodka helps to unloose inhibitions and to free the guests from their suburban snobberies as well as giving scope for some well observed passages on social aspirations. The action builds up to a dramatic curtain when Dad's mistress appears and accuses him of deserting her. By the end of the play Felix decides he must go, although there is a strong hint that he will be reunited with the daughter who loves him. In the meantime, although he has shaken the family out of its narrow little ways, they, too, have done something for him. 'You give me everything,' he says. 'I have a home – there are people around me, loving me. I have learned to laugh again. Nothing I can give can pay for that.'

Robert Newton made one of his earliest appearances in *I Lived With You*, and Ursula Jeans showed again the physical attractiveness and the gift for subtle comedy which distinguished her acting. Ivor himself received an ecstatic welcome back to the London stage and had to take ten curtain calls. When he made his first-night speech the ovation lasted some two minutes – and that is a very long time indeed for applause alone. The critics were very favourable – 'I can imagine nothing more likely to be popular than a theme of Dostoievsky treated in the manner of Ian Hay!' commented Agate – and only an unexpected heat-wave cut short the run of *I Lived With You*. Ivor took it on a provincial tour during the autumn and was rewarded with 'House Full' notices in all the towns. Every night he was obliged to make a curtain speech and every night hundreds of admirers besieged the stage door. 'You're wonderful!' screamed hordes of girls milling around him in frenzied adoration. Unlike Gladys Cooper, who regarded fans as an unseemly intrusion on her private life, Ivor loved them. He was never too busy to sign an autograph book or to pause for a friendly remark, and even after battering his way through a crowd of screaming importunates, exhausted and breathless, he kept his smiling composure. They were, after all, the customers. What is more, he really enjoyed touring the provinces, especially when the town he was visiting included a fairground or an amusement park where he could indulge, over and over again and long after his companions had given up, in the vertiginous delights of the roller-coaster.

Before going on tour he had already launched the second play he wrote during his Hollywood stay. *Party* is a good-natured skit on Mrs Patrick Campbell and Tallulah Bankhead. It is very much a play for the profession and he originally designed it as a Sunday night performance at the Arts Theatre before an audience of stage folk. Leslie Henson saw it, and, impressed, booked it for a public run at the Strand. Since it was rather short Ivor added a sequence in which guest stars, among them Douglas Byng, did a number of turns to entertain the company. Ivor took over the leading male rôle and so achieved another of his ambitions: since he occupied The Flat on top of the Strand Theatre he was now, as it were, living over the shop.

Even in the nineteen-thirties Mrs Patrick Campbell was a legend – a legend and also a back number, for although she had been the greatest actress of her time she was, as Noël Coward described her, 'impossible'. When very young she married a remote and ineffectual army officer who, before his early death, gave her little else besides two children and a name she was to make famous. She had always been 'artistic', and since money was scarce she decided to go on the stage. Without the advantage of any formal training she soon discovered a natural talent for acting. Passionate eyes, black hair and a dominating presence established her as an English Sarah Bernhardt, with whom indeed she acted, notably in *Pelléas et Mélisande*, when Sarah forgave the unfortunate practical jokes she would play in performance because, she said, Campbell was a 'grande artiste'. She was the first Eliza Doolittle in *Pygmalion* and Bernard Shaw claimed to be in love with her, though from the long correspondence they exchanged he emerges with little credit. 'Some day you'll eat a pork chop, Joey,' Mrs Pat told the vegetarian Shaw at rehearsals, 'and then God help all women!'

Having gained money, a reputation and the awed respect both of her colleagues and of high society, she threw it all away. A strain of perversity impelled her to savage anyone who helped her. When seriousness was called for she would laugh, and if a situation demanded gratitude she would be haughty. Sometimes known as 'the Pat-Cat' because of her barbed retorts, she could never resist a witticism, hurtful though it might be, and again and again throughout life she destroyed her own chances with her ready tongue. Eventually few managers would employ her and she was reduced to long provincial tours. John Gielgud once congratulated her on a performance which had been a *tour de force*. 'I suppose,' she replied, 'that is why I am always forced to tour.' She hoped to find happiness in a second marriage and what she called 'the deep deep peace of the double bed after the hurly-burly of the chaise-longue', but this too was denied her. Given her experience of men it is not surprising that she preferred animals. She carried everywhere with her a small Pekinese dog whose hair liberally bespattered her expensive gowns. The most famous in this long series of pets was called 'Moonbeam'. A New York taxi driver who conveyed her and Moonbeam was annoyed to see a small puddle on the floor. 'All right,' he grumbled, 'who's responsible for this?' Mrs Pat snatched up Moonbeam. '*I* am!' she boomed, and made off. She could always make a perfect exit, even from a taxi.

Many anecdotes and epigrams are attributed to 'la petite Campbell', as Sarah Bernhardt fondly called her, and most of them are true. She it was who, told of a gay affair between two actors, made the famous remark: 'I don't care what people do, as long as they don't do it in the street and frighten the horses!' Of a beautiful singer she commented: 'Ah, yes – *me* in a spoon'. On rivals whom she disliked she could be merciless, as when she said of Marie Tempest: 'If you prick her, sawdust comes out.' An admirer who congratulated her on the striking voice she created for one of her most successful rôles as a Jewish matriarch was told: 'My dear, nothing could be easier, I simply copied King Edward.'

While Ivor was rehearsing *Party* he often saw Mrs Pat with the sly intent of gathering material for the play. He was not disappointed. At supper one evening they were joined, to their despair, by an earnest entomologist who could not stop talking about ants. They were his passion and he dilated voluminously about these astonishing insects which had, he told them, their own social services, their own hospitals, their own sanitary system. Even Mrs Pat was dazed into silence for a moment. Ants, the unwelcome guest continued, had their own architects, their own engineers, police force, army . . . Mrs Pat recovered herself. 'No *navy*, I presume?' she enquired in tones that filled the restaurant.

Such was the character on whom *Party* is based, and she was played, as 'Mrs MacDonald', by Lilian Braithwaite, while the Tallulah Bankhead part of 'Miranda Clayfoot' was given to Benita Hume. The pastiche of Mrs Pat's wit does not always come up to the original, although there are some good attempts. The action takes place at a first-night party given by Miranda and two women arrive wearing the same dress. 'Darling, don't upset yourself – it's really rather a bit of luck,' says one. 'Who for?' asks the other, to be met with the reply: 'For you. There's always the chance that someone will think you're me.' Then Mrs MacDonald speaks with a character called Strube. 'I'm afraid, Miss Rube – ' 'Strube.' 'Strube – Oh, well, I expect you know best . . .' Miranda is involved in the following repartee:

Miranda	And Venice – I bet you went to Venice.
Rosie	Yes, we went there.
Miranda	I don't see what they mean by Venice – it's just like any other Italian town, only flooded.
Rosie	Yes, but flooded with great care.

From which it will be seen that *Party*, as a portrayal of a *monstre sacré*, does not quite have the impact of, for example, Noël Coward's *Hay Fever*, where the character Judith Bliss, as played by Marie Tempest, is a much more vivid depiction of the species. Yet Ivor was successful again and despite the parochial nature of the subject, an essentially theatrical one, the general public supported it with enthusiasm and the rights were bought by Hollywood to provide a vehicle for Joan Crawford – who never made the film. During the run Mrs Pat came backstage to see Lilian Braithwaite. 'Oh, Lilian,' she graciously announced. 'You make me so much nicer than I really am!' In the New York production she herself acted the rôle of Mrs MacDonald, smoking one of the Havana cigars she favoured and cuddling Moonbeam in her arms.*

In the following year, 1933, Ivor celebrated his fortieth birthday with three plays on the London stage. The first of these, *Fresh Fields*, presented Lilian Braithwaite (Lady Lilian Bedworthy, an echo of Restoration comedy) and Ellis Jeffreys as the impoverished daughters of a duke trying to keep up appearances in their Belgravia mansion. Lady Lilian earns a little money giving beauty hints in a women's magazine. Her secretary reads out one of the enquiries: 'I am 34 – no one ever seems to want to kiss me – I have a very spotty skin. What should I use?' Lady Lilian dictates her answer: 'Prussic acid.' Beauty hints are not enough, however, to keep the two sisters in the style they think their due, so they take in as paying guests some rich Australian relatives headed with vulgarian brio by Minnie Rayner. There follows much snobbish fun at the expense of the Australians and, as ever, a great deal of talk about money. 'Poor Alec's saving up to pay his death duties,' observes a visiting noble-woman played by Martita Hunt. 'Well, there's one cheque he won't have to sign,' a friend commiserates. 'My dear,' she is told, 'whoever signs it he'll turn in his grave.' In the end Lady Lilian succumbs to the rough-and-tumble charm of Minnie Rayner's Australian brother. 'I'm only trying to bring a little friendliness into the atmosphere,' he says as he gathers Lilian into an ape-like embrace. 'Friendliness! Rape!' she exclaims, sinking gratefully into his arms.

Ivor wrote *Fresh Fields* in nine days while on the provincial tour of

---

* Philologists may also find *Party* of interest since it contains an early use of the slang term 'wimp' – though not in the sense people give it today. One of the characters explains: 'My name for people with familiar faces but unfamiliar names.'

I Lived With You. He began it one Friday morning in Manchester and by Saturday of the following week had completed it in Birmingham. This was the shortest time it had ever taken him to write a play and what resulted became one of his most successful, as *Fresh Fields* had a run of fifteen months. Backstage, however, there were moments of tension and disharmony largely caused by the two leading ladies. Between Lilian Braithwaite and Ellis Jeffreys a rivalry existed which showed itself in well-bred skirmishes and murmured innuendoes. Both actresses were more or less of an age but Lilian sought to give the impression that she was much the younger. 'Poor old Ellis had quite a time remembering her lines tonight,' she would say with an air of benevolent concern. Or: 'It's such bad weather for Ellis, I hope the old darling will be able to get home all right.'

The mainspring of Lilian's discontent was the difference in their salaries. Having received eighty pounds a week in her last play, this was the sum she contracted for *Fresh Fields*. Next day Ellis's agent was in touch. For years, he said, his client had been paid a hundred pounds a week and she would take nothing less. Moreover, she had been a star for a very long time while Lilian had only been a leading lady. This was untrue but by then Ivor needed Ellis badly for the part and her terms were agreed. Lilian found out and was exceedingly vexed. The delicate task of mediating between the two players fell to Richard Rose, the young American whom Ivor had befriended in New York and who was presenting *Fresh Fields*, as he did a number of Ivor's other plays. He would arrive in Lilian's dressing-room and proffer for her inspection a note of the evening's box-office takings. Placing a monocle in her eye with graceful precision she would scrutinise the figures and then remark innocently: 'Lilian has made some more nice pennies for you tonight, Dickie dear.' She had the last laugh. Within a few years she became Dame Lilian Braithwaite D.B.E., an honour which King George VI neglected to confer on dear Ellis.

A week after the opening of *Fresh Fields* Ivor appeared in another new play called *Flies In The Sun*. This time he took the leading rôle opposite Gladys Cooper in what was to be the last of the ventures she embarked on under her own management. It proved disastrous. For his subject Ivor had chosen a silent film star faced with ruin because of his poor speaking voice, a fate which had recently struck John Gilbert who was known until the advent of sound as 'The Great Lover'. The story was set on the French Riviera and developed among wealthy characters who might have strayed out of a Scott Fitzgerald novel. It was a milieu Ivor knew very little about and he did not write convincingly. Gladys Cooper was delighted with the chance of playing, for once, a wicked lady instead of the good sweet women she had been limited to until then, and Ivor, as a drunk and disillusioned film star who shoots himself at the end of the second act, also hoped to break away from type-casting. Both were disappointed, since their admirers, having looked forward to another sentimental comedy with the two idols as romantic lovers, refused to accept them in this unpleasant light. The situation was not improved by Ivor being obliged to work all day in the studios filming *I Lived With You* and then to rush back for his evening performance. *Flies In The Sun* closed after only a few weeks and Ivor took failure in the same equable way as he took success. 'I'm sure I'll always have to write a romantic part for myself,' he said with a shrug of his shoulders. 'That's what the audience wants and that's the only way I can have a success.' He never spoke of it again.

Immediately he set to work on another play in the setting he knew best of all: that of the theatre. *Proscenium* is about a young man who marries a famous actress older than himself. At first overshadowed by her prestige, he gradually emerges as a fine actor in his own right and his performance as Romeo brings him independent fame. His wife, realising that their situations are now reversed, unselfishly stands aside and arranges for him to accept a glittering offer from America. Apart from an unnecessary sub-plot – the young man is revealed to be the son of a gallant lieutenant-colonel who a generation ago had also been in love with the actress – the construction of the play is solid and the dialogue, especially at climactic moments between the twenty-six-year-old hero and his wife of forty, is admirably paced. A more Strindbergian writer might have given a sombre ending to *Proscenium*, but Ivor, always an optimist, preferred the happier view, and while the scenes between husband and wife are powerful enough, he could not resist a final curtain that held out hope of brighter things. He also, in a prologue to the play, appeared as the hero's father, white-haired, trimly moustached, and gave one of his strongest performances. People who had known his father were struck by the resemblance to Dave which the son showed. Here was proof that Mam's bold claim to have given Ivor his good looks might not be so well justified as she imagined.

Proscenium gave Ivor a chance to realise Shakespearean ambitions which he had always cherished. Clad in tunic, tights and pointed slippers, he mimed through an interlude during the third act

called 'A Masque of Romeo and Juliet'. It was accompanied by the
lovely incidental music Fauré wrote to a French adaptation of *The
Merchant of Venice*. Ivor had, too, many opportunities for comment
on the theatrical way of life. 'You can't tell me anything I don't
know,' snaps the gifted young woman who plays Juliet. 'Oh yes I can,'
replies her partner. 'You're a self-satisfied, malicious, cruel little –
bitch – but you're a *great* actress.' The leading lady's new production
inspires this exchange:

Mrs Grey	Oh, she's great as the injured wife – though what she knows about being injured, or being a wife at all, puzzles me.
Bessie	That's acting, that is –
Mrs Grey	That's right!

And when the American producer offers to stage *Romeo and Juliet*
in New York, he expresses one of Ivor's firmest beliefs: 'I want to give
people the chance to dream again – and I want to show them that
there is an art beyond the reach of mechanical devices and black and
white shadows chasing each other round a white sheet . . .'

Fay Compton played the ageing wife and, for the hero's mother,
Ivor persuaded Zena Dare to join the cast. She and her sister Phyllis
had for years been celebrated stage beauties. Having made their first
appearance at an early age, before they were twenty they commanded
a large following of admirers. In the first decade of this century their
photographs could be seen everywhere: on playing cards, on magazine covers, on boxes of chocolates and on postcards. During the
1914–18 war soldiers bought pin-ups of the Dare sisters by the hundreds of thousands and used them to decorate trench and billet. Zena
and Phyllis could remember the day of the stage-door Johnny and of
the young men who brought their favourite actresses flowers and
champagne and took them out to lavish suppers. Quite a few of these
performers married into the aristocracy, which is what Zena did
when she fell in love with the 'sweet and funny little face' of Lord
Esher's eldest son. She thought she had left the stage until, in 1933,
Ivor asked her to play his mother in *Proscenium*. He would only be
twenty-five in the play, he explained, which meant that she would be
about forty-five – and that, he added with all his persuasive charm,
was the most attractive age for a woman. 'Darling,' she answered, 'if
it's a good part, I'll play your grandmother. Of course I'll play it.' This
she did, and although, throughout rehearsals and before making her
entrance, she suffered from appalling nerves, the adroit technique

she displayed on stage revived her pre-war celebrity. She, too, joined the Novello 'repertory company' and became one of the happy band for whom he wrote tailor-made parts. Her one stipulation was that they should be 'little and amusing', and she must be the only actress ever to have asked for her rôles to be kept as short as possible: most of them usually complain that they have too few lines to speak. Besides appearing in Ivor's plays she went on acting until her eighties and, for six and a half years, played Professor Higgins's mother in *My Fair Lady* without missing a single performance.

Another of Ivor's favourite women took part in *The Sunshine Sisters* which he put on at the end of 1933. This was Dorothy Dickson, a former star of the Ziegfeld Follies who, with her husband Carl Hyson, enjoyed popularity in both New York and London. In Jerome Kern's *Sally* she sang 'Look For The Silver Lining' with a vivacity that established her as the central figure of many subsequent revues and musical comedies. 'I must write a play for my Dottie,' said Ivor. 'She has more star quality than anyone I know.' He produced *The Sunshine Sisters* for her and for another of his old friends, Phyllis Monkman. With Joan Clarkson to make up the trio of down-and-out music-hall performers who give the play its title, the plot concerned a young man played by Jack Hawkins and his rash decision to put them up in the home of his mother, an eccentric duchess. She is in the charitable habit of rescuing waifs and strays, and when she gets it into her head that the girls are reformed prostitutes she opens up intriguing opportunities for complications. They failed, however, to amuse, and the play did not succeed. 'I made a big mistake,' said Ivor. 'If only I'd set it to music it would have been a great musical comedy.'

Still, *The Sunshine Sisters* at least helped him to create a record. During the short time it ran he could claim the rare privilege of having three plays featuring simultaneously in the West End, since not far away from the Queen's Theatre which billed *The Sunshine Sisters* were the Criterion with *Fresh Fields* and the Globe with *Proscenium*. This hat-trick at the end of 1933 marked the conclusion of a prolific twenty-month period after his return from Hollywood during which he had staged no less than six plays and taken the leading rôle in four of them. He had, beside all this, made films of *I Lived With You*, *The Lodger* and *Sleeping Car*. The last-named, a comedy with Madeleine Carroll, Stanley Holloway and Kay Hammond, presented Ivor as a French sleeping-car attendant who embarks on an arranged marriage with an American heiress. The shooting of the film was, according to Madeleine Carroll, a lugubrious affair. 'The only laugh I got was over a face-slapping scene,' she confessed. 'Ivor Novello hated having his face slapped, I got the giggles, and we had seventeen takes.'

After all this he felt that he deserved a holiday and, with Bobbie, Lloydie and Richard Rose, he set off from the November fogs of London on an extended cruise to warmer climates. In Barcelona, their first port of call, Ivor's instant reaction was to find out where the nearest matinée was playing. To his delight he discovered a local opera company was doing *Madame Butterfly* that afternoon. The hotel concierge warned him that they were very bad and that the district was the poorest in Barcelona. Ivor was not deterred: any theatre was better than no theatre at all, and while the others went sightseeing he made his way to the little run-down opera house.

Amid the chipped and crumbling plaster he saw a heroine six feet tall and of inordinate tonnage that suggested a massive Brünnhilde rather than Puccini's delicate little Cho-cho-San. She had, moreover, laryngitis and was obliged to speak her lines instead of singing them. The tenor was a small man with eyes too close together and gestures reminiscent of a clown in a Mack Sennett film. At the end, when the heroine stabbed herself, she fell on the stage in such a lump that the boards trembled. Yet despite the awfulness of the performance, despite there being only six players in the orchestra, the audience was deeply moved and tears ran down the faces of women sitting around Ivor. It all went to prove, he thought, the indestructibility of Puccini's music.

The holiday-makers travelled on to the Holy Land where Ivor led them tirelessly from the Manger in Bethlehem to the Church of the Holy Sepulchre and the Mount of Olives. In Cairo, his energy undimmed, he dragooned them around the Pyramids and took them out into the desert for a midnight picnic. When they reached Venice they met Noël Coward who was also on holiday. Coward's friend, Admiral of the Fleet Sir Dudley Pound, often entertained with his wife on board the flagship, and Noël was asked to invite as many people as he liked to a big cocktail party. Ivor, of course, was included and so were a large number of other guests. 'Noël,' said one of the ladies, 'I have a dreadful feeling we've asked too many queer people.' Noël reassured her. 'If we take care of the pansies,' he replied, 'the Pounds will take care of themselves.'

By the time Naples was in sight Ivor had become restless for the London theatre again. He left the cruise and went to Rome for a short but intense bout of opera-going which included *Aida* and *Turandot* before returning home once more. There was a film to be made, a version of Dodie Smith's *Autumn Crocus* with Fay Compton as his leading lady and Jack Hawkins in the supporting cast. It was the story of a spinster on holiday in the Tyrol who discovers romance for the first time with a dashing foreigner. Ivor, as usual, was playfully attractive in the role, although, at the age of forty, he seemed a little mature to be wearing lederhosen. It was, in any case, to be his last film. He had no regrets about his decision to concentrate henceforth entirely on the theatre. While by no means ungrateful for all the cinema had given him, he left it with a feeling of relief. 'I love seeing films,' he said, 'but I hate doing them. I believe I always have, anyhow, after the first novelty of seeing myself on the screen wore off. I hate the hours one has to keep. I have never been able to get up in the morning without a feeling of impending death. I don't like going to bed early . . . That first shot at nine o'clock in the morning, usually in evening clothes, with the memory of a nice warm bed almost too close, is my idea of one of the lesser-known forms of Chinese torture.'

He spoke of the difference between films and the stage in terms every actor will recognise: 'On the stage every performance is an event, because you have a living, breathing audience to conquer. You *know* immediately whether you are doing something that pleases or offends, and you can adjust yourself accordingly. But the camera, which is never supposed to lie, makes no response whatsoever, and, even if the director seems pleased, he is only one man. Just compare that reaction with a Saturday night at Drury Lane with two thousand five hundred people showing their interest by their laughter, their silence, and their deeply appreciated applause! Also, there is something so final about performing for the screen. Once it is – as they say – 'in the can', that is the end of *that*. You have no opportunity to perfect or alter. It is there for good and all, whereas on the stage every performance means spiritual and mental growth of some kind.'

He lost no time in getting back to the live theatre and, in September 1934, put on a new play he had written while on tour with *Proscenium*. The title, *Murder in Mayfair*, tells the whole story, and as the hero wrongly accused of the killing Ivor gave what is thought to be one of his best performances. Despite handicapping himself with a 'French' accent, the portrait he drew was, in the general opinion, entirely consistent and marked by nervous sincerity and concentration. Every mood of the character's temperament was worked out and his interaction with the other players – they included Fay Compton and Zena Dare – was subtly varied. Bobbie Andrews, in the part of the guilty one, was less convincing, for, as James Agate said, he had 'bounced up and down with a tennis racket on too many of Marie Tempest's sofas to steep his hand in murder.' The rôle of the *femme fatale* was taken by Edna Best, pert and adorably snub-nosed. She had but recently been divorced from the actor Herbert Marshall and found a certain consolation, as far as he could oblige, in Ivor. During a Christmas spent at Redroofs she shared a guest-room with an actress friend. Late one night she vanished and returned with the dawn, bright-eyed, to tell her friend: 'I've been with our host!'

After the successful production of *Murder in Mayfair* Ivor started thinking of other directions he might take. One Sunday, after lunch with Richard Rose, he spoke about his music. 'I've neglected it for ten years,' he said, 'and it's high time I began again. After I've written this next play I'm going to try to write an operetta.'

He went to the piano and improvised.

'That's wonderful,' said Rose. 'Put it down on paper and keep it for that musical you've just been talking about.'

The notion grew. Why not write a big musical and star in it himself? Rose went on excitedly. He could play the romantic lead and get an actress with a beautiful voice to play opposite him. There would be other actors singing too, and choruses and ballets.

'How did you happen to think of that?' Ivor asked.

'You write good plays and lovely music, and there's no reason why you can't combine the two.'

Before this alluring new project could be set up, however, an idea for another play was clamouring to be released. It was a successor to *Fresh Fields*, or rather a follow-up which aimed at capitalising on Lilian Braithwaite's triumph in that piece, and he called it *Full House*. Once more the actress was cast as a sharp-tongued woman of the upper class who is short of money and desperate for schemes to make it. Again she had a sister, played this time by Ursula Jeans, and again the juvenile lead was Bobbie Andrews. Heather Thatcher, one of the few actresses to wear, like Lilian herself, a monocle in private life, appeared as a horsey young woman from the shires. There was a scene where Ursula Jeans, her rival in love, put the jodhpur-clad Thatcher across her knee and spanked her vigorously. This dramatic moment sprang from a passage-at-arms between the two characters when the horsewoman, disapproving of the other's excessive make-up, tells her to wipe all the 'muck' off her face. 'There – is that artificial?' says the latter, doing as she is told. 'Yes – it won't come off – it's enamel.' 'It's not enamel. It's me – my skin's famous.' 'Anything's famous if it's been there long enough.'

Apart from this a feeling of *déjà-vu* hovers about *Full House*: whereas in *Fresh Fields* the impecunious gentlewoman took paying guests and arranged for presentations at court, in *Full House* she turns her home into a gambling club. The impression is strengthened when Ivor plays a favourite joke, used before in *Party*, of two women wearing identical dresses at a social function. The play was really an occasion for Lilian Braithwaite to show the practised ease with which she could transform the flimsiest trifles into an evening of gracious entertainment, like a glass of champagne enjoyed for its fleeting sparkle and then forgotten.

Full House began its run in the August of 1935. Although it had fair success in London and the provinces it was overshadowed by a production which had taken place a few months previously and which originated from Richard Rose's conversation with Ivor about a musical play. One of Ivor's closest collaborators in this venture, which is the subject of the next chapter, was a young man by the name of Christopher Hassall whom he had met early in 1934 and engaged as his understudy in a tour of *Proscenium*. Hassall, brother of Joan, later a distinguished engraver, was the son of John, the artist who, although he produced many other accomplished works, remains best-known for the famous poster of an elderly fisherman skipping vigorously above the caption 'Skegness is so bracing'. Christopher had not long since departed reluctantly from Oxford, where his English literature tutor was Lord David Cecil, and been obliged to scrape a living on the stage for which his obvious good looks seemed to fit him. Ivor heard him (it is said) humming a tune by Fauré as he wandered down a corridor in the Globe Theatre. He recognised the melody and was intrigued enough to give Hassall a small part in *Murder in Mayfair*.

They were on tour with *Proscenium* in Oxford when Ivor was injured by a piece of stage machinery and the call went out for the understudy. Hassall was appalled and confessed to the stage manager that he wasn't at all sure he even knew his words. Fortunately Ivor decided to go on and the unwilling Hassall was saved from an ordeal which would certainly have found him wanting. Ivor forgave him since he was the only member of the *Proscenium* cast who knew anything about music, a subject they often discussed for hours on end. It was Ivor who introduced him to the music of William Walton and early Schoenberg. More practically, Ivor gave the struggling young actor an overcoat and three shirts, a lurid bottle-green in colour, which he had acquired in Hollywood but which he thought a little 'arty' for the provinces. On tour he always ensured that Hassall got at least one square meal a day.

News of Ivor's accident brought an anxious Eddie Marsh to Oxford. Having found out that the damage was not serious, Eddie retired to his hotel room and busied himself with the proofs of Winston Churchill's *Marlborough* which he was currently engaged on 'diabolising'. Around midnight Ivor called him down for a cold supper to meet Christopher Hassall. The twenty-two-year-old boy had written some poetry which the connoisseur Eddie, he explained, might like to see. Eddie walked into the room 'planting his feet with gingerly deliberateness, keeping them close together, not turning out the toes, as if practising some orthopaedic exercise,' Hassall remembered. The thick eyebrows shot up, the voice fluttered, the eye-glass dangled. At odd intervals he took out his watch and consulted it worriedly. For reasons of health his doctor had restricted him to one cigarette every forty minutes. When the vital moment arrived he squeezed his cigarette into a blunt little holder and enquired: 'Ivor, isn't there any port?'

Next day he lunched alone with Christopher and they found they both had a taste for eighteenth-century poetry. Later the young man visited Gray's Inn with some of his own poems. Eddie glanced at them and impulsively caught at his guest's hand: 'Dear boy,' he said, 'you're a poet.'

Gradually he drew out the shy would-be poet's story, how he'd been forced to leave Oxford through lack of money, how he had literary ambitions, how he lived from week to week as a reluctant actor, and how he lodged in an attic over a Kensington shoe-shop at 17/6 a week. Next day Eddie lunched with David Cecil, another of his many friends, and heard favourable things about the latter's former pupil. Soon Eddie was calling his protégé 'Chris' and writing to Ivor: 'He doesn't seem very happy on the stage, do you think he is cut out for it? Of course his heart is set on writing – but that won't earn him a living, at any rate not for some time. *How* difficult life is, is it not?'

Some of the 'murder money' was discreetly handed over and Chris became a frequent visitor at Gray's Inn where he sat up late talking poetry and literature and retiring at last to sleep in the bed Rupert Brooke had occupied, an item of furniture reverentially spoken of as 'Rupert's bed'. Eddie was enchanted with Chris. Like Rupert, like

Ivor, he was very handsome with his dark hair and sympathetic smile, and, equally important, he had talent. As often happens with elderly queens in this situation, Eddie wanted to take Chris under his wing and unofficially to 'adopt' him as his son. Always respectful of social convention, he took care to meet the Hassall parents at what Chris described as 'a strange and touching encounter'. In his diary Eddie noted simply: 'John Hassall's studio has not been dusted for 39 years.'

Another grand passion had come into his life. So it had into Ivor's, and while the discovery of Chris was to give Eddie all the familiar and unselfish pleasure of grooming fresh talent, it supplied Ivor with a collaborator who soon became one of his best-loved friends.

Part Four

GLAMOROUS NIGHTS

'Ivor Novello said to me at lunch, "It's obvious, James, that musical comedy bores you stiff. Would you like me to write to your editor asking him not to send charming Mr Agate, whom we all adore, to musical pieces which he dislikes and doesn't understand?" The trouble is that I understand too well both the disease and the cause . . . The essence of your musical play is tears in waltz-time.'

James Agate

1

DRURIOLANUS

'*Drury Lane, Theatre Royal* First theatre opened on 7 May, 1663, as
Theatre Royal . . . Capacity: 2,247 . . . Stage: 42' wide × 80' deep.'

Diana Howard: *London Theatres & Music Halls, 1850-1950*

AMONG THE characters of a Somerset Maugham short story there is a
gentleman of saintly appearance and benevolent mien. His hair is a
distinguished grey, he has a gentle manner and he speaks as if confer-
ring a blessing on his hearers. You would think he was a bishop at
least. He turns out to be a card-sharper by trade. In the same way
no one could possibly have thought that Harry M. Tennent was a
man of the theatre. To judge from his bird-like air and reflective way
of speech he might have been a professor. On the other hand his very
straight back and trim tall frame suggested a retired soldier, though
one of cultured interests. He was, in fact, a composer and had written
popular songs, including one for the American crooner Rudy Vallee,
and was later to set lyrics by Christopher Hassall. After working for
Broadwood's, the piano firm, he joined Moss Empires and then
Howard & Wyndham, the producing company which specialised in
theatrical tours. At first nights he wore a dinner jacket of elderly vintage and a tie which was never quite straight. Actors and producers
liked him because he was a man of honour and because his advice
was sound. A deceptive air of helplessness made people anxious to
help him. Each morning he hopefully tackled *The Times* crossword
and, nearly always, relied on friends to come to his assistance and
finish it for him.

In the nineteen-thirties he set up his own production firm. H. M.
Tennent Ltd., the M being his second name of Moncrieff, and took
into partnership a young man called Hugh Beaumont, or 'Binkie' as
his mother used to call him. Although Harry was an Eton and Oxford
man and his partner the illegitimate son of a Welsh timber merchant,
it was Binkie who supplied the driving force that made H. M.
Tennent the most powerful organisation of its kind between the late
nineteen-thirties and the mid nineteen-sixties. Binkie once lived in

the same Cardiff street as Ivor and had known him when they were lads. At the age of twelve, already stage-struck, he began as a call-boy at the Cardiff Prince of Wales Theatre and learned very fast. He had the eyes of a poker player, cold and icy blue, and they were never more expressionless than when he was conducting one of those intricate negotiations at which he excelled. His skin was very white and he always dressed immaculately in suits of light grey or dark blue, the ties an impeccable match, unlike those of Harry Tennent. His quick brain was powered by long draughts of revoltingly weak China tea, often stone-cold, and by Du Maurier cigarettes – the empty packs were useful for making notes which he later passed on to his secretary so that she could type the innumerable letters he sent.

While Harry concerned himself with the firm's property interests Binkie looked after artists and contracts. The office was at the top of the Globe Theatre in cramped quarters reached by a tiny lift almost as fearsome as the one that led up to Ivor's flat over the Strand. Many stars of the time profited from Binkie's flair and organising skill. For the less well established it helped if you were male, good-looking and young, since his taste inclined to men and he had the power, if denied, to keep you out of the charmed West End circle. He was, indeed, a formidable character and he terrified people. Donald Sinden tells the story of a hopeful actor who had been interviewed by one of H. M. Tennent's executives and who afterwards entered the tiny lift and shut the gate. No sooner had he done so than it rattled open again and Binkie himself appeared. As the lift jerked downwards the actor respectfully flattened himself against the wall, hardly daring to breathe in the presence of the great man whose nose almost touched his. They reached, at last, the ground, and the actor squeezed ahead to open the door of the foyer. Outside a chauffeur waited beside a car. 'Can I give you a lift anywhere?' enquired Binkie graciously. The actor, at the end of his tether, stammered: 'N-no thank you – but that is unkindly common of you.'

H. M. Tennent Ltd. had already been associated with Ivor in *Proscenium* and *Murder in Mayfair*. Harry often met Ivor socially and, as one composer to another, talked music to him. In 1934 Harry found himself general manager of the Theatre Royal in Drury Lane. The old place was in a bad way. *Cavalcade* had been the last play capable of filling its huge auditorium, and although the pantomimes Harry commissioned from Julian Wylie did good business no one yet had found anything else that pulled crowds during the other nine months of the year. Noël Coward was too busy with other things to attempt a successful repeat of *Cavalcade*. Perhaps, thought Harry, Ivor might have some ideas.

They lunched together at The Ivy, then a preserve of the theatrical profession, where Ivor, known as 'The Guv', Noël as 'The Master', and Binkie as 'The Boss', always had a right, along with other important persons, to the best tables in an area known as the Royal Circle. These faced the door while the rest were allotted in a descending scale of priority to lesser breeds. On that day Harry looked more lugubrious than ever and resembled, Ivor thought, a picture of a llama which hung on the wall of his Strand flat and revealed to the world a neck of considerable length topped by a long mournful visage. Over coffee Harry lamented the state of Drury Lane and bewailed the lack of good musicals from America.

'What do you expect if you persist in going to America for plays?' said Ivor. 'Now, if you'd asked me . . .'

'And why should I ask you?'

'Well, I've got plans for Drury Lane,' replied Ivor, who up to that moment had not had a single notion in his head.

'Do you mean to tell me that you have a play which would suit?'

'Well, I've got an idea.'

As Ivor later told MacQueen Pope, who then handled publicity for Drury Lane and H. M. Tennent Ltd., that moment resembled the instant when, it is said, a drowning man sees his whole life pass in review before him, except that, in Ivor's case, what flashed through his mind was a kaleidoscope of all the musical plays he had ever seen.

'Let me hear it then.'

'Are you really interested?' said Ivor, playing for time. 'Well, you know, it's difficult to tell it in cold blood.'

Having gained a few seconds to put in order what few ideas he had, he launched impromptu on the outline of a plot. It would be a mixture of operetta, musical play, melodrama, spectacle and romance. The setting would be an exotic Ruritanian kingdom and the heroine a gypsy-born prima donna who was mistress of the monarch. Ivor did not know much about politics, least of all the foreign variety, but even he had heard about Magda Lupescu, at that time the unpopular *maîtresse-en-titre* of the Rumanian King Carol. He visualised an assassination attempt, a rebellion, a spectacular shipwreck that would give scope for the machinery at Drury Lane, and a gypsy wedding. For good measure he threw in a climax that featured the marvellous new invention of television.

In the full flood of fantasy he went on to demand a large orchestra, a big cast of revolutionaries, palace guards and gypsies, and all the lavish staging Drury Lane could provide. He lit another cigarette and asked breathlessly: 'Will it do?'

Harry, wide-eyed, said: 'It sounds just like it.' Abruptly he recovered from the spell of Ivor's enthusiasm. 'Of course, I can't say yes myself,' he added cautiously. 'I must put it to the board. When can I have it on paper?'

'Oh, tomorrow,' said Ivor nonchalantly.

As he went back to The Flat his elation dissolved into a state of terror. What had he let himself in for?

Then he collected his thoughts together and started writing a synopsis. It was not, in the end, very much different from what he had regaled Harry Tennent with over lunch. The hero he visualised was Anthony Allen, inventor of a new television system which no one seems anxious to finance. Anthony disappears for a while and goes on a pleasure cruise to the land of Krasnia. (The language spoken is a peculiar form of English in reverse, according to notices at the Krasnian opera house which read 'ON GNIKOMS'.) The political situation there looks difficult: King Stefan VIII is infatuated with his beautiful mistress, the prima donna Militza Hajos, while his villainous prime minister, Lydyeff, is plotting a revolution which will overthrow the monarchy and give himself dictatorial powers. Lydyeff knows that Militza is his real enemy, for if he can eliminate her then the pliable King Stefan will easily be made to abdicate. Anthony Allen spends an evening at the première of a new operetta starring Militza. He sees a man in the audience take out a gun and aim at the singer. Fortunately he jostles the man's arm and the shot goes wide. A grateful Militza hears the story of his invention from him and gives him a large cheque to help develop it. The scheming Lydyeff now appears and tells Militza that she must leave the country immediately on the instructions of King Stefan. Outside angry crowds are demonstrating and singing a revolutionary song. Militza steps on to the balcony and replies defiantly with the Krasnian national anthem. She tells Lydyeff that she is off for a brief trip on the *Silver Star*, the ship carrying Anthony Allen, and will be back for the next performance of her operetta. On board she comes across Anthony who warns her of his suspicion that there is a conspiracy to murder her. They are about to put off for the shore when a bomb explodes and the *Silver Star* begins to sink. Somehow they struggle to dry land, the ship having subsided on a mud-bank, and during their ordeal the two castaways fall in love. Militza is a gypsy by birth and when they come to a Romany encampment they are married in traditional ceremony by exchanging their blood. While their love flourishes the prime minister in Krasnia works on King Stefan to persuade him to abdicate. Without the support of Militza's strong character Stefan is lost. Lydyeff threatens to shoot him if he has not signed the abdication document by the time he has counted up to ten. Lydyeff reaches the fatal number and a shot is heard. But it is Lydyeff, not the King, who falls dead, and his executioner is Anthony who has once again come to the rescue. Militza arrives leading a band of loyal followers who have defeated Lydyeff's revolutionaries and ensured the survival of the monarchy. Stefan now sees that Militza is indispensable to him and offers to make her his queen. She, sacrificing her love of Anthony for love of country, accepts the proposal. A grateful Stefan promises Anthony all the money he needs to make his invention a success, the only proviso being that the first picture shown on the screen should be of Militza. The hero recognises that patriotism is greater than love and nobly renounces her.

Having put together this glorious farrago Ivor thought hard about a title for it. He needed something short but something also that would convey the idea of romance, excitement, mystery. A word much in vogue at the time, though old of origin, was 'glamour'. It stood for enchantment or a magical spell, it suggested alluring charm. And when were glamorous things most likely to happen? Not during the obvious glare of daytime but at night, of course! Put the two things together and you have *Glamorous Night*.

The synopsis, which he had prepared in twenty-four hours, went off to the Drury Lane board and Ivor, having risen as usual around midday, waited anxiously for the expected telephone call. When it came he heard Harry Tennent relaying the news that all was well and that the board had given him a totally free hand. Ivor always believed that it was the title above all which influenced the decision.

Within a fortnight he had completed the script. He still needed someone to write the lyrics of the songs and he thought of Christopher Hassall as a collaborator. The poet, a little disturbed at being picked out, was summoned to drink coffee. Had he ever written any lyrics for plays before? No, he had not. He had, to tell the truth, only seen one musical play in his life. Never mind, he was told, that was all to the good since he would not be hampered by convention, and anyway he knew quite a lot about music. Ivor dug out a bit of crumpled paper and gave it to him. On it was the melodic line of a tune. 'See if you can get the words "Glamorous Night" into it,' he ordered.

Chris obliged with the words 'Deep in my heart', which are attached to the lingering anacrusis introducing the famous tune, and ended, giving double value, 'Magical Night! Glamorous Night!' Ivor was delighted: he had found his lyricist, and from then onwards an incessant stream of music manuscript flowed in the direction of the attic where Chris lived. He ate when he could, drank Guinness for nourishment and tea for refreshment, and smoked ceaselessly. He also cut himself often while shaving. 'When,' asked Ivor, 'are you going to bring me a lyric not covered with Guinness, tea and blood?'

Sometimes Ivor would try out melodies at the piano with Chris in attendance, rejecting or preserving as a result of discussion together. There were occasions when Chris could think of no words at all. A slow waltz tune defeated him completely until Ivor suddenly thought of 'Fold your wings', after which the refrain came with ease. Another writer's block emerged at the number that became 'Shine though my dreams'. No one could provide a verse for this *Tosca*-inspired motif. One day at Brighton Ivor had a sudden idea: 'I've just thought of a scrumptious title – do write it down – "Shine Through My Dreams".'

In the second week of October, 1934, Eddie Marsh was the first person to hear Ivor read aloud the script of *Glamorous Night*. He was supremely happy that Ivor and Chris were enjoying a successful collaboration but he felt anxious about the play. His approach was that of the scholar, the literary man, and he applied the rules of logic and artistic convention to what he heard. In a scene that was often repeated he would protest: 'Really, Ivor, you simply *can't* say that!' Ivor, the instinctive showman, would smile and reply: 'But the extraordinary thing is, Eddie, I can.' Usually he was proved right, for he knew much more than Eddie about effective curtain lines and dramatic situations.

Eddie was not the only one to offer well-meant advice. Mam often intervened with ideas of her own and at Redroofs weekends she enjoyed outlining her forceful views on the many ways in which *Glamorous Night* could be improved. One night, after an especially long tirade, Ivor took Chris aside and mumured; 'Don't ever listen to what Mam says. Follow your own instinct. That's what I've always done.'

The lyrics Chris produced were excellent of their kind. In this case words must fit the music well and, simple enough to be quickly absorbed and understood among all the distractions of what is passing on stage, must at the same time have a certain poetry about them. A good example of this is the chorus he wrote for the gypsy wedding scene which begins 'Gods of the gale and the wild flowing stream'. For the blues number he evolved a skilful pastiche, 'Shanty Town, my heart is callin'', and in the love songs he evoked a light sentimental strain that deftly avoided excess. There were moments, too, when he showed an ironic wit not at all usual in musical comedy, as in the chorus sung by the Palace Guards:

> Princes of Destiny,
> Guards of the Commonweal,
> The latest thing in sex-appeal . . .

Critics tend to forget that a composer who works in the theatre is not writing a sonata or a symphony. The music he composes is intended to be theatrically effective, and for that it has a rôle to play as much as the scenery, the costumes and the acting. It can only be properly judged when heard in its context. No music could be more theatrical, in the correct sense of the word, than Ivor's. The sweep of the melodies is generous and unforced, the flow of tune is spontaneous and directly appealing. It came across the footlights with an impact that went immediately to the heart of the matter. Perhaps the secret of Ivor's skill lies in the way he adroitly combines all the traditional elements of Edwardian musical comedy with something that is uniquely his own. Thus the Palace Guards' Chorus mentioned above turns into an obligatory march as hale and hearty as the Robbers' Chorus in *Chu Chin Chow*. The *valse lente* of 'Fold your wings' looks back to the popular works of Sydney Baynes, a composer of waltzes that were heard often in ballrooms at the turn of the century. Yet the idiom is transformed by Ivor's very personal touch. Everywhere there are signs of his musical background. The introduction to the Palace Guards' Chorus includes poignant harmonies that might have been written by Fauré, and Militza's 'When the gypsy played' turns into an allegro moderato which descends from Brahms of the *Hungarian Dances* and Liszt of the *Rhapsodies*. At the end of Act I the audience sees Militza in the première of her new operetta where the music takes on the expansive lushness of a Puccini.

The same artful blend of old and new characterises the plot. This is, in effect, little more than the conventional Drury Lane formula of romance and spectacle. Yet while there was plenty to amaze – carriages drawn by real horses, a foundering ship and scenes that utilised for once the whole extent of Drury Lane's vast stage – there were novel factors that Ivor alone was responsible for introducing. The hero was not a dashing youth but a mature engineer who, moreover, did not live happily ever after with the heroine, but, at the end, in a mood of resignation gave her up for another. Even so, Ivor ensured himself a dramatic final curtain by appearing in a simple dark suit that stood out amid the blazing uniforms of the others, a solitary figure who dominated everyone else. Another innovation was the opening scene, now cut from the printed acting edition, which began, not with the expected flamboyant flourish, but with a view of quiet suburban streets to emphasise the hero's commonplace origins. There were, too, the novelty of television, something people then knew very little of, and the excitement of Militza's beautiful image flashed on a gigantic screen. Never had the substantial resources of Drury Lane, hydraulic lifts and all, been so ingeniously exploited as in *Glamorous Night*.

Ivor himself was to play the non-singing rôle of the hero. Other members of his troupe included two opera singers, Trefor Jones as the tenor who partners Militza in her operetta, and Olive Gilbert from the Carl Rosa touring company. She too sang in the operetta and was to appear in all his other musical plays. Minnie Rayner, an established member of Ivor's repertory company, had the comic part of Militza's maid, and Barry Jones played King Stefan. Another well-known actor, Lyn Harding, was engaged as Lydyeff. His mellow voice had won him Shakespearean rôles in the past, and his strong presence made him a natural 'heavy'. One of the characters, a black stowaway on the *Silver Star*, was interpolated for no other reason than that Ivor had recently heard Elizabeth Welch give her show-stopping performance of 'Solomon' in a production of Cole Porter's *Nymph Errant*. The indestructible Miss Welch, who was born in New York City and who settled over here in the nineteen-thirties, brought to 'Shanty Town' all the emotional power and urgency which have made her so vivid a figure in West End cabaret and theatre. She more than justified the quite extraneous addition Ivor made to Act II of *Glamorous Night* which consisted of a cabaret aboard ship with a rumba and, of all things, a skating waltz on deck. He had been awaiting the chance to use this latter for years, it having been originally composed in 1913 for his unproduced *The Fickle Jade*.

The biggest casting problem was that of Militza. Some months previously Ivor had seen Mary Ellis in a Cochran musical and had been struck not only by what Graham Greene once described as her 'dae-monic good looks' but also by her acting skill. In her dressing-room one evening she found an immense bouquet of lilies accompanied by a note bearing the signature of Ivor Novello. The name meant little to her, although she vaguely remembered something about 'Keep The Home Fires Burning'. The run of the musical ended and she began packing her bags for a two-year stay in Hollywood where she had been offered a Paramount contract. Just then the telephone rang. It was Ivor talking about his new play at Drury Lane. She was tempted but explained that she was about to leave for Hollywood. His seductive Welsh voice trilled relentlessly on: never mind, he would persuade the studio to let her come back in time for the opening, he would arrange everything with Paramount, her agent, Drury Lane. 'I felt I had no way of handling it, so I did what I still do, at stressful times – I relaxed completely, and let it happen if it could, and should,' Miss Ellis now recalls. Which it did.

She was born, of French and Spanish ancestry, in New York, and it is not surprising that she knew little of Ivor since her versatile career had up to then been largely confined to her native country. As a girl she discovered vocal talent that won her engagements at the Metropolitan Opera House where she made her debut in Puccini. There she sang with Geraldine Farrar in Charpentier's *Louise*, with Caruso in Donizetti's *L'Elisir d'Amore*, and with Chaliapin in Moussorgsky's *Boris Godunov*. Having distinguished herself in opera she took to the non-musical stage and became a member of the famous company run by the leading American actor David Belasco. With this brilliant showman she played New York and toured America in *The Merchant of Venice*. From Shakespeare she turned to musical comedy and sang the title role in the 1924 première of *Rose-Marie*. She then wearied of Broadway and returned to the 'straight' theatre with parts in Shakespeare, Chekhov and O'Neill. From the nineteen-thirties onward, being then married to the English actor Basil Sydney, she commuted between New York and London and gained a reputation in both capitals as an actress of accomplishment and beauty. Among her leading men was Owen Nares, a celebrated matinée idol of the time. Their popularity was shown by a feature in an illustrated magazine displaying photographs of them in romantic poses. It was coyly entitled 'The Gentle Art Of Making Love'.

Ten years after *Rose-Marie* C. B. Cochran told her she ought to be singing again and brought her back to music in one of his own pro-ductions. Ivor saw her and instantly decided that she and no one else would be the heroine of *Glamorous Night*. The deal was done and she set off for Hollywood to make a film with Carl Brisson, although she was not allowed to forget her next engagement: day by day big parcels arrived from London containing the latest instalment of the script and records of Ivor playing the numbers she was to sing. Each week, too, the postman delivered bundles of lyrics from Christopher Hassall for her to get by heart.

On the sea journey back from America she made herself word-perfect in the script. At Victoria Ivor awaited her and rushed her to Drury Lane where the whole cast assembled to welcome her with champagne. She was struck by 'the blaze, the excitement and the enthusiasm which Ivor created. He had complete faith in himself and what he was doing and in the people he had chosen to do it with him. Because of this, everyone felt bound to do their utmost for him. . . . Despite his huge success, he remained unspoiled. His mischievous grin, his acceptance of criticism, his unstinting praise of things that pleased him, counteracted any flaws in his personality. Highly emotional, non-intellectual, he had read everything, seen everything.' There was, at Redroofs, an unusually long sofa, big enough for Mary and Ivor to recline on it feet to feet and listen to the new records he had bought. At weekends, between rehearsals, they would lie there while the sound of Schoenberg, Richard Strauss, Mahler and Ravel filled the room. Mary became one of Ivor's closest women friends. She had little success in explaining to her puzzled mother just why their association could not have a romantic ending.

Having assembled his cast and secured the leading lady of his dreams, Ivor engaged as director the German-born Leontine Sagan with whom he had already worked on *Murder in Mayfair*. He had seen her production of *Children in Uniform* and thought her one of London's finest directors. She was at first, or claimed to be, uneasy at the thought of doing a big musical show. 'You will have to tell me all about it,' she said, 'as I really know nothing about this aspect of the theatre.' Her modesty was needless. She soon demonstrated a genius for organising and shaping the crowd-movements which were an important part of *Glamorous Night*, and she was pitiless when rehearsing the effect she wanted. 'Why do you do it like that?' she would demand of an actor. 'You are such a stupid man – you do such stupid things. I have shown you time and again – still you are stupid.' When the thing was at last done properly she erupted into praise as lavish as her rebukes had been devastating. Her moods varied from the dove-like to the tigrish. Her voice, depending on her temper, could be sweet or rasping. The cast, who treated her with a fearful respect, nicknamed her 'Madame Hitler'.

The Drury Lane management kept their word and allowed Ivor to spend money freely. Miss Sagan travelled abroad to study ideas for Krasnian dress and returned with all sorts of notions and crates of costumes as well. Her companion on the trip was Oliver Messel, the artist who had recently designed a string of famous Cochran revues. For *Glamorous Night* he conceived a lavishly baroque opera house, a glittering palace, a rock-girt gypsy encampment, and a ballroom with soaring pillars and rich drapes. His must surely have been the most rococo imagination ever to survive schooling at Eton.

Rehearsals continued over a period of five weeks. The first night was scheduled for 2 May, 1935, and long before curtain-rise a flood of bouquets rolled in at the stage-door. Everyone sent everyone else a telegram, and Ivor, who never missed a detail, even sent one to his publicity manager. While the celebrities, who had come to look at each other, gathered in the foyer, Ivor slipped in quietly at the back door. He was calm and a little subdued, although, as he afterwards confessed, his hands trembled with emotion.

For once theatrical superstition was proved wrong. Rehearsals, though exhausting, had gone well and the première went even better. Ivor's first entrance evoked a tornado of cheers and clapping, and the mood of the audience continued enthusiastic for the rest of the evening. The mob stoned Militza's villa with bloodcurdling energy, the ship sank amid terrific explosions and a cloud of smoke, the gypsies curvetted in a blur of exhilaration, and, at the end, the glamorous image of Militza dominated the theatre. The curtain rose and fell many times. Enthralled by the beauty of Mary Ellis and her perfect roulades, by the dazzling spectacle and by the perfect illusion which Ivor had created, the audience called again and again for the man who had devised, written, composed and acted in *Glamorous Night*. He came forward, and, modestly, almost humbly, made a simple little speech of thanks which only served to increase the hysterical applause. He knew, as an astute showman, that there are times when you bang the drum and others when you let the audience do it for you.

Critics, in the main, were generous. *Glamorous Night* was doubtless punk, said one, but it was 'inspired punk'. Another remarked: 'If it is nonsense, it is glamorous nonsense, and for those who are ready to be entertained, it is the best show of its kind Drury Lane has had for years.' Even James Agate resigned himself to the ineffectiveness of critical opinion when faced with overwhelming popular acclaim such as *Glamorous Night* had achieved, and he contented himself with a breath-taking pun at the end of his remarks on the gypsy wedding scene: 'Mr Novello, making the best of lots of worlds, here gives us the best thing in the show, and the fact that the atmosphere is a little derivative should be put down to the Euclidean rule that composers truthfully setting the same thing must resemble one another. There is no reason why this rule should not apply to the gypsies of Borovnik, or why Mr Novello for his Borovnikian dances should not borrow din from *Prince Igor*.'

The ticket agencies picked up large blocks of seats and the box-office was faced with daily queues. Although the hot summer of 1935 tended to lower sales of cheaper seats, capacity bookings were soon reached and the production began to recover the expensive outlay to which Drury Lane had committed itself. Ivor made more out of it than the management. He received seven-and-a-half per cent on the first £3,500 of the takings and ten per cent on anything beyond that. Those were the terms of his contract as leading man. Since, as author and composer also, he was entitled to the same share, he regularly drew fifteen per cent and, in good times, as much as twenty per cent of the gross. Even if the management of Drury Lane were not doing so well as that, they were still indebted to Ivor for having put the theatre back on the map.

Soon after *Glamorous Night* opened King George V and Queen Mary celebrated their Jubilee. Ivor and Mary Ellis, leaning dangerously out of the windows of The Flat, were able to glimpse the royal procession with its coaches and bands marching through Aldwych and the Strand down below. That weekend, at Redroofs, a patriotic Mam arrayed in green velvet jumped to her feet every time she heard the National Anthem on the radio and hastened to drink a loyal toast from her glass of brandy. Since the familiar tune recurred at ten-minute intervals she was obliged, at the last, to remain beaming and red-faced in her seat.

Their Majesties later conferred prestige on *Glamorous Night* by attending one of the performances. Ivor and Mam were invited to a Royal Garden Party at Buckingham Palace.

'And you write the story and music and act the principal part yourself!' said the King. 'Don't you find it very tiring in this hot weather?'

'Not when *you're* in front, sir,' replied Ivor with the polished skill of a Ruritanian courtier.

'Well, I can tell you this,' the King went on in an exchange of dialogue which might have come from one of Ivor's own romantic plays. 'We enjoyed ourselves enormously, with one reservation – we could have wished a different ending. We found it a little sad, the Queen and I; in fact you made the Queen cry. Make the next one with a happy ending, please.'

Such was the accolade for a venture that rescued Drury Lane from bankruptcy and established Ivor as the theatrical phenomenon of his time. Eddie Marsh was overjoyed. The two people he loved most, Ivor and Chris, had won a success undreamed of. Throughout the various episodes which led up to *Glamorous Night* Eddie had been associated with every stage in its development. He was in touch with Ivor two or three times a day, he sat through the dress rehearsal until after midnight, and he spent hours afterwards at The Flat nearby. He was there until half-past four in the morning after the première and waited anxiously for the early editions of the newspapers so that he could read what the critics had to say. During the run of *Glamorous Night* he saw the play eight times, proudly noting at his last visit: 'Ivor and Mary gave of their best for my sake.' Whatever happened now, whatever failures or tragedies might lurk in the future, nothing could ever dim the triumph of that first night for Ivor. 'It was,' Eddie wrote, 'the night of his life.'

2

THE HAPPY HYPOCRITE

Mr Aeneas Is the expression exactly as your Lordship would wish?
Lord George It is scarcely a mirror of true love. It is too calm and
contemplative.

The Happy Hypocrite, Act II

GLAMOROUS NIGHT ran exuberantly throughout the summer and into
the autumn. It seemed that nothing could stop its progress. Every
night, and twice daily when there were matinées, the S.S. *Silver Star*
went under dramatically and the machinery at Drury Lane func-
tioned with a smoothness that gratified the Master Carpenter. 'I want
a scene where a big liner explodes and sinks in flames,' Ivor had
explained. 'All right,' said the Master Carpenter, a man not given to
eloquence, and he forthwith delivered exactly what was required.
Only once did things go wrong, and that was not the Master Carpenter's fault. The incident occurred when Ivor had to shoot Lyn
Harding who played the scheming prime minister, Lydyeff. Ivor,
loathing guns, would point the weapon vaguely in the direction of his
enemy and hope for the best. One evening he fired and Lydyeff
collapsed on the floor with a realistic shout of agony. There he lay, as
the script demanded, senseless and, apparently, dead. After the curtain fell Lydyeff rose clumsily to his feet and roared in the tones of an
anguished King Lear: 'Take that young man's gun away. He does not
know how to handle a rifle.' Because of frequent shooting a portion
of cartridge had worn loose and penetrated low down in the villain's
back. An X-ray showed that the jagged piece of metal was too near
the kidneys for an operation to retrieve it, and until the end of his
days Harding carried around with him this unique souvenir of
Glamorous Night. At subsequent performances Ivor always pointed
the gun in the air and shut his eyes.

The callboy in a theatre is usually the person who knows, from
the nature of his job, most of what is going on. He is always to hand,
in the corridors, in the dressing-rooms, everywhere behind the
scenes, hearing all that is said and much that is not. It was from the

124

Drury Lane callboy that Ivor first heard a disturbing rumour. What a pity, he was told, that the show had to come off.

Ivor was baffled. He asked the management for an explanation and learned that *Glamorous Night* was indeed to end before Christmas so that the annual pantomime could be put on. When the board of Drury Lane made their agreement with him they were not to foresee that this musical play would become so successful. Anything can happen in the theatre, and they had thought it prudent to hedge their bet by ensuring the one factor on which they knew from experience they could rely. Angry and bitterly disappointed, Ivor proposed to take a cut in his percentage of the receipts on condition that *Glamorous Night* ran until February of next year when Mary Ellis was committed to a Hollywood film. Then, in accordance with 'an idea I've long since cherished', he wrote to Jack Joel, chairman of Drury Lane, he suggested a spring production of *Romeo and Juliet* with himself and Edna Best. It would, he said, 'not only be extremely distinguished but a big popular success,' and what is more, Shakespeare having been dead for centuries, the author on this occasion would not be claiming royalties or a percentage of the gross. Ever since the mime episode in *Proscenium* Ivor had been obsessed with *Romeo and Juliet*. The suggestion was turned down. He was later able to exorcise his *idée fixe* quite harmlessly at a Shakepeare Matinée where he played the balcony scene with Jean Forbes-Robertson as Juliet.

He renewed his assault on Drury Lane with an offer guaranteeing any losses if *Glamorous Night* were allowed to run on into the next year. In addition, he continued, he would from his own resources cover the profits that might have been made on the pantomime. Both proposals were rejected. Ivor did not give up. If *Glamorous Night* was out of the question, he said, he would put forward ideas for a new show to be launched in the following year. With his usual speed he assembled a spectacle which he entitled *Careless Rapture* and, accompanied by Christopher Hassall who wrote the lyrics, went round to play the score and act the dialogue for the benefit of the Drury Lane board. It was a mournful occasion from the very start. As Chris distributed copies of the lyrics among the assembled businessmen he felt, he afterwards said, like a verger handing out hymn books at a memorial service. The atmosphere, bleak and unfriendly, was as if a corpse lay in the next room and as if no one there had been mentioned in the will. All Ivor's jokes fell flat and his music was heard in silence. Grimly he pressed on to the end. Then he picked up his papers and left, vexed, his pride wounded. Harry Tennent rang him later that day. Drury Lane did not want *Careless Rapture*.

Ivor tried to forget the disappointment in his other numerous activities. He supervised the preparation and rehearsals of his new play *Full House* which has been described in the previous chapter. When timings allowed, the cast of *Glamorous Night* attended a performance of *Full House* as Ivor's guests, and, in a return of compliments, the players in the latter visited a matinée of the former. Another project which helped to allay his regret over *Careless Rapture* was a dramatisation of Max Beerbohm's story *The Happy Hypocrite*. While still an undergraduate at Oxford Beerbohm had evolved a theory which shaped the rest of his life. He believed that the human personality is a mere bundle of unorganised impulses. A man needs therefore to adopt a mask which represents his ideal, his notion of what, so far as his abilities and limitations allow, he might aim to be. His life will acquire beauty and meaning if he consistently acts up to the ideal of the mask, and over the years his personality will absorb its qualities so that the face he presents to the world will be the man himself. This, as we have seen, is what Ivor did when, early on, he determined to create a personality which should be consistently charming and benevolent. Soon these qualities were second nature to him, and, just as a carefully nurtured attitude of irony protected Max from unwelcome things, Ivor's charm shielded him and enabled him to enjoy the sort of existence he wanted for himself.

The mask theory provides the basis of *The Happy Hypocrite*. The tale is a pastoral set in Regency days and is told with lightness and delicacy. The beautiful dancer Jenny Mere catches the eye of Lord George Hell, a wicked and debauched nobleman. He falls in love with her, but, since his face is ugly, deformed with horrible passions and likely to repel her, he puts on a saintly mask for his wooing. After she has fallen in love with him the mask is stripped away. It reveals, not his old repulsive self, but a visage as saintly as the mask. By assuming virtue Lord George has in time achieved it. A friend once discussed the tale with Max and said to him: 'It would be easy, if by just putting on a mask of goodness and a mask of beauty, you could achieve both.' 'But oh,' Max replied, 'you have to live up to the mask, you know. Lord George lived up to his mask. His love for Jenny made it possible for him to do it. If you live up to a good mask long enough, don't you know, perhaps it will become first nature to you instead of second or third.'

In 1900 Max had written a one-act version of *The Happy Hypocrite* which Mrs Patrick Campbell used as a curtain-raiser. It was not

Ivor in the film of *The Rat*, 1925

Gladys Cooper as Ivor first knew her

Ivor with Madeleine Carroll in
Sleeping Car

Ivor in his early twenties

Constance Collier

Ivor in *Perchance to Dream*, 1945

Ivor's favourite photo of himself

Eddie Marsh in old age

Ivor with Vanessa Lee

Ivor shortly before his death (*Camera Press*)

Ivor as Shakespeare's *Henry V*

Portrait by Angus McBean, London

unsuccessful, and having laboured as a reluctant drama critic himself, Max was amused to find his work on the wrong side of the footlights. 'The public, after all, is the *final court of appeal*,' he observed, relishing the irony. 'The public is on my side.'

Thirty-six years later Clemence Dane turned the story into a three-act play. Her collaborator was Richard Addinsell who provided the incidental music. He had earlier deserted law, which he read at Oxford, to become a composer of theatre and film music. His 'Warsaw Concerto', originally played in the movie *Dangerous Moonlight*, is still often heard, and its pastiche of Rachmaninov is the work of an ingenious musician. Clemence Dane, a pseudonym of the author Winifred Ashton, wrote many novels and plays in her time, one of them at least, *Will Shakespeare*, deserving revival. Everything about her in priviate life was large, her figure, her presence, and the voluminous gowns that enveloped her majestic amplitude. At her flat in Covent Garden she entertained a wide circle of friends, among them Ivor and Noël Coward. She was prized by Noël for what he lovingly called 'Winifred's Garden of Bloomers', a never-ending series of double-meanings which peppered her conversation but which were uttered with seemingly complete innocence. 'It is well known,' she boomed in a crowded Old Vic foyer, 'that Shakespeare sucked Bacon dry.' She assured a friend worried about the plight of goldfish in a pool exposed to the blazing sun: 'Oh, they're all right now! They've got a vast erection covered with ever-lasting pea!' On a weekend at Binkie Beaumont's country house she greeted her host with: 'Oh the pleasure of waking up to see a row of tits outside your window.' While dining with the Governor of Jamaica and his lady she remarked of a mutual acquaintance: 'Do you remember the night we all had Dick on toast?' This partiality of hers for the idiom of outdated schoolgirl slang made her the original, whether she knew it or not, of the medium Madame Arcati in Noël's *Blithe Spirit*.

Usually she managed to retain her 'Bloomers' within the limits of everyday conversation, but there were times when they ran over into her novels and she could write: 'He stretched out and grasped the other's gnarled, stumpy tool.' A keen painter and sculptress, she later took up clay modelling and encouraged her friends to practise the art with her. She gave joyous instruction on how to manipulate the skewers, knitting needles and other necessary impedimenta: 'You must wipe your tool! You cannot work with a dirty tool! Now then, stick it right up, ram it, ram it and work away, either from the back or the front, whichever comes easiest! Some people use a lubricant, I've used honey in my time! And remember, when you've finished you must withdraw it wig-gle wag-gle, wig-gle wag-gle, ve-ry ve-ry gently.' Another of her achievements, and not a minor one, lay in persuading Noël Coward to read the Bible. The language of the King James version was magnificent, she assured him. He obeyed her advice, and for weeks afterwards the playwright, more to be associated with the fleshpots of Shaftesbury Avenue than with the asperities of the Old Testament, sat up in bed drinking Bournvita and poring over the news from Gath.

Clemence Dane's play of *The Happy Hypocrite* was, like every-thing else she wote, effective and workmanlike. It held a double appeal for Ivor, first because of the mask theory which coincided with his own experience, and second because the rôle of Lord George Hell gave him an excellent acting opportunity. He was perpe-tually irritated by people claiming that without his good looks he would never have succeeded on the stage, and as Lord George he thought he could prove them wrong. For the part of Lord George's mistress he engaged Isabel Jeans,* and for Jenny Mere he chose a young actress whose dark hair and fine-cut beauty made her an exquisite heroine. At his suggestion she changed her name to Vivien Leigh. He lavished great pains on the hideous appearance of the character he played. At no time did he wear a complete mask. In later scenes he used three different half-masks which left mouth and chin free, and for the most part he relied on a complicated make-up and nose-tubes to present the red-faced and bloated lord. His publicity manager was horrified by the transformation and asked him why he was deliberately obscuring the famous profile that had won him so many admirers. 'You've said it,' Ivor laughed. 'There'll come a day when the profile won't be so maddeningly perfect, when I shall no longer be young – and I don't want to give up acting. So I'm going to prepare the public for it by degrees. See, duckie?'

Max Beerbohm was charmed out of his Italian exile and brought over to one of the rehearsals. At a press conference in the dress-circle bar of His Majesty's where the play had been scheduled to open he delighted everyone with the stories he told so well, so wittily and

---

* She died in 1985 at the age of ninety-three. Apart from a brief spell in Hollywood she never deserted the area of Shaftesbury Avenue, where her talent for the nuances of comedy and for 'placing' a line made her, said *The Times*, 'one of an aristocracy of players'.

often a shade indiscreetly. Then, as he was about to leave, he turned round and disappointed all the journalists by remarking: 'Of course, gentlemen, nothing I have said is for publication. You understand that, don't you?'

He came to the first night in Easter Week, 1936, standing rather apart from the crowd and looking, someone said, 'in it but not of it', and quite happy to be outshone by Mam with her silver hair and grey gown and cloak of velvet. Ivor acted extremely well and showed, for once, that he need not rely entirely on his profile. There were those, indeed, who thought that he gave the best performance of his career. Under the headline 'An Easter Garland', James Agate wrote: 'Mr Novello plays Lord George with great sincerity. His make-up for the first act is very effective and exactly gives the note of Caligula with a touch of Sir John Falstaff. He acts all the latter part of the play with a disarming simplicity; to have such a profile and pretend not to know it would write him down as an artist of enormous sensibility. It is a beautiful performance throughout.'

Ivor could act! It was a revelation the critics found hard to bear, but they took it manfully and did not hesitate to agree. On the one occasion, however, when critical opinion was unanimously favourable, the public thought otherwise. *The Happy Hypocrite* ran for a few weeks and then had to close. The only person not to be surprised was Max Beerbohm.

3

EARTHQUAKE WEATHER

'Be here at ten o'clock on Thursday morning, they're delivering the earthquake.'

Ivor to Dorothy Dickson at rehearsals of *Careless Rapture*

BOBBIE ANDREWS always thought that *The Happy Hypocrite* was the best thing Ivor had ever done. It cost a lot of money with its fanciful scenery, costumes, large cast and orchestra, but if it brought him little cash it earned him a great deal of credit. A short while before the play closed he and Bobbie went to a matinée of *Rise and Shine*, the piece which Drury Lane had chosen to succeed their pantomime. At the interval Ivor slipped backstage. When he returned he whispered to Bobbie: 'Guess what! They've offered me the Lane for *Careless Rapture*.'

The theatre resembles politics in that today's master can be tomorrow's suppliant, and as both activities depend on the public's favour situations are apt to be reversed with startling speed. Having rejected *Careless Rapture* out of hand Drury Lane now discovered that *Rise and Shine* was not fulfilling the promise of its title. The doomed play had a run of forty-four performances only, and to save the theatre from going dark once again the management called on Ivor. This time, he resolved, he would be in full control. The financial responsibility would have to be largely his, and, through his private company, he agreed to meet seventy-five per cent of the production and running costs, profits to be shared in proportion. Ivor Novello, the romantic hero, was also Ivor Novello the realistic businessman: there was to be no flat rate for his services as composer and actor, and he insisted on a sliding scale according to the gross. Every detail was carefully listed, even down to the wording on posters which should read:

In Association with Theatre Royal, Drury Lane Ltd.,
Ivor Novello
Presents
Careless Rapture

While rehearsals were going on the billing was to be:

In Active Preparation
Careless Rapture
Devised Written and Composed by
Ivor Novello.

Every economy, he stipulated, should be practised, especially concerning the orchestra, which at rehearsal consumes vast amounts of money when kept waiting around. If the orchestra was retained unnecessarily, warned Ivor, it would be 'over *my dead body*'.

He came back, like visiting royalty, to Drury Lane and was hailed everywhere as 'Guv'nor'. Minnie Rayner joined him and so did other faces from *Glamorous Night*, among them Olive Gilbert and Peter Graves. Having had a small part in the earlier musical Graves was now promoted to Ivor's understudy and from time to time played the leading rôle. His father was Henry Algernon Claud, seventh Baron Graves, whom he succeeded as eighth holder of the title. He worked, at first, in an estate agent's office but then decided, rightly, that the theatre offered a likelier opening for his debonair talent. Dorothy Dickson was reunited with Ivor as his leading lady, and he wrote in a part for his friend Zena Dare. Once more the presence of Leontine Sagan brooded over the stage at Drury Lane, terrifying the cast with her rages and as often calming them with words of extravagant praise.

Ivor had found his title in those lines of Browning:

That's the wise thrush; he sings each song twice over,
Lest you should think he never could recapture
The first fine careless rapture!

His plot he had distilled from a riotous imagination guided by instinct for what would make a good stage picture. An Englishwoman travelling in China had recently been kidnapped by bandits, and for weeks the newspapers were full of speculation about what had become of her. Very well then, he would use this topical item as he had used Madame Lupescu for *Glamorous Night*, and he would have the hero and heroine of *Careless Rapture* seized by wicked Chinese thugs. Was not China the place where they often had earthquakes? He would go one better than the sinking ship in his first musical play and would stage an earthquake. Now China was also the country of pagodas and temples where mysterious rites were held, and that would give him an opportunity for at least one big scene, a willow-pattern setting in white, that could do duty as the final act. China was doubly topical, for Lehár's operetta *The Land of Smiles* had recently established itself as a popular draw. How, though, was he to get his characters to China?

The story he evolved to bring this about featured the impetuous young Michael who falls in love with a stage singer called Penny. She is, however, already engaged to Sir Rodney, a well-off businessman and none other than the half-brother of Michael, the latter, it must be added, an illegitimate child, 'a happy bastard' as the *Tatler* facetiously called him in its review. Michael lives abroad on an allowance paid by a family anxious to keep his existence dark and is only permitted to stay in England for short spells. He sees Penny at her farewell performance, gets her to elope with him, and whisks her off to Hampstead Heath for the fun of the fair. Sir Rodney tracks them down and tells Penny of Michael's true identity. The boy, he thunders, has forfeited his inheritance because he has stayed too long in England. The next act takes us to China. Why? Because Sir Rodney is sponsoring an exhibition there and Penny is taking the lead in an amateur production of *The Rose Girl*, her big hit. Michael turns up disguised as a Chinese prince (a tilt at *The Land of Smiles*) and is recognised by Penny who thereupon faints. Nature replies with an earthquake which devastates the town where they have been staying. They escape in the company of Sir Rodney and are captured by bandits. After much plot and counter-plot Michael and Penny make their getaway and leave the wicked brother still in the hands of their captors. They come back to the town and are married in splendour on the Bridge of Lovers.

So full of enthusiasm was Ivor for *Careless Rapture* that he determined to sing in it. A teacher of voice production came to give him lessons in his dressing-room whence there emerged as a result the most peculiar sounds. These coincided each day with children coming home from school to the block of artisans' dwellings that stand beside the theatre. When they heard the disjointed squawks ringing out across the yard their usual chatter was hushed and they stood and listened in wondering silence. Then they joined in with bloodcurdling howls of imitation that made Ivor realise it wasn't such a good idea after all. If he could not sing, he thought, then at least he could dance. During the scene where Michael and Penny fall asleep after their flight from the earthquake there is a Dream Ballet which enacts various legends against the background of an imposing Chinese temple. The early days of the run found Ivor cavorting around in an appalling costume of black trunks, leather armlets and welly boots that showed off his slim thighs. As a musician he knew enough about rhythm to keep time but otherwise the technique of ballet was foreign to him. After a few performances he gave up and sent on a professional dancer in his stead. 'All those old ladies out there thinking doesn't Ivor dance beautifully!' commented a malicious observer from the wings at one of the matinées. Until he withdrew, however, he adopted the same defence mechanism that he employed so successfully with Noël Coward. Anyone looking in at his dressing-room to comment on this outlandish performance would be greeted with a broad grin and the immediate remark: 'I *knew* you'd love it, ducky!'

The music of *Careless Rapture*, for which Chris Hassall wrote the lyrics, includes a singing lesson, that favourite standby often utilised in opera as well as in operetta. Ivor shaped the simplest of materials to produce a charming effect. Olive Gilbert had a song called 'Why Is There Ever Goodbye?', one of the best things in the score, a wistful refrain led up to by a carefully worked-out introduction with some ingenious modulations. Penny's big number, 'Music In May', goes with an attractive lilt and carries conviction as part of *The Rose Girl* operetta in which she is starring. She also sings 'Wait For Me', a humorous item that enables her to deplore, quite wittily, her unpunctual habits. The music for the ballets, one in *The Rose Girl* and the other in the Chinese temple, is spiced with harmonies that are picturesquely 'oriental' though bland enough not to frighten conventional ears. For the Hampstead Heath scene Ivor wrote a deft fantasia on Cockney songs that wove 'Knocked 'Em In The Old Kent Road' into the texture. A distinct curiosity is a dance called 'The Manchuko' which was performed during the Chinese scenes by Dorothy Dickson and Walter Crisham. The latter was an American dancer whose lean features and lissom form recalled Watteau's portrait of the melancholy Gilles. *Careless Rapture* introduced him to a fruitful career on the London stage, even though 'The Manchuko', a piece of exoticism intended to rival other speciality dances of the time like 'The Piccolino' and 'The Continental', never really made its mark. Mention of 'The Piccolino' situates *Careless Rapture* in its period as much as the names of two characters in *The Rose Girl*, who, inspired by contemporary slang, are listed as 'Lord Twirp' and 'Lady Twirp'.

Careless Rapture opened at Drury Lane in September, 1936, and reaped even greater acclaim than its predecessor. The curtain rose on a glittering beauty parlour, the epitome of nineteen-thirties chic, where Ivor as Michael has pursued his half-brother's reluctant fiancée. From there the action moved to the presentation of *The Rose Girl* in which long lines of top-hatted and tailed gentlemen sang with Penny against a backdrop of skyscrapers and flashing searchlights reminiscent of the Twentieth Century-Fox film trademark. The first big spectacular came in the sixth scene of Act I with a boisterous evocation of Hampstead Heath fair: amid helter-skelters and sideshows of every kind stood a genuine roundabout, garish, phantasmagorical, revolving at dizzy speeds. A crowd of pearly kings and queens sang 'Winnie Get Off The Colonel's Knee', one of the pastiche music-hall songs Ivor had written not so much tongue in cheek as with nostalgic affection. This was probably the scene he enjoyed most, for he genuinely liked riding on fairground machines and did not need to counterfeit pleasure as he whirled round with the heroine. In China, where the second act transported Drury Lane, there were slim pagodas and distant prospects of formal gardens with clipped trees and exotic flowers. The scene changed to a crowded street through which priests reverently bore a palanquin. Thunder was heard and the High Priest spoke an incantation. More peals of thunder broke out, lightning flickered and buildings trembled. As the crowd dashed about in panic shop fronts crumbled into dust, telegraph poles splintered, columns crashed and the great arch at the centre of the stage split asunder. Only a few moments earlier Dorothy Dickson had spoken the line: 'My maid says it's earthquake weather.' Whenever, in future, anything in her professional or private life threatened to go wrong, this was the hallowed remark she and her friends would utter.

Act III, if not quite so exciting, had many good things. Michael and Penny fall asleep at the foot of a giant idol which dominates the Temple of Nichaow and dream a ballet recounting ancient legends. By way of mountainous paths and subterranean caverns they get back to the devastated town where, for the purpose of the finale, the Bridge of Lovers has been left unharmed by the earthquake. Here, in an ensemble of dazzling white, they are married before a cortège of almond-eyed virgins. The audience was dazed by the speed at which Ivor took things and had little chance to query the logic of what was occurring before their astonished eyes. Under the persuasive spell he wove they cheered wildly and demanded curtain after curtain. They were what gossip columinists describe as a 'brilliant' gathering and included Marlene Dietrich, whose arrival earlier had caused a sensation. It is said that Mam, who occupied her usual seat in the royal box, was so annoyed at being overshadowed that she deliberately pushed a box of chocolates over the edge and spoilt Marlene's entrance. If the story is not true it ought to be.

For ten months *Careless Rapture* filled every seat in the house. Given Drury Lane's capacity, which is roughly double that of the average London theatre, this represents a run of nearly two years and, moreover, does not take into account the long provincial tours that followed. There was no doubt that in Ivor Drury Lane had found its salvation and the management asked him to produce a successor. He responded with *Crest Of The Wave*, a title very appropriate to the situation in which he now found himself. While Garrick, Sheridan and other accomplished men of the theatre had brought success to Drury Lane, none of them did so with the versatility Ivor showed as creator, composer and actor. He now demanded, and received, a fifty-fifty share of the profits, Drury Lane being only too pleased to grant him everything he wanted.

Having engineered a sinking ship and an earthquake Ivor decided to add to his list of natural calamities with a train crash. This was the high point of *Crest Of The Wave* which also proposed a film sequence in Versailles, a fiesta in Rio de Janeiro, a cruise liner being transformed visibly into a battleship, and a Gothic cathedral peopled by ghosts. The plot, so thin that it threatened on occasion to vanish utterly, concerned the impoverished Duke of Cheviot who retrieves his family fortunes by going to Hollywood and becoming a highly paid film star. Not content with playing the hero Ivor doubled besides as the villain, a faded Hollywood star who plots the train crash which he hopes will finish off the Cockney heroine in love with the nobleman turned actor. 1937 was Coronation Year and Ivor paid his tribute with a prologue in which the ancestral Knights of Gantry, duly helmeted and cloaked, line up before the castle and sing 'Rose of England'. The melody, of the same swaggering cut as 'Keep The Home Fires Burning', is the most durable item in *Crest Of The Wave* and comes over with real vigour. Another attractive number is the mazurka danced by Walter Crisham and Dorothy Dickson as part of the 'Versailles in Tinsel' scene. Ivor, always ready to pay for the best, commissioned Lydia Sokolova to choreograph it. He bubbled over, as usual, with all sorts of ideas which ranged from the clever to the idiotic. One of them was to show Grauman's Chinese Theatre in Hollywood on the night of a big film première. He asked Angus McBean the photographer to build masks of famous Hollywood

stars arriving for the film so that he, Ivor, could stand behind the scenes
and imitate them speaking to each other. He rather fancied his talent
as a mimic, though to the unbiased hearer the voices he imagined as
being those of Clark Gable and William Powell emerged as the all too
recognisable tones of Ivor Novello. Much persuasion was needed to
make him drop the idea, and long into the night of the dress rehearsal,
over ham and a tired lettuce, a friend argued staunchly against it. At
last, around four in the morning, Ivor gave way.

The first night of the new production came almost exactly a year
after the opening of *Careless Rapture*. Ivor spent the morning in
Bond Street choosing presents for the company. To Dorothy Dickson he gave a lapis lazuli solitaire ring, to Ena Burrill, who played a
villainess, he presented a cross of emeralds on a gold chain, and to all
the other members of the cast he offered a keepsake of what everyone
hoped would be his Drury Lane hat-trick. It is typical of the warm
atmosphere Ivor created around him that his fellow players
responded no less generously. From Leontine Sagan, his producer,
he had a walking-stick carved in rare South American wood, from
Marie Lohr, who played the statuesque Duchess of Cheviot, a model
yacht with sails of mirror glass, and from his leading lady Dorothy
Dickson a gold-mounted crocodile-skin blotter. After he had done
his shopping he went back to The Flat and slept tranquilly for two
hours. He ate a light meal and walked round the corner to Drury
Lane. In his dressing-room he found even more gifts, some of them
embodying the title of his new play: a china fish poised on a block of
sea-blue crystal, a lifebelt in red, white and blue carnations (he liked
the thought but hoped he would not need it), tie-pins, a set of green
and gold liqueur glasses, a bottle of Chartreuse, and good luck figu-
rines of pink jade. Beside his make-up mirror and spilling over onto
the floor lay five thousand telegrams from well-wishers.

Long before the finale and ritual ovation it was obvious that the
Novello formula had scored a third consecutive hit at Drury Lane.
Formula is, perhaps, too precise a word to define the bulging rag-bag
of variegated goodies which he opened up with a flourish and
strewed generously before his audience. The most exciting of all was
naturally the train crash. Over the stage rumbled the Transcontinen-
tal Express at great speed with passengers sitting at the lighted windows. On it tore into the night when suddenly a gigantic explosion
was heard and the train vanished in a cloud of smoke and flames.
After the fumes lifted they revealed a crumpled mass of scrap iron.
The crash brought, each night, a moment of anxiety for the junior

stage manager. The shipwreck in *Glamorous Night* had found him immured in a cabin at rehearsals while the special effects team exploded thunderflashes and fire-crackers all around to test how safe the devices were. When *Careless Rapture* was being prepared it had been his job to lie on the stage during the earthquake so that the areas where débris fell could be marked and safe spaces allotted for the cast. All these trials he survived without harm. Then, for *Crest Of The Wave*, he was supervising the train crash and a steel wire that carried the scenery and trees revolving madly to give the illusion of motion abruptly snapped and cracked back into the wings. It missed him but caught another member of staff in the face and scarred his eye irretrievably.

The other big scenes were harmless compared with this. 'Versailles in Tinsel', which took the place of the 'operetta-within-an-operetta' favoured by Ivor, presented Olive Gilbert singing 'Haven Of My Heart', an opulent production number that has not been heard a great deal since. The Fiesta, which the hero visits while on his way to Hollywood on a luxury liner, was filled with castanets and guitars and sombreros and swirling dresses. Walter Crisham, who had already danced with Dorothy Dickson the charming mazurka in the film director's dream of Versailles, popped up here again to throw off a dazzling tango. The best numbers in an unequal score were the romantic 'Why Isn't It You?' and 'If You Only Knew'. There is also something to be said for the last scene of all, which, rather than ending with a bang, drew to a tranquil close in Gantry Castle where the Cheviot family and their tenants gather on Christmas Eve to the gentle sound of carols.

Ivor did not forget to give his audience a little humour as well. He was always at his best in light comedy and the opening scene of *Crest Of The Wave* presented him with an opportunity for it. Even in those days the owners of stately homes allowed the public in at certain times. At Gantry Castle the 'open' day is Wednesday but on this particular occasion the family have forgotten about it. The Duke, his sister-in-law and his younger brother are surprised sitting round the breakfast table by two sightseers. The Duke and his relations immediately freeze and pretend to be waxworks. 'That's the one I like,' says the first sightseer pointing at a motionless Ivor. 'But doesn't he look cross, though.' Ivor's younger brother was played by Peter Graves who had been promoted to major rôles and even, in *Crest Of The Wave*, sang a song called 'Clementine'. Other members of the Novello 'gang' were not neglected. Minnie Rayner acted the heroine's

cockney mother, and although Olive Gilbert had no big part to play
she sang two substantial numbers. Ivor engaged an 'outsider', Finlay
Currie, as a blustering Hollywood executive. In a flamboyant straw
hat and dazzling tie the Scottish actor gave a typical display of the
spluttering irascibility which was his trademark.

After the first night Ivor went back round the corner to The Flat
and threw a supper party for various lords and ladies and assorted
friends. Eddie Marsh was there – he would never have missed anything like this – pouncing on the early editions of the newspapers as
they came in and digesting all that the critics had to say. 'One staggers
out sated and a trifle stunned, observing, with a bloated species of
relief, as one does at the end of a long Christmas dinner with the
family, that this occasion is over for another year,' wrote the
Observer. 'How bare the narrative seems! How richly Drury Lane
has clothed it! . . . The train crash of tradition is perhaps the best of
all. . . . A boyish and simple evening,' said *The Times*. The *Tatler*
declared that 'Ivor Novello has again rung the bell with a resonant
clang. Time rolls on, and he continues to fill Drury Lane with a consistency that no other author, actor or manager has been able to
achieve.' It added that he had drawn to the Lane 'thousands who
enter a theatre hardly ever'. James Agate, who loathed musical
comedy, bluffed his way out with some colourful writing. 'The audience largely consisted of Privy Councillors, Elder Brethren, Hereditary Legislators, Film Stars, Mannequins and lovelies. As the
conductor advanced to his rostrum a Parsifalian hush reigned,
broken only by the crackle of a too-stout shirtfront and the rustle of
an ill-mannered ruby. A Mongolian would have realised that this was
the drama nearest to the British heart, the white elephant for which
stables of porphyry and rose-pink marble are presently to be
erected.' He continued with a summary of the plot and observed,
shrewdly, that the Fiesta was a simpler version of the second act in
Carmen. 'I declare the music, dancing (by Mr Walter Crisham), and all
the acting to have sparkle – altogether a very jolly show if only one
could look on it in any old clothes, with leave to smoke, and without
the silly pretence that Here We Have an Artistic Event of National
Importance. Not that Mr Novello pretends. He knows better. *The
Happy Hypocrite* taught him not to trust the British public with anything except sheer unadulterated bosh. Then who does pretend?
Why, the Privy Councillors, Elder Brethren, Hereditary Legislators,
Film Stars, Mannequins and lovelies!'

Although *Crest Of The Wave* ran for little more than six months at

Drury Lane it had been a happy production. Rehearsals had been long and tedious, and at one of them a weary chorus boy remarked: 'I wish I was a woodpecker. I'd get my supper off the scenery.' Immediately Ivor called a break. On another occasion, when everyone lay about exhausted during some technical delay, Ivor came on and started to play the piano. Old tunes and new floated through the empty theatre, and then he switched to a number which had been dropped from *Careless Rapture.* The cast had not forgotten it and gradually joined in. 'Ah, boys and girls, do you remember it?' said Ivor. 'Will you sing it with me?' They did, and when the time came to start rehearsing again they threw themselves into the work relaxed and contented. Later on during the run of *Crest Of The Wave* they all subscribed to a present for him. It was a silver cigarette case on which was engraved a map of London's theatreland. Each of the theatres where Ivor had put on a play was marked by a jewel. Dorothy Dickson organised the presentation, and Ivor, much moved, told them that, despite his habit of often losing such things, this cigarette case he would always preserve and carry near his heart. He kept his word.*

When *Crest Of The Wave* had ended its London run he decided to take it on a tour of the provinces. In those days touring was big business and an important branch of the theatre world. If you mounted a play in the West End and lost money on it you were often able to recoup your outlay and even make a good profit by sending it out on tour afterwards. There were impresarios like the Edwardian George Dance who grew very rich on touring alone and never produced anything in London, his policy being to let others take the risks. *Crest Of The Wave* did make money in London but, like other Novello productions, took still more in the provinces. Touring, for Ivor, was like a state visit during which crowds gathered to cheer him at stage doors and theatres. They jostled each other to touch him, to see him at close quarters, to fight for his autograph. When he appeared a form of hysteria seized them and they swamped him in their enthusiasm. It was all quite different from the average actor's experience of touring which meant, usually, cheap digs and loitering at Crewe railway station for a late connection on dank and dreary Sunday mornings.

The *Crest Of The Wave* tour was managed by Tom Arnold. He had

---

* When he died it was offered to the Victoria and Albert Museum for the theatre archive but was rejected. It now reposes in a glass case, along with many other theatrical treasures, at the Garrick Club.

known Ivor for some time but this was their first business association and it worked very well, probably because the differences in their personalities only served to complement each other. Ivor was a manager as well, although his ideas sometimes verged on the grandiose and impractical. It was at this point that Tom Arnold was able, with tactful logic, to steer him in safer directions. They became close friends in private life and business, and Tom Arnold was to present all Ivor's musical plays from then on. Another welcome result of the tour was Ivor's discovery of a new star. He had decided to cast Esmond Knight for his own part in *Crest Of The Wave* and needed to find someone to follow Dorothy Dickson. At Peter Graves's suggestion he auditioned a dancer called Roma Beaumont. She did her piece and then, convinced she had failed, went to her dressing-room. Ivor called her back. 'Do you want to play this part?' he said. 'Oh, yes!' 'Then you shall.' When the tour reached Birmingham Ivor himself joined the production and went straight on without rehearsal one Monday night to play opposite a somewhat apprehensive Miss Beaumont. At the end he took her hand and told the audience: 'Tonight I have found my new star. I shall write my next play for her.'

4

A WORM I' THE BUD

Gray. Have you ever thought of doing Shakespeare?
Norma. Never – no money in it.

Proscenium, Act I, Sc. ii.

CREST OF THE WAVE and *Careless Rapture* brought Ivor large earnings and compensated for what he lost on his production of *The Happy Hypocrite*. In the financial year covering *Glamorous Night* he made nearly twenty-four thousand pounds. During the period from 1937 to 1938 he was able to recover from the unsuccessful Beerbohm play and to make something close on fifteen thousand. These figures, of course, need to be multiplied by eight or ten to give an idea of today's purchasing power. He was a rich man.

He enjoyed not only money but the love of many close friends and the adulation of millions. His homes in London and at Redroofs were the perfect setting for him, and in each a devoted staff looked after him with affectionate care. He had the gift of friendship and inspired loyalty from everyone who worked for him. At Drury Lane, where he alone was responsible for co-ordinating actors, orchestra, chorus and stage management, he ruled with an authority as genial as it was absolute. His generosity was famous and his compassion was freely given. Off the stage as well as on he shed a radiance which people found irresistible. His energy was formidable, and, at least in the nineteen-thirties, he seemed to have put behind him those heart troubles which in his youth had so worried Eddie Marsh. He loved the life he had made for himself and asked for no other sort of existence. At the first night of *Careless Rapture*, while everyone else was jittery with nerves, he exulted to Dorothy Dickson: 'Can't wait to get out there, can you?' 'No!' she replied as he kissed her on both cheeks.

The picture is one of unalloyed happiness and complete fulfilment. Was there no flaw, no imperfection, however slight, in the pattern? There was. As *The Happy Hypocrite* showed, Ivor sometimes cursed the destiny that had burdened him with exquisite looks and charm. He knew that however hard he worked, however good his acting, any success he achieved would be attributed to physical advantage rather than dramatic ability. Another, more serious fear was that one day the inspiration which enabled him so fluently and easily to compose music and write plays might suddenly dry up. There were sombre visions in which he saw himself bereft of ideas and powerless to attract audiences into a theatre. Would the time ever come when he was played out, a back number dimly recalled as once the most successful theatrical figure of the age?

Professional doubts of this sort did not, however, last for long, and were usually dispersed by a session at the piano when tunes bubbled up as freely as ever and the words sprang without effort into his mind. Much more distressing were the failures in his private life. The general public was less knowing than today, and it is doubtful if many of his female admirers can have realised that he slept with men. To his bed came actors who were appearing in his plays, chorus boys, and any other presentable male who happened to stray within his circle. One of the latter was J. R. Ackerley, subsequently literary editor of *The Listener* and author of those classic books *My Father and Myself*, *We Think The World of You* and *My Dog Tulip*. In his youth Ackerley, who was very handsome, had written for the theatre, and it was presumably at this time that he became acquainted with Ivor. Somewhat ungallantly he was to record that Ivor's equipment did not strike him as very impressive.

Theatrical gossips often commented on the fact that the people Ivor engaged for his plays comprised, at least so far as the men were involved, an unusually high proportion of gays. He himself was only too aware of this and shrugged it off with private jokes, as when he rechristened *The Dancing Years* and called it, among his intimates, *The Prancing Queers*. Bizarre stories were told about him in London society. Somerset Maugham once remarked in old age to Winston Churchill: 'Winston, your mother often indicated that you had affairs in your youth with men.' 'Not true!' said Churchill. 'But I once went to bed with a man to see what it was like.' 'Who was it?' 'Ivor Novello.' 'And what was it like?' 'Musical,' replied Churchill committing a pun, since 'musical' was then the cant word for gay. The source of this extraordinary anecdote is the late Alan Searle, for many years Maugham's secretary and companion. Since both he and Maugham, who told it to him, were skilled raconteurs given to embroidering their tales for artistic effect, it may not be taken too seriously, if only because it would cast the highly respectable Eddie Marsh, then Winston's secretary, in the rôle of pimp.

There were many men in Ivor's life. One of the earliest was Alec Robertson and one of the longest-lasting was Bobbie Andrews. Another of his infatuations was a young man who, pursued also by the dramatist Terence Rattigan, encouraged rivalry between the two by granting his favours in shrewdly judged rotation. Yet another was Christopher Hassall, 'dearest Chris', whom Ivor loved both for his talent and his beauty. Their relationship, a deep and professionally rewarding one, continued after Hassall's marriage and caused much distress to the latter's wife. Ivor would ring up and have long conversations with him while she, unable to avoid overhearing what passed, would flinch at the passionate terms of endearment that were used. Long rows between husband and wife followed. Chris, remarks his son, 'loved to be loved', and Ivor was unscrupulously single-minded in lavishing attention upon him. Although really an intellectual, a writer who valued his poetry far more highly than the pop lyrics he was able to turn out with such facility, Chris was also a suppressed romantic who could not resist Ivor's blandishments. Ivor gave him something that his wife, even though the mother of his two children, was powerless to bestow. His daughter Imogen, a beautiful actress who later committed suicide, was like him, his son recalls, in that she, too, loved to be loved.

Ivor struck Hassall's son 'as being ever so Italian – basically dishonest with himself, and ever so slightly corruptible, not venially but emotionally . . . Novello, you see, always knew what he wanted. He was as sure of himself as any Welshman can be. He had no scruples about taking whom or whatever he wanted, instinctively, and possibly guilelessly, and without a qualm.' So the marriage teetered on from dispute to dispute as Chris, forever torn between Ivor and his wife, could not make up his mind which to choose. Her situation was yet more unenviable in that Eddie Marsh also claimed his share of Chris and was perpetually demanding more and more of his time. Like Ivor, when Eddie called or telephoned he would ignore her completely. The children left home as soon as they could, and, bitterly wounded, unable to stand any more, she divorced Chris and slipped out of his life. Yet the dismal tale did not end there. Now and again she would receive desperately pleading telephone calls from Chris beseeching her to come and meet him at Victoria station where, over a cold cup of tea, he plaintively held her hand in his.

The failures in Ivor's private life did not refer to episodes like the above. The gay side of his existence was wholly successful. As a famous man of the theatre he could command all the indulgence he

wanted in this respect, and the complications he inspired elsewhere
were no concern of his. The darker aspect of things became apparent
in his relationships with women. He liked them, appreciated their
views and enjoyed their company. From Mam onwards women were
very important to him. Constance Collier taught him the art of
writing for the stage, Gladys Cooper gave him expertise in acting and
Clemence Dane helped improve his acquaintance with history and
literature. He delighted to tailor rôles in his plays for Lilian Braithwaite, Olive Gilbert, Dorothy Dickson, Minnie Rayner and, above
all, the beautiful Mary Ellis. Had he been a true bisexual he would
have been equally happy sleeping with either men or women. Unfortunately he was not. Feminine beauty appealed to him as much as the
male sort, and he was as likely to fall in love with a woman as with a
man. While he could fulfil himself in the company of a man, he was to
find, over and over again, that when the crucial moment arrived with
a woman he could not. This was a cause of black frustration and misery. He longed desperately to have a family. Children he loved, and
with them he was at his most endearing. In those days when it was
generally believed that children should be seen and not heard, Ivor
took the opposite view, treated them as equals, entered into their
little world with genuine enthusiasm and was rewarded by their
affection. The thought that he would never have a son or daughter of
his own filled him with despair, and standing as godfather to his
friends' innumerable offspring was but a poor substitute.*

One of his doomed infatuations centred on the Norwegian
soprano Kirsten Flagstad. In the mid nineteen-thirties she startled
London with a series of Wagner performances at Covent Garden
which placed her, in the view of connoisseurs, on the same level as
the greatest prima donnas of the past. Over the years she learned to
control her ample powers with infallible instinct and her resilient
voice was equal to all the tremendous demands Wagner made on it.
He, of all composers, was probably Ivor's favourite. There was in his
music a passionate emotion and strength to which Ivor surrendered

---

* The biographer is restricted to discoverable facts whereas the writer of
fiction is hampered by no such thing. *The Painted King* (Heinemann,
1954), a novel by the late Rhys Davies, is a brilliant psychological study of
Ivor as man, actor and playwright. The reconstruction of Ivor's love life
with women, although based on no apparent testimony, is convincing and
has a pathetic ring of truth. Perhaps Davies, a fellow Welshman writing
three years after Ivor's death, had found someone willing to kiss and tell?

utterly. Often he would slip out between acts of the play he might be doing and hurry up Bow Street to catch a glimpse of Flagstad during her Covent Garden seasons and to hear the surge of music which to him was irresistible. It is significant that Flagstad, whose Brünnhilde was reckoned the best in her time, had all the large and stately attributes of the typical Wagnerian heroine. She was, like Mam, a dominating figure both on stage and off, and Ivor became obsessed by her. As an honoured guest she came back to The Flat for late-night parties and made the walls resound with the commanding tones of Isolde or Senta. But of course, as always, the liaison could not go much further than the stage of intense admiration on Ivor's part.

He found the remedy for his disappointments in work. It is difficult to understand why people sometimes described him as 'lazy' when one thinks of the twenty or so plays both musical and otherwise which he wrote and acted in, the many films he made and the music he composed so tirelessly. Perhaps he was 'lazy' in that he never bothered to revise or polish and was too easily satisfied with the first idea that came to mind, but in the matter of sheer productivity few could equal him. The manuscripts of plays which for various reasons he never produced or published run to a considerable number. Among them are items with titles such as *Love Story*, *Silver Wedding*, *The Mother Country*, *The Gate Crasher*, *Love Will Find a Way* and *The Argentine Widow*. It is not, however, surprising that they failed to see the light of day since, from the nineteen-twenties and on, it would have been physically impossible for him to bring them out, given that he was appearing nearly every night in one of his own plays and often had several of them running at the same time. One wishes, nonetheless, that somebody would stage the pastiche he wrote of Oscar Wilde and called *Lady Fandermere's Wynd*, subtitled: 'As played by a touring company in the Nineties'.

A lady journalist who once proposed to interview him was disconcerted when he said: 'I'm afraid it will have to be terribly early in the morning.' Well, Mr Novello was a busy man, she reflected, and she steeled herself. 'Would you mind calling at no later than eleven o'clock,' he warned her, naming an hour which was, for him, early. An actor's day, he contended, should lead up to the evening performance, and only afterwards could he allow himself to relax. He rose towards midday and, over tea, read and dictated letters. At Redroofs he made for the fumed-oak piano and started improvising. Christopher Hassall would sit and listen while a recording machine absorbed the music. After the disc was cut and prepared, Chris put it on the gramophone and played it back. 'I think,' Ivor would say, lighting a cigarette, 'this is going to be *it*.' Or he might decide: 'That was foul! Let's have some coffee.' Coffee he drank in vast quantities, usually the 'instant' sort, and he smoked Turkish cigarettes at a rate of about sixty a day. He wore an ancient dressing-gown with sleeves so long that they fluttered and capered like a bird as his hands flew up and down the keyboard. 'Isn't this heaven?' he would say. 'Can there be anything more enjoyable than what we're doing? How perfectly frightful to be anyone else. I can't wait to play this to Mary!'

Suddenly his face would go blank, he would stop in mid-sentence, would switch off and walk away leaving Chris to struggle with words for the new lyric. He had the ability to sleep at any time of day and his hour-long nap every afternoon was sacrosanct. An idea for a play or a scene would strike him in the middle of a party, whereupon an absorbed look spread over his features and he would vanish, to be discovered hours later scribbling with pencil in his large fluent handwriting on a rapidly growing pile of manuscript sheets. That was how he conceived the notion of *Fresh Fields*. He had invited Minnie Rayner to Redroofs one Sunday and she arrived with a gang of twenty cronies. He prudently retreated and, in bed, thought up the plot of his new play.

His afternoon nap was fitted in between writing, composing, seeing people, casting a new production, rehearsing or studying a part. When he had no matinée of his own he would visit the cinema, for he was a keen film fan, or go to see a new play. Early in the evening, at the hour when actors get restless and thoughtful about their performance, he would eat a light meal, an egg or salad, some fruit or coffee, among the green painted walls and beige curtains of his dining-room in The Flat. If he was playing at Drury Lane there was only a few minutes' walk to the theatre. When the curtain fell for the last time he quickly took off his make-up. It was invariably light for his complexion had no need of heavy greasepaint. Chris Hassall used to say that even offstage Ivor gave him the impression of always being made-up and ready to go before the footlights: it was his dark colouring, his gypsy look that created the illusion. Once in his street clothes again he would linger for another hour or so at the theatre talking with his company and discussing how the play had gone and what the audience was like. If he were host at a supper party afterwards, as often happened, he would take his guests to one of his three favourite restaurants, the Ivy, the Savoy Grill or the Caprice where a 'Bombe Ivor Novello' immortalised him in ice-cream.

Yet although he always wanted to be surrounded by a crowd of people he was happiest entertaining them on his own ground at The Flat. There the married couple who ran the household would provide a hot meal for ten or even twenty. After dinner people sat round in the drawing-room which contained a book-case slyly designed to house his collection of more than three thousand gramophone records. Next door was the music room with its white pine panels, white alabaster lamps and, on the mantelshelf, two pigeons in white porcelain beneath a tinted mirror. Beside the satin-curtained windows, on a dais, stood two pianos, a grand and a little 'yacht' piano. They were played late into the night and into the early morning. By one or two o'clock Ivor was ready for bed. He dropped off with no trouble at all and slept as deeply and happily as a child.

'What fun it all was,' Ivor said to Chris when, during the war, the latter was called up and the composer was bereft of his lyricist. 'You'd bring in a lyric and give it to me, and I'd say "No, it stinks". Then you'd clutch your head, alter a word and I'd read it again and say "It's heavenly . . ." That's the way to work.' The toil of collaboration was often lightened by Ivor breaking out into hilarious imitations. He would 'do' a well-known actress playing Shakespeare without the slightest knowledge of what it all meant and making up the words as she went along until both he and Chris choked with laughter.

Another of his turns was Mrs Patrick Campbell, a monstre sacré who never ceased to fascinate him. Having already featured her in *Party* he decided to make her the central figure of another play which he wrote while *Crest Of The Wave* was still running. He entitled it *Comédienne* and gave the leading role to Lilian Braithwaite. The play came out in the summer of 1938 and everyone knew who had provided the inspiration for it. 'Donna Lovelace' is an elderly actress who has been great in her time but who is now the scourge of West End managers. No one will employ her and her 'wicked sense of humour' frightens off any attempt to help. She is, as an American once described Mrs Pat, a sinking ship firing on her rescuers. A young dramatist is encouraged by one of her admirers from the palmy days to offer her the lead in his new play. At rehearsals she is unpunctual, quarrelsome and generally unbearable. When her authority is challenged by a younger actress she declares: 'I think, my dear child, *you* should remember who I am.' 'I'm remembering who you *were*!' comes the retort. The reason for her disgraceful behaviour is a fear of failure which shows itself in being unable to remember her lines. The play is well received but Donna's notices are uniformly bad. She prepares for retirement and muses: 'I may even write a book of reminiscences – there are dozens of people I simply can't wait to offend.'

The structure of the play includes another of those fussy sub-plots Ivor liked to add, in this instance based on the fact that the young playwright is the illegitimate son of Donna's former husband. The ending, too, is improbable in that a wealthy publican, another of her admirers from way back, suddenly appears and offers to finance her in box-office poison like Ibsen, so she sits down and drives a typically hard bargain over contracts, terms, percentages. Still, Molière is notorious for the unlikely dénouements he cobbled up in his plays, so perhaps Ivor is not to be unduly criticised if he did the same thing.

As a representation of Mrs Pat and her ilk *Comédienne* is not without flaws. It is very unlikely that she would have gone under at rehearsals and, most uncharacteristic of all, been delighted at her failure because it means that the play will now be acted throughout America by a rising star instead of a waning one and that the author whom Donna naturally favours will be successful. All these faults were camouflaged by a bravura piece of acting from Lilian who even imitated the accents and intonations of her model. She had an excellent foil in Kathleen Harrison as her acid-tongued cockney dresser, the sort of rôle Miss Harrison played to perfection. 'Oh, Gawd defend me from 'ighbrows – she'd have been worth a fortune if she'd stuck to her line,' says this hard-headed critic of the drama. 'Something they can understand – a bit of a laugh, a tear or two, a big scene at the end of the second act (and she can do it!) and a nice him and her embrace to bring the curtain down.' In its rough and ready way this is a fair analysis of Mrs Pat's career which zig-zagged dramatically between the popular stuff she did for money and the Ibsen and Maeterlinck which she preferred to do as an artist. James Agate summed up *Comédienne*: 'There is a brilliant cast – Miss Fabia Drake deserves special mention – which gets itself on the stage as unobtrusively as possible, and as expeditiously off again, thus leaving the coast clear for Miss Lilian Braithwaite, whose Donna is as *mobile* as the original. But why Lovelace? Everybody must find his own answer to this. Mine is that I could not love the copy so much, loved I not the original more!'

The writing of *Comédienne* may have stirred once more Ivor's acting ambition to the extent of ignoring the cynical exchange quoted at the head of this section. Two months after his new play had been launched at the Haymarket he himself appeared in the title rôle of Shakespeare's *Henry V* at Drury Lane. Astonishment was the general reaction. His business partner Tom Arnold was not a little disturbed, although he was eventually won over by an agreement that he would be commissioned to present the lucrative pantomime there at Christmas. No one really paid much attention to Ivor when he spoke of his wish to do a Shakespeare season somewhere or to stage a programme of avant-garde items at a little theatre like the Arts. He was, however, genuine in his desire, and, as a complete change from his usual line, he decided to follow *Crest Of The Wave* with a major production of *Henry V*. As his director he engaged Lewis Casson who had impeccable Shakespearean references. He put himself under Casson's guidance and accepted humbly, as he had when venturing into the cinema for the first time, all the expert advice that was given him. 'I thought he played beautifully,' said Lewis Casson's wife Sybil Thorndike. 'He was such a sensitive actor; I think he could have done big things – he would have been a lovely Hamlet.'

Long after the rest of the company had gone home Ivor went on rehearsing alone with Casson, worrying at the sense of difficult lines and slaving to assign them their precise rhetorical value. His Princess Katherine was Dorothy Dickson, who, thought Sybil Thorndike, gave an 'awfully good' performance. Another unusual and successful piece of casting was Gwen Ffrangcon-Davies, who played the chorus as a boy, an idea of Lewis Casson which she carried out well. If Ivor lacked a majestic presence and that 'touch of Harry in the night', he made up for it with a commanding and incisive voice and movements that were fluent but kingly. He did best in the quieter, more reflective moments, which were, said Ivor Brown, 'modest, careful and well graced'. Another Shakespearean authority, Alan Dent, noted that Ivor 'plays the king with far more zest and poetry than his more serious admirers could have anticipated'. The most formidable Shakespearean of all, though criticising Ivor's light timbre, admitted that he could 'end by being a very good, complete Henry'. James Agate went on: 'He has fire where fire should be; the prayer before the battle and the reading of the list of the dead are movingly done; and the soliloquy beginning 'Upon the King...' has an entirely admirable cogency.'

Henry V had originally been planned for a ten-week season after which Ivor hoped to put on *Much Ado About Nothing*, *As You Like It* and perhaps *Romeo and Juliet*. The opening weeks played to excellent business with good houses at matinées and evening performances. By the third week attendances had dropped so badly that Ivor was obliged to end the run. This was due to no fault of his own but to the international crisis which supervened and closed down other theatres as well. War threatened, sandbags were brought out, men started digging air-raid shelters in Hyde Park. Ivor reluctantly put up closure notices for *Henry V* and five hundred people lost their jobs. The production had cost him fifteen thousand pounds which he was never to see again. He did not regret it, for he had proved his mettle once again as an actor.

Then Mr Chamberlain negotiated in Munich with Herr Hitler. The news was full of war and rumours of war. Bobbie Andrews joked in mock horror: 'If there's a war they'll find out how old I am!' There was not, for the time being, and Mr Chamberlain returned from his journey declaring that he had obtained peace with honour. Like many people at that time Ivor was delighted and welcomed the announcement. Noël Coward, a vehement anti-appeaser, belonged to the minority who execrated the result of the prime minister's errand and saw the episode as a humiliation. He happened to be with Ivor at the Tivoli cinema when a newsreel showed Chamberlain descending from the aircraft and jubilating in what he claimed as a triumph. Ivor burst into tears of relief. Noël, boiling with anger, hit him savagely.

Part Five

BUFFETS AND REWARDS

'Lunched one day with Marie Tempest and Willie Browne, and we agreed that Ivor Novello's nose and chin are still the world's handsomest outline. Told Ivor this, and he said the word "still" was unnecessary.'

James Agate

1

DANCING THROUGH THE BLACK-OUT

'Of all my plays, *The Dancing Years* has proved to be the one that could go back and back again to the various cities. It has played Manchester, for example, eight times, and I sometimes wonder whether it is not the nostalgia that comes when we remember the time of mutual danger that brings people so often to see it.'

Ivor Novello

MAM, TOO, had her views about Munich. Lately she had been quiescent and preserved herself from mischief by organising and running what she called her 'Welsh Singing Grandmothers' Choir'. This comprised friends whom she had known for many years. They had grown old along with her and she brought colour into their lives with tours all over the country. By now, though, musical tastes had changed. Audiences did not wish to hear the Welsh Grandmothers, and the large numbers of unsold seats became an embarrassment. Mam nevertheless contrived to get full houses by giving tickets away in profusion to passers-by, taxi-drivers, hotel employees and anyone within sight. Finally even those who had free passes were unwilling to attend her concerts. Ivor persuaded her to renounce these performances and to concentrate on private lessons. She did not feel well and he sent her to Redroofs for three months' convalescence. Even so he suspected that she was plotting another escapade. 'Mam is certainly being a good girl and doing just what the doctor ordered,' he confided in Richard Rose, 'but she's being so quiet that I'm not completely sure she's not up to something.'

A few days later she rushed into The Flat and caught him over breakfast. Her eyes shone and her voice trembled with excitement. She had never looked in such tremendous form.

'Darling,' she exuberated, 'the most wonderful thing has happened. We're going to sing for Hitler in Berlin. I'm going to take sixty of my girls with me and our slogan is going to be "Singing For Peace". We're going to start at The Hague and give two concerts in Holland and two in Belgium on our way to Berlin. When we sing for Hitler in the stadium there we're going to change from our Welsh costumes into white angel dresses for our Grand Finale and release hundreds of pigeons, each one carrying on its leg a little message of peace.'

Ivor choked on his coffee and, aghast, tried to talk her out of the crazy scheme. She would not listen. Everything was arranged, she continued, and one of her greatest fans, a noblewoman, had agreed to finance the trip. Now she must rush off because she had a big press conference at the Waldorf Hotel next door. She kissed him wetly and flew out through the door.

No more was heard from her until Ivor learned that the expedition had set off for Holland. After two days a telegram arrived: 'Concert halls filled to capacity. Deafening applause. Greatest success of my career. On to Berlin. Send me four thousand pounds immediately.'

The message was what Mam would have liked to think had happened. Only the demand for money was real. A telephone call to Amsterdam revealed that the concert had been cancelled for lack of an audience and that the Dutch, like the English, were impervious to the vocal delights promised by the Welsh Singing Grandmothers. Ivor sent Fred Allen bearing a cheque to Holland with instructions to pay Mam's debts and to escort her and her sixty Welsh Grandmothers back home. She protested violently and only by dint of long and furious argument was she persuaded to embark.

For weeks afterwards she stayed locked in her house and would see no one, Ivor included. In due course she appeared at Redroofs, vivacious and jolly as if nothing had happened. When the Munich crisis deepened she looked out of the window, saw trenches being dug and sandbags trundled into position, and commented thoughtfully: 'If they had let us go to Berlin all this would never have happened.'

Her bitterness was understandable. After years in the spotlight, after making music and hearing applause everywhere in England, she had been relegated to obscurity. What else was there left for her to do? An inspiration, one of her less harmful ones, irradiated her brain. She was the mother of the famous Ivor Novello. Surely that was a rôle she could play with elegance and distinction? Henceforward, at first nights and gala performances, she would take her seat in the royal box of the theatre. Her entrance would be an affair of splendour, and she would create such an impression that the audience would be forced to pay homage. So it came to pass that in future Ivor's first nights were graced by Mam queening it in the royal box. She made her entry, went to the ledge, bowed and threw kisses to the people below. Her silver-white hair, her ice-blue satin gown and her ostrich feather-fringed cape were accompanied by an enormous bunch of Parma and Russian violets.

'Isn't Mam marvellous?' Ivor would say on these occasions, nobly quelling signs of the deep nervousness she caused him. 'Have you ever seen anyone her age with such vitality and enthusiasm? She's absolutely incorrigible.'

On Mondays, after a weekend at Redroofs, Ivor's Rolls-Royce waited to drive her back to London, where, she said, she had pupils awaiting her. Large safety pins held two silver fox furs in position, the wind blew her white hair about and the train of her velvet tea-gown flopped on the path. Maids loaded up the car with baskets of food and vegetables for her London home. She asked for a bottle of champagne and two glasses so that she and her travelling companion could 'get warmed up for the trip'. On the journey she chattered and laughed with gusto. Her voice trailed away, her head fell forward and she dropped off to sleep. In London the Welsh Grandmothers attended her. They gently took her from the car, undressed her and put her to bed. No pupils expected her, indeed none had for years, and there were no more concerts to be launched. Yet to admit as much would surely have killed her, and both she and Ivor knew it.

She was determined to play the last remaining part left to her in life with all the energy she could summon from her tired old body. As Ivor's mother she went to his first nights and parties wearing dresses that sparkled and capes that floated regally about her. Her aspect was gracious but commanding, and although little clouds of powder flaked away from her red cheeks and her eyes watered rheumily, everyone agreed that she was quite, quite wonderful. She was at Drury Lane in all her splendour one March evening in 1939 for the première of *The Dancing Years*, Ivor's latest musical show. It was not such a spectacular affair as the others had been, and contained no earthquakes or train crashes. Indeed, his new play, although romantic, carried echoes of the outside world, its ugliness and its tragedies. While on holiday the previous year he was shocked to hear about a friend's experience in Vienna. This friend had gone to his favourite record shop and been unable to buy any music of the great Viennese composers thought to have Jewish blood. The Nazi ban was absolute. What, said Ivor, would have happened if, as a writer of popular music, he himself had been Viennese and of Jewish descent?

When touring *Crest Of The Wave* in Liverpool the same year he heard from Peter Graves that his old friend Viola Tree had just died. Her wit and her gangling presence had delighted him for many years,

and her death saddened him. To cheer him up Graves took him to a
new film about Johann Strauss called *The Great Waltz* starring the
exotic soprano Militza Korjus. As they watched the film, stray
notions began to run through Ivor's mind and he thought of his
recent discovery, Roma Beaumont. At the end he said to Peter
Graves : 'I've got an idea. Do you think Roma Beaumont can look
twelve?' Graves replied: 'She's only twenty. I'm sure she could.'
'Ring her up and ask her to lunch,' said Ivor, 'and I'll fiddle with her
hair.' They had lunch, the hair was fiddled with, and that afternoon
Ivor wrote the first scene of *The Dancing Years*.

The period covered extends from 1911 to 1938 and the plot is
directly concerned with Nazi persecution of the Jews. Ivor's original
idea was to open with a prologue in which the composer hero, Rudi
Kleber, by now an elderly man, is condemned to death by the Nazi
authorities for having helped Jews escape from Austria. The Drury
Lane management disapproved of introducing politics into light
entertainment and wanted to drop the scene, but Ivor insisted and
finally, in the first run of the piece, it was put at the end where Rudi is
given a last-minute pardon. The rest of the plot, which opens in
carefree Vienna before the first World War, tells how Rudi, then a
young, penniless and unknown composer, becomes attached to
Grete, his landlady's twelve-year-old niece, and swears that he will
ask no one else to marry him until she is old enough to give him first
refusal. He then meets the operetta star Maria Ziegler who,
impressed by his talent, helps him to his first success and, having
fallen in love with him, deserts her rich and influential protector
Prince Charles Metterling. Some years later Grete returns from England
where she has established herself as an actress in musical comedy.
The idealistic Rudi has not forgotten his vow, and when Maria over-
hears him propose to Grete she rushes away in a fit of jealousy and
returns to Metterling – not, however, having stayed long enough to
learn that Grete turns Rudi down. The years dance by and Rudi
achieves an international reputation for his music. By chance he
comes across Maria again and realises that he still loves her, as she
him. Moreover, at the time of their break, she had been pregnant by
him, and she now introduces him to their son Otto. But everything
has come too late, and Rudi sees that it is impossible for her to
renounce her marriage and her family. They part, and the final scene,
which has already been described, is played out in a mood of
autumnal resignation. It has since been cut from the acting edition
with the result that Ivor's original intention is nullified. During the

scene of Rudi's parting from Maria, however, he was able to add a speech that ran: 'We shall see great changes and feel it here – times of unrest and anger and hatred in the world – and these things are strong. We shall almost forget to laugh and make music, but we shan't quite forget, and some day we'll wake up, as from an evil dream, and the world will smile again and forget to hate, and the sweetness of music and friendliness will once more be important . . .' The words may read a little sentimentally, but, spoken by Ivor with all his warm sincerity, they impressed on audiences the message that music, art and all that goes to make up the nobler side of humanity can rise above the horrors of everyday life.

Christopher Hassall again wrote the lyrics and had particular difficulty over one intended for an Edwardian musical comedy number sung by Grete. He had never seen, let alone heard, anything of this period, so Ivor went to the piano and played and sang for hours on end the favourites which he knew so well from *The Merry Widow*, *The Arcadians*, *The Quaker Girl*, *San Toy*, *Floradora*, *Chu Chin Chow*, *Merrie England* and all the other musical comedies which had been an unforgettable part of his youth. After this entertaining lesson Chris was able to find lyrics for what he entitled 'Primrose', a pastiche in words and music of any typical dance number from any Edwardian musical comedy. Or was it only a pastiche? The inspiration is so fresh, the rhythm so alert and the tune so captivating that it embodies the very spirit of the real thing.

In composing the music Ivor followed a long-established method. He never wrote his own orchestration and left this task in the able hands of the professionals Harry Acres and Charles Prentice (conductor of the Drury Lane orchestra), whose skill was always acknowledged in the programme. As he said to Alec Robertson, it was melodies people remembered, not the scoring, and of melodies he had an unlimited store. In any case, he did not have the time for orchestration. After improvising at the piano and, with Chris, deciding on the best tunes, he recorded them, played them back, and wrote down the melodic line. He did not have the time, either, to harmonise them – something he was perfectly able to do if necessary – and he would send his manuscript and records to the musician Leighton Lucas who did the job on his behalf. For years Lucas had worked with him like this in a smooth and happy collaboration. Lucas, who was known elsewhere as a conductor distinguished for his performances of modern French music and as a composer of ballets and chamber works, had largely taught himself without much aid from others. He began his career in a novel way by dancing in Diaghilev's ballet company and then by acting at the Birmingham Repertory Theatre before discovering his true niche in music. He wrote a great deal of incidental music, among it the classic film suite *Target For Tonight*. One of his best scores was for Alfred Hitchcock's *Stage Fright*. He gave Ivor a copy of the theme music and inscribed it with amused irony: 'For Ivor – for once sending you *my* music – affectionately, Leighton.'

The score of *The Dancing Years* achieves a degree of consistency which is not always to be found in Ivor's other musical plays. This is as well, given that, in the absence of elaborate stage effects, the audience's attention is focused more closely on the music alone. Publishers have a shrewd idea about the relative popularity of the songs they print – they need it if they are to keep afloat in a toughly competitive business – and the piano selection from *The Dancing Years* bears this out. The cover shows the familiar Chappell design of curtains opening beneath the masks of tragedy and comedy, the beam of spotlights, and, in the pit, silhouettes of conductor and orchestra, the whole being tinted in a delicate shade of turquoise. For years this distinctive cover was to be seen on the pianos of amateurs everywhere, and it signalled the presence of one of the hundred and twenty or so musical stage-works to which Chappell had the rights, Ivor's, of course, featuring prominently. The *Dancing Years* selection contains no less than ten numbers, each one of them tailor-made for success. From 'Lorelei', supposedly a concerted number in the operetta composed by Rudi, comes 'Three Cheers for a Lovely Party', a tripping little melody full of innocent high spirits. 'Waltz Of My Heart', a valse lente sung by Maria, has a romantic languor which contrasts with the brisk rhythms of the traditional march ensemble 'Uniform'. The intimate tone of 'I Can Give You The Starlight' has made it one of Ivor's most popular songs. The big production number is 'My Life Belongs To You', a grandiose declaration nourished by memories of Puccini. Then comes 'Primrose', which has already been mentioned, and 'My Dearest Dear', a meditative tune which surges to an impassioned climax in Ivor's best manner. The quieter pieces include 'The Wings Of Sleep', an affecting berceuse, and 'Let's Say Goodbye', which are liable to be overlooked in the company of more flamboyant tunes. 'Leap Year Waltz', mercurial and fast-moving, is only one of the dance numbers Ivor scattered throughout the score with a generous hand, the others being a polka and a galop. He wrote, in addition, a 'Masque Of Vienna' and Rudi's operetta sequence which are thought through and worked out with a rigour unusual for him.

Ivor played Rudi and, for the operetta, came down from the stage, took over from Charles Prentice and himself conducted the scene. Maria could be played by no one other than Mary Ellis. 'I had always wanted to follow up Mary Ellis's fine triumph in *Glamorous Night* with another part where she could show her fine range of acting and exceptional singing,' Ivor remarked, 'and it seemed to me that a Viennese prima donna in the early 1900s would be ideal for her. I further reflected that it might be a good angle that the public should see a composer playing a composer, and that therefore when they heard my music on the stage they would subconsciously identify it with that of Rudi Kleber, and thus give an air of reality to the play.'

Mary Ellis, of course, fulfilled all his hopes, as actress and singer, although once again, as in *Glamorous Night*, she found an Ivor Novello score more demanding than that of any opera. The reason for this paradox is that, in opera, one sings continuously and can therefore remain at a consistent pitch of endeavour, whereas in musical plays the long stretches of dialogue mean that one has to keep switching into high gear as the next number looms ahead and then switching off before doing it all over again five minutes later, a technique which can be very exhausting. She had also discovered that the best way of attacking Ivor's music was to treat it as if it were opera. This was one of the reasons for her triumph in *The Dancing Years*, where her artistry gave to his music a bloom and a freshness for which he was ever grateful.

Roma Beaumont, too, made her mark and, with 'Primrose', stopped the show cold. The 'gang' was well represented by Minnie Rayner as a comic maid, Olive Gilbert doubling as Maria's singing teacher and as a character in Rudi's operetta, and Peter Graves as a young nobleman fallen on hard times who, we are left to suppose, eventually marries Grete. At the end there were deafening cheers, many curtain calls and many bows, with Ivor delivering one of this modest little speeches to an audience emanating waves of friendliness and admiration across the footlights. The *News Chronicle* grasped Ivor's dual intent and observed that 'when, in the last scene of all, in the captured Vienna of 1938, Mr Novello, now artistically decrepit, defies the conquerors . . . and brings the house down – why, this is only to show that Mr Novello is astute enough to make the best of both worlds, the tinkles of 1911 and the tragedies of our own day.' The *Evening Standard* said: 'Mary Ellis has never been better: a

tender, passionate and utterly lovely performance. And Miss Roma
Beaumont, as Grete, captured our hearts from the moment she
took the stage.' Even James Agate in the *Sunday Times* had grudging
approval for a type of theatre he detested: 'General opinion insists
that the latest is the best to date of all the Tales from the Novello
Woods. So be it! It is certainly an excellent example of that form of
entertainment which should be called Magnoperetta – meaning the
filling of the vast Drury Lane stage and the still vaster British bosom
with the grand passion's small change. Mr Novello is the usual
velveteen hobbledehoy who pursues, or is pursued by, Miss Mary
Ellis's wayward warbler. Always in the same waltz-time, and I
suspect to the same waltz. The scenery is pretty enough to eat, the
chorus is agile, there is a pleasant newcomer in Miss Roma Beaumont, there is no wit, and there is, thank heaven, no humour!'

The morning after a first night of kisses and hugs and embraces
among a jubilant cast brought overwhelming demand for tickets at
the Drury Lane box-office which had trouble dealing with the long
queues that stretched out of and around the building. *The Dancing
Years* was a complete success. It had gone smoothly from the very
beginning except for the management's timidity about the Nazis and
for a disconcerting incident at rehearsals. The latter occurred when
the producer Leontine Sagan decided that Ivor spent too much time
on stage playing the piano and suggested that he do less of it. This was
one of the rare occasions when his friends saw him really angry. He
smiled and disagreed. She insisted, claiming that too much piano
would bore the audience. His smile became fixed and his blue eyes
froze. In a steely voice he said: 'Leo, I know *exactly* what my audience will stand from me. I know they like to hear me play. And I shall
go on playing.' Even Leo was silenced.

The Dancing Years should have run a very long time at Drury
Lane. Bookings for spring and the early summer remained buoyant
and houses were full throughout most of August. As the international
crisis became worse, however, fewer and fewer people wanted to visit
the theatre. Ivor decided that he must close down, and on 31 August
The Dancing Years played for the last time at Drury Lane. The vast
auditorium, which when full could take over six hundred pounds
worth of tickets, was reduced that evening to little more than forty-
nine. At the first interval Ivor invited people in the circle and gallery
to come down and join those in the stalls. As the small gathering hud-
dled together he sat at the piano and, playing the part of Rudi, found
his fingers straying nostalgically into 'Glamorous Night' from his first

success at Drury Lane. Mary Ellis could not hold back the tears and fought to control herself. Then Ivor remembered what he should have been playing and switched to the correct tune.

Mam responded to the outbreak of war in a last defiant gesture by writing what must have been one of the worst songs ever concocted. It began:

> We must all fight for victory,
> We'll fight to beat the foe;
> We must all fight for victory,
> To victory on we go.

Ivor could not do much better, and with lyrics by the journalist Collie Knox he produced a song called 'We'll Remember The Meadows'. Although the music was accredited to the 'Composer Of "Keep The Home Fires burning"' it never reached the popularity of his First World War ballad.

For a time all places of entertainment were closed. A month after the declaration of war provincial theatres reopened and Ivor went out on tour with a new play he had written. Originally entitled *Second Helping*, it was a bedroom comedy starring himself with Isabel Jeans and Dorothy Dickson. Next year he brought it back to London under the title of *Ladies Into Action*. Bobbie's sister, Maidie Andrews, and Peter Graves and Finlay Currie joined him, and Dorothy Dickson's rôle was taken by Lilli Palmer. 'It is one of those comedies,' said James Agate, 'in which everybody does a great deal of getting into bed, and nobody seems to get out of it!' He had praise, though, for Lilli Palmer's 'platinum incandescence' and Isabel Jeans's 'sense of glittering enormity'.

That summer, at Redroofs, Ivor thought of reviving his play *I Lived With You* in the nearby Theatre Royal, Windsor. At a break in the dress rehearsal news came over the radio that France had fallen. The long silence that followed was broken by Ivor. 'How terrible, terrible,' he said. Ever the professional, he added: 'I suppose that means there won't be a soul in the house tonight.' John Counsell, director of the Theatre Royal, took him up on this: 'My dear Ivor,' he said, 'if there was a German machine gun mounted in the foyer and others at every entrance to the theatre, your fans would somehow contrive to find a way in.' He was right, and a few hours later the Theatre Royal was probably the only place in England to have a house packed to the rafters.

Encouraged by the success of *I Lived With You*, Ivor gave John
Counsell a new play he had written called *Breakaway*. Originally
intended for Edith Evans and Marie Tempest, *Breakaway* was done
at Windsor with Olga Lindo and Frances Rowe in the main rôles and
Peter Graves as juvenile lead. The play travelled no further than
Windsor and, a rarity for Ivor, did not reach the West End. He,
meanwhile, spent three months touring *I Lived With You* in the
provinces and came back to London in August, 1940, at the height of
the blitz. On the evening of the 26th, when one of the worst all-night
raids took place, he and his company were at the King's, Hammersmith. Amid pandemonium at curtain-fall as bombs crashed down
and rocked the theatre, Ivor announced that he and the cast would
remain there and carry on until the morning if necessary. The audience agreed, and, rather than risk going home, stayed to sing songs
with Ivor at the piano and to watch an entertainment improvised by
other members of the company. Only at six in the morning, when an
eerie silence implied that the raid was over, did he leave the stage.
Next week he was due to play the Wimbledon Theatre, but Nazi aeroplanes got there first and dropped a bomb on it. He cancelled the
tour.

By now all but a dozen London theatres had been closed down by
air-raids and it was futile to contemplate doing anything at all in the
West End. He decided, instead, to take *The Dancing Years* on a
provincial tour. So great was its reputation throughout the country
that Tom Arnold found no trouble at all in booking dates over a
period as long as eighteen months. Provincial audiences were keen
to see Ivor in a production that carried with it all the prestige of Drury
Lane, and the tour opened to acclaim in Manchester. It went on to
Edinburgh, Glasgow, Leeds and Birmingham where seasons of up to
half a dozen weeks were booked and where it more than once
returned to satisfy a public demand that seemed limitless. 'I love the
hustle and bustle of a tour,' Ivor once said. 'Why, every Monday night
is a First Night . . . Touring to me is absolute delight. It is like one con-
tinuous house party, with a nice fat cheque at the end of the week; it is
a wonderful way of making new friends and keeping old ones, and it
does definitely build up a public that remains faithful.' He had also
found that while on tour, away from the hectic social life of London
and a clamant telephone, it was easier for him to get on with writing a
new play.

Even the grim conditions of wartime travel failed to shake his
enthusiasm. At night the black-out was omnipotent and impenetra-

ble. Slow and uncomfortable trains ambled through darkened stations and loitered for hours in unrecognisable parts of the country. Food was short and not particularly appetising when available. Oranges and bananas were unknown. Often members of the cast were suddenly called up for military service and understudies had to be abruptly thrown into the breach. Sometimes the company slept on the floors of church halls, schools and, once, a police station. Late at night after the performance there were long journeys home to bed by way of blacked-out streets. Somehow the company managed each time to create the atmosphere of glamour and romance that audiences longed for. One evening in 1942, Ivor summoned the cast on stage and made an announcement that brought cheers from them. They were going back, he told them, to London, where a revival of *The Dancing Years* was planned. It opened there in March and instantly repeated the triumph of Drury Lane. For the next two years the show played over a thousand times and was only taken off in 1944 when Germany's new 'Secret Weapon', the flying bomb, succeeded in closing London theatres.

On Sundays and at other moments when he was not committed to performances at the Adelphi Ivor appeared in troop concerts and helped organise entertainment for isolated gun batteries and remote encampments. He was too old for military service but contributed to the war effort nonetheless with frequent tours of army camps and, above all, with *The Dancing Years* which, like *Chu Chin Chow* in the earlier war, became something of an institution to be visited again and again by men on leave and their families anxious for light and colour and music.

The Christmas of 1942 was celebrated as usual at Redroofs. A Christmas tree glittering with baubles stood in the hall and everyone received presents. Ivor's jeweller had given him a Siberian amethyst. As Ivor travelled down in the car on Christmas Eve after the performance he was eating sweets and gave one to Harry Sinclair, a protégé of his who played many of Ivor's leading rôles on tour. Barry instantly handed it back saying: 'You've given me your amethyst.' Eddie Marsh who was with them delightedly seized the chance of a neat Biblical quotation and remarked: 'If his son ask him for bread, will he give him a stone?'

At the Christmas dinner Eddie sat next to an actress, 'a bright bird-like little creature with a most inconsequential mind'. He happened to be discussing Ibsen's *Ghosts* with Barry Sinclair, and the little bird chirruped: 'Are you interested in straight plays as well as musical shows?' It reminded him, he later told Chris Hassall, of an old and very deaf friend he had met at a recent first night. 'I haven't seen you for *years*,' he said to her. She answered: 'The same to you and many of them.'

It was a peaceful and enjoyable Christmas, though Eddie fretted about Ivor's health. He seemed tired and, just before bedtime, was sick twice. A holiday was what he badly needed, and although success buoyed him up Eddie had the impression that he was heartily bored with acting in the eternal *Dancing Years*, or 'The Advancing Years', as he sometimes ruefully called it. He preferred to dwell on a scheme he had been thinking about for running opera seasons after the war. The idea would be to produce works in the original language, beginning with the three big Puccini operas and following them up with *Carmen*.

Yet there were, as always, much fun and laughter. When Eddie awoke at nine on Christmas morning he rang the bell for Mabel the maid to bring him his breakfast. A figure came in, drew the curtains and, with Mabel's voice, said: 'Get up, you lazy bugger!' A startled Eddie shot upright amid the blankets and saw Ivor standing before him.

2

ARCH OF TRIUMPH – AND DISASTER

'We gather he will be well-treated, with books and good food and of
course his own clothes – but imagine Ivor, of all people, cut off from
affection and gaiety and friendship. Bobbie is afraid he will give up all
for lost and never have the heart to go back to the theatre.'

Eddie Marsh

THE NEW YEAR of 1943 was seen in at The Flat with great rejoicing for
Lilian Braithwaite who, in the honours list, had been created a
D.B.E. She was 'Dame Lilian' now and revelled ignobly in the
thought that she had caught up with her old rival Marie Tempest, a
Dame of some years' standing. The award only served to intensify the
state of war between them. At a recent dinner party Marie had been
congratulated on a tiara she was wearing. 'It is sweet, isn't it?' she
bubbled. 'I inherited it from my great-grandmother. She had a beautiful voice and was often summoned to Court to sing before the King.'
Afterwards, as the guests went home, Bobbie Andrews mused: 'I
can't figure out whose Court Marie was talking about. Do you think it
could have been Henry the Eighth's?'

But Dame Lilian it was who delivered the *coup de grâce*. 'Great-
grandmother fiddlesticks!' she snapped. 'She bought it last winter at
a little jeweller's in Wardour Street. He'd been trying to sell it to me
for years but I didn't think the stones were very good. She'd have
been much wiser if she'd kept her pennies in the bank for her old age,
which should be arriving at any moment now. When I was a little girl
with my hair in braids she'd been acting for many years.'

Someone else who had been around for years was Mam. Even she
was flagging now, though, and she would doze for hours in a comfortable chair, her white hair straggling untidily, a bottle of something not too far away. Her attempt to make Hitler see reason with
Welsh folk-songs had ended in disappointing failure and war had
curtailed her rôle as Ivor's mother at first nights. The last mani-
festation of her lively spirit was the voluminous autobiography she
published in 1940. She called it, with typical bounce, *The Life I Have*

Loved, and made it very clear that her foundations were laid in the 'rich soil of Glamorgan'. Proudly she wrote of her Welsh ancestors that they 'lived among Nature's wonders, and walked with God, taking Him into their everyday lives as a matter of course, like His fresh air and sunshine, rain and storm.'

Ivor contributed a foreword, having taken the precaution of not reading her book in advance lest he should be tempted to criticise what had been a labour of love. He remarked: 'If she has been too indulgent towards me, her son, I can only bless her for it. If she thinks that my plays are the best of all plays, far from allowing my natural modesty to delete those glowing opinions, I can only wish that she were the dramatic critic of every leading newspaper.'

He added: 'Her life has been curiously selfless – she has never saved a penny – and, in addition to having no sense of money at all, she has a sound conviction that what is hers is also somebody else's. Some years ago it was calculated that she had given hundreds of thousands of singing lessons, and I feel quite sure that each lesson – even if it didn't turn the pupil into a Melba or a Caruso – sent her or him away with a better knowledge of how to live.'

In February, 1943, at the age of seventy-nine, wild, feckless, improvident Mam died peacefully while asleep. Only Ivor's closest friends and business manager knew what anguish and embarrassment and inconvenience she had cost him over the years. With perfect loyalty he never mentioned any of these things in public. However outrageous her behaviour he was attached to her by a bond that could not be shattered. He recognised in her some of the qualities she had bequeathed him, among them toughness and independence, and they were too much alike, this squat pugnacious woman and her lean handsome son, for them ever to part. Her death, though not unexpected, caused him agonies of distress for he truly loved her. On a dank February afternoon she was buried at Golders Green and her ashes put next to those of Dave. When Ivor telephoned Eddie Marsh with the news of her death and described himself as 'knocked sideways' he was not exaggerating.

The shock of Mam's death and the rigour of a hard winter laid him low with a severe attack of bronchial pneumonia. At the age of fifty he was gravely ill for the first time in his life. His rôle in *The Dancing Years* devolved on Barry Sinclair and Ivor spent five depressing weeks as an invalid at Redroofs. From his big bed he looked out at the leafless trees stirring in the east wind and meditated plans for the future. Mary Ellis wrote to tell him that she was thinking of playing in a new musical about Lola Montez by Eric Maschwitz, lyricist of 'These Foolish Things' and author of many stage plays.* Ivor replied saying that he thought it a good idea. He signed his letter as 'Ivor – the Rudiest Boy in Krasnia'.

Later, when he had recovered and gone back to London, Tom Arnold who was presenting *The Dancing Years* gave him the Lola Montez script to read. Ivor did so and remarked that it needed a great deal of rewriting which, perhaps, he might do himself. Better still, suggested Tom Arnold, why not write a completely new show for Mary Ellis? Ivor temporised until one day soon afterwards an idea came to him. He had been reading about Mary Garden, the beautiful Scottish soprano lately retired at the end of a long and unusual career. From her native Aberdeen she went as a child to America and thence to Paris where, in a dramatic debut, she replaced at the last minute the principal singer in Charpentier's opera *Louise*. From then on she sang many leading rôles in Paris, London and New York, establishing herself more by virtue of a dominant personality as hard as Scotch granite than by her vocal resources. Debussy, her admiring friend, chose her to sing Mélisande in the first performance of *Pelléas Et Mélisande* and was, as a result, challenged to a duel by the librettist Maeterlinck who wanted his mistress, another prima donna, to have the part. There was, as can be seen, much dramatic material in the life of Mary Garden, fascinating woman and powerful character. Debussy was among Ivor's favourite composers, and had not Mary Ellis made her debut also in Charpentier's *Louise*? He decided to write a musical play inspired by Mary Garden's example, although very little of her stormy and romantic existence was to be found in what he produced.

Arc De Triomphe is the story of Marie Forêt, a girl from the Auvergne who travels to Paris in 1906 with the ambition of becoming a great prima donna. She impresses a famous singing teacher and he takes her as his pupil at a low fee because of her obvious talent. One of her neighbours in the modest quarter where she lodges is a penniless young song-writer and actor called Pierre. Despite her good-natured contempt for his light songs by comparison with the opera

---

* One of these was based on the life of Chopin. James Agate cast his review in the form of a judge's summing up: 'Members of the Jury,' he began, 'the charge against the prisoner at the Bar, Eric Maschwitz, is murder, in that on 29th day of September, 1942, at the Cambridge Theatre, in a piece entitled *Waltz Without End*, he destroyed the reputation of Frédéric Chopin.'

she worships, his charm conquers and she falls in love with him.
They are separated by the impresario Adhémar de Jonzé who has
plans for Marie and sees her love affair as an obstacle to the splendid
career that lies before her. Under his guidance she wins stardom at
the Paris opera while Pierre emigrates to America and turns into a
film star. At the outbreak of the 1914–18 war the lovers are reunited,
although Pierre now realises that de Jonzé's hold on her is complete.
Pierre goes off to the trenches, is badly wounded and dies in hospital
with Marie at his bedside. The jealous impresario, aware that he will
never win Marie's heart even though he has made her a star, tries to
keep her out of the important new opera *Joan Of Arc*. His plot is
foiled and Marie achieves the greatest success of her life as the Maid
of Orleans.

The most typical item in the score of *Arc De Triomphe* was 'Man
Of My Heart', a slow waltz recalling its sumptuous predecessors in
Glamorous Night and *The Dancing Years*. 'Shepherd', the little
tune with which Marie captivates her singing teacher, had an attractive innocence and a pastoral tone quite different from the urban
sophistication of 'Paris Reminds Me Of You' and 'Easy To Live With',
the number that helps Pierre in his wooing of the heroine. Among the
big set pieces were an apache ballet in the Café de l'Europe et de
l'Asie and a pageant on the Seine which provided an occasion for
Elizabeth Welch to deliver, with mellow intensity, two specially written songs including the Cole Porterish 'Dark Music'. The grand finale
showed a scene from the opera *Joan Of Arc* which ended *maestoso*
in 'France Will Rise Again'. At rehearsals Ivor was in good form and
humorous vein. Having come to the finale 'France Will Rise Again'
he announced the title and added, under his breath, 'unless we're
very careful.'

Arc De Triomphe opened at the little Phoenix Theatre in November, 1943, with a production by Leontine Sagan. It was not quite
what Ivor's admirers expected, although spectacle was supplied by
the fancy dress ball which took place on a barge moored in the Seine.
Mary Ellis wearing costumes designed by Cecil Beaton had as her
lover Peter Graves, an attractive and debonair hero. Her singing
teacher was Harcourt Williams, the Shakespearean actor who as age
crept on made a speciality of sweetly doddering old gentlemen, and
the possessive impresario was acted by Raymond Lovell, plump,
brooding, and expert at implying sinister reserves beneath an urbane
manner.

During preparations for the show Ivor's treatment of his designer was amusingly characteristic of the way he handled people. A model set was brought for Ivor's approval and he, clasping his hands in delight, said it was marvellous, wonderful, it showed real genius, one wouldn't have thought it possible! The designer basked in the warmth of his admiration. Then Ivor flashed his broadest smile. Of course, he might be wrong, he usually was, but could he make a small suggestion? Perhaps one of the doors might be moved. Suppose a table was put here instead of there? Why not change the position of the window? Would it be possible to introduce a piano on the left? What did he think about hanging curtains to the right? In the end the whole set was completely changed, but it was all done with such kindly good humour that the designer went away feeling that he had given of his best.

Although *Arc De Triomphe* had a fair run of some two hundred performances it did not do as well as the Drury Lane successes. One reason was that the hero died at the end of the second act. Sixteen weeks into the run Ivor remedied this by bringing him back alive, yet audiences went on dwindling. Despite the lovely voice of Mary Ellis and the polished acting of Peter Graves, Ivor's following remained unsatisfied. They wanted Ivor, Ivor alone, and would be content with nothing else. In vain did he add a new scene and contribute another number for Mary Ellis. It was a very good number but it failed in *Arc De Triomphe*, so he took it out and revived it some years later in *King's Rhapsody* when it became one of the hit songs, thus proving the old rule that certain items, whatever their quality, will only 'go' with certain shows. It was called 'The Mayor of Perpignan' and had a witty lyric by Christopher Hassall which began:

> The Mayor of Perpignan had a wife,
> And the whole of Perpignan
> Loved the wife of the Mayor of Perpignan
> But they never loved the Mayor of Perpignan ...

and ended:

> Oh! Madame la Maire, never let your husband know
> That his only son and his only one belongs to Madame la Maire,
> Not the Mayor of Perpignan.

Ivor consoled himself with the thought that in *Arc De Triomphe* he had, with the Joan of Arc scene, taken a step towards fulfilling what was always Mam's ambition for him, that of writing an opera. More and more these days his thinking was directed towards the world of opera – his plan of mounting a season after the war ended was evidence of this – and one day perhaps he would himself compose a full-length work. He was encouraged by James Agate, who, though usually cool about his work, described *Arc De Triomphe* as 'musicianly'. It did not perturb Ivor that the show gained only a modest success. He could well afford it since his income in the financial year from 1941 to 1942 had amounted to over sixteen thousand pounds. In the following year it topped more than twenty-four thousand, a figure which by standards of the time meant great affluence.

In June 1943 he appeared at the Albert Hall with George Robey and Violet Loraine to sing at a charity event called 'Seventy Years of Song' organised by C. B. Cochran. The stars of the old *Bing Boys Are Here* performed 'If You Were The Only Girl In The World' and Ivor gave the audience 'Keep The Home Fires Burning', now some twenty years old but still as popular as in the days when it first came out. For Christmas at the Adelphi he presented a stage version of *Alice In Wonderland* adapted by his old friend Clemence Dane with music by Richard Addinsell and designs by Gladys Calthrop, Noël Coward's associate, which brought alive the familiar Tenniel illustrations. Roma Beaumont was a little weary of playing a twelve-year-old girl in *The Dancing Years* and had said so to Ivor. To make up for it he promised her 'something lovely', which turned out to be the part of Alice. Zena Dare was the Red Queen, and, as the White Queen, Sybil Thorndike suspended from wires flew over the stage with gallant aplomb.

Throughout the war, like millions of his compatriots, Ivor cheerfully sustained bombs, black-outs and rationing. What he could not do without was his Rolls-Royce, the sleek limousine, his initials 'I.N.' painted red on the door panels, which took him at weekends to and from Redroofs. During the week he stayed at The Flat, but after the Saturday evening performance he needed the peace and refreshment of a country home which had become still more attractive to him after his recent bout of pneumonia. Petrol was severely rationed and for a time he ran the car on gas. Even this was denied him when the authorities banned all private transport. He applied for a licence and made out a case that, since he was helping to keep up public morale, surely he could be allowed the small amount of petrol needed to take him once a week the four miles from Maidenhead to Redroofs? The application was refused. All this happened in 1942, and that Christ-

mas, in his crowded dressing-room at the Adelphi, he complained
about the official decision. The wretched car was no use to him, he
joked, he would give it away, to the Red Cross, to anyone!

Among the people there who heard the remark was one of his
admirers, a lady known as Grace Walton. Ivor, as we have seen,
always had time for his fans, and invariably treated them with
politeness. Miss Walton was first pointed out to him as frequently
occupying the same stall during the run of *Crest Of The Wave*. Afterwards, in a crowd of other admirers, she would come and say goodnight to him at the stage door. She made the acquaintance of Minnie
Rayner and, helped by the latter's credentials, was able to get a personal introduction to Ivor who was struck by her interest in the theatre.
When he took *Crest Of The Wave* on tour, he was startled to see her
sitting in a front stall, not once but in several of the towns on his itinerary. Miss Walton explained that, as private secretary in a big
commercial firm, she travelled a lot on visits to branches throughout
the country.

She saw him in *Henry V*. She saw him in *The Dancing Years* over
and over again. She followed his route on tour and often sat in the
same stall night after successive night. She wrote to him and mentioned the little problems of her daily life. Ivor could not but be
touched by this devotion, and when she asked for the privilege of
speaking to him occasionally for a few minutes at a time he willingly
granted it her. She became a regular visitor to his dressing-room
when *The Dancing Years* settled in at the Adelphi, although she was
never alone with him, few people ever were, and there were always
lots of others around to observe this quaint, rather touching little
woman who looked at Ivor with adoring eyes.

When Ivor made his joke about giving away the Rolls Miss Walton
put forward a suggestion: since her firm's business involved a great
deal of travelling she might arrange its transfer to them. Ivor was
impressed by the offer but insisted that his chauffeur Morgan should
continue to drive the car and that he would go on paying Morgan's
salary if the firm could not afford it. Morgan had worked in his
service for twenty years and he did not want him to be the loser. The
Rolls was duly transferred, the insurance handed over and the re-
registration carried out to the satisfaction of Ivor's business manager
Fred Allen.

At this point Miss Walton coyly promised Ivor 'a nice surprise'. It
happened, she explained, that her firm had a branch at Reading.
What could be easier than for Ivor to have a lift to Redroofs on Satur-

day evenings? It sounded too good to be true. Why not? she replied.
The Rolls could be kept at Redroofs over the weekend and driven
back on Monday. During the week it would be used as the property of
a firm engaged on war work. Ivor could, at any time, have hired a private car with the aid of a doctor's certificate which would not have
been difficult for him to obtain given his state of health, but Miss Walton's proposition was so much simpler. He accepted gratefully. He
had, for years, left the routine details of his life to an efficient staff,
and this small matter seemed no different from other minor details.

Some months later, on 8 October, 1943, the managing director of
the firm rang Ivor and asked him to call urgently. When Ivor arrived
he was told that the firm had been unaware of the arrangement by
which the Rolls was transferred to them and had only just found out.
The lady he knew as Grace Walton, moreover, far from holding an
important position, was only a clerk on their staff. Her real name was
Dora Grace Constable. Why had she done this thing? The reason,
she said when questioned, was that she had become utterly infatuated with the composer of *The Dancing Years*.

Through his solicitor Ivor immediately told the Petrol Board of the
situation. Enquiries began, the police were called in and statements
were taken. On 24 March, 1944, a polite but determined gentleman
in civilian clothes who could have been nothing but a police officer
called at The Flat and insisted on seeing Ivor. He was shown into the
bedroom, for Ivor was not yet up, and handed over a document
charging him with unlawful conspiracy to commit offences against
the Motor Vehicles (Restriction of Use) Order 1942 and summoning
him to appear at Bow Street on a date in April. Receipt of the
summons, it added, should be acknowledged to the Clerk of the
Court by signing a tear-off slip and returning it. A helpful footnote
advised that the correct postage, if the envelope were unsealed, was
one penny.

Ivor panicked. What he thought was simply a matter of an over-
enthusiastic fan had now become a criminal affair. He told his solicitor but otherwise kept silent and did not inform his associates who,
most of them, learned of the incident from newspaper reports. It was
all too ridiculous. How could he possibly be found guilty of committing a crime? He did not know that three factors weighed heavily
against him: the magistrate in charge of the case, a veteran noted for
his fierce sentences, loathed the theatre, detested homosexuals and
abominated law-breakers.

The morning of 24 April arrived and Ivor took his seat at Bow

Street police court while a vagrant accused of stealing some knives and forks was dealt with and remanded. A foot or so away from Ivor sat the plump, thirty-five-year-old Miss Constable. She seldom looked at him. The public seats were crammed with spectators, mostly women, who listened closely as Ivor and Miss Constable were charged. Both pleaded not guilty. The policeman responsible for serving the summons gave his evidence and said that Mr Novello had suggested the possibility of keeping the matter quiet. The magistrate scribbled a note. The prosecution opened its case and relied on Miss Constable's statement that Ivor's car was to be used for work of national importance. The actor, she said, was 'elated' when the trans-action went through and promised her anything in the world she wanted. She settled for a pair of earrings which had belonged to Mam and were worth about twenty-five shillings, or one pound twenty-five pence.

Mr Novello's story, said prosecuting counsel, was 'incredible'. He must have known that the arrangement was a subterfuge to get round the law. Had not Miss Constable declared: 'He is trying to put all the blame on me. That is grossly unfair. He was willing to do anything crooked so long as he had the use of the car'? Later Miss Constable had told a Fuel Inspector that if she could not do anything to assist Mr Novello it would go 'far towards losing his friendship which I deeply value'. Miss Constable, wisely, chose not to give evidence.

Ivor, pale and nervous, entered the witness box. As in the case of Bardell versus Pickwick the most innocent situation could be depic-ted unfavourably and the lightest remark clothed with ominous meaning. Letters written to Ivor by Miss Constable were quoted and, in suggestive tones, counsel enquired if he was 'well acquainted with her'. She was, Ivor replied, a fan, and 'We appreciate fans very much.' He did reasonably well during examination by his own counsel, but when the turn of the prosecution arrived he began to falter. With no script to support him, no well-timed curtain to bring the scene to a close, he lost his way and floundered. It was the worst performance of his life. The magistrate gave his verdict. Miss Constable was sent away with a fine of fifty pounds and twenty-five pounds costs. She went out in tears and holding a handbag over her face. The accused, Ivor Novello, was sentenced to eight weeks' imprisonment subject to appeal, twenty-five pounds costs and bail in his own surety of twenty pounds.

Ivor and his friends were stunned. 'If I were *conscious* of anything wrong,' Ivor told Eddie Marsh, 'surely you know I would have told *you.*' He went on, confiding in his oldest and most loyal friend: 'How can anyone suppose I would have knowingly run such a risk for so little?' Eddie was beside himself with anger and railed at 'the most monstrous miscarriage of justice' perpetrated by a 'grotesque old judge, who looks as if he came out of Punch and Judy . . .' In an attempt to rectify it Eddie visited every person of influence, and he knew many of them, who might be able to help. He even called on his old employer Winston Churchill at Downing Street and in impotent rage thumped the prime ministerial desk with his fist. Churchill offered sympathy but could do nothing else. Eddie was so upset that his normally clear handwriting began to waver and the numerous letters he wrote became wandering and uncertain.

Spring was normally Ivor's favourite season but this year April and May were a time of strain and worry. It cost him a great effort to go on appearing in *The Dancing Years* and each time he went on stage he felt the audience was thinking of him as a convicted criminal who had gloried in the luxury of his Rolls while the rest of them had been struggling for buses and trains. Offstage he was lacklustre and depressed. He rarely laughed and he slept badly. However much his friends assured him that all would be well, however often his legal advisers went over the case and dug out favourable items for the pending appeal, his eyes did not lose their despondent look nor his mouth the tight-lipped rictus that distorted it.

The appeal was heard at Newington Butts on 16 May. Ivor created just as bad an impression as he had earlier for he was not a ready speaker who could express his thought in few words, and he was disconcerted by the rapid volley of questions the cross-examiner put to him. Eddie Marsh gave evidence of character for him, and so did Lewis Casson and Sybil Thorndike. The one moment of humour in a dismal morning came when Lewis Casson was asked if he agreed with what his wife had said in evidence. 'Certainly,' he replied. Counsel went on: 'I suppose you always agree with your wife?' A pause and a smile were followed with: 'Well, no, not always nor of necessity.'

At lunch-time the court adjourned. The defence had concentrated on Miss Walton's capacity for self-delusion and her tendency to romanticise. In the past, it was revealed, she had told her fellow-workers that she was engaged to be married and that she had had a play produced. Counsel remarked on her alleged statement to Ivor that 'I have consistently lied to you about my position in the firm.' The ploy was ungallant but offered the only valid means of defence. It did not impress the Appeals Committee. When the Court reassembled the verdict laid down that the appeal should be dismissed although the prison sentence was reduced from eight weeks to four.

Ivor was led out by two warders. At the door he turned and threw his arms open wide in a gesture of despair. Eddie Marsh, Sybil Thorndike and a few other friends went downstairs to see him. He looked, Eddie told Christopher Hassall later, 'unutterably sad, aged and broken, but he summoned up smiles for us and pressed our hands.' The prisoner was taken off to Wormwood Scrubs. 'It was certainly the most painful thing in my life,' Eddie wrote to his artist friend Paul Nash. 'He had certainly been most imprudent and far too happy-go-lucky, but if there's one thing in the world I'm certain of it is that he had neither intention nor consciousness of doing anything wrong, and now he bears his misfortune with exemplary courage and fortitude.'

Although the blow had fallen Eddie still hoped to soften it. He visited the Home Office in the company of his doctor and saw the head of the Prison Department. They told this man about Ivor's bronchitis and pneumonia, of the strain he had gone through over the past two years and of how, his constitution being what it was, he would give no sign of an imminent breakdown until, suddenly, the collapse declared itself. The high official heard them with attention. The Home Office was as much concerned for its own sake as for Ivor's. Public opinion would be outraged if such a national favourite as Mr Novello were to crack up while in their charge. He said that the prison doctor would be fully informed.

Ivor's day began at half-past six in the morning with an uneatable breakfast. For the old lags who surrounded him the existence was, perhaps, an improvement on what they knew outside since at least they were sheltered from the weather and had regular food. For Ivor, used to silk pyjamas, late rising and the ministration of a devoted entourage, it resembled the seventh circle of hell. He was given work in the prison library and a genial padre commissioned him to make scrapbooks from illustrated magazines for the benefit of the many illiterates there. When the authorities gave him a mailbag to sew he broke down. The padre intervened and arranged for him to take choir practice in the chapel. Music revived him, and teaching the prisoners new anthems and accompanying them at the piano helped to ease his misery.

At the end of the second week, however, he collapsed in a fit of bitter tears. The padre found him moaning on the floor of his cell.

Ivor could see no future for himself. When he left prison, he said, he would retire from the theatre and live on his savings. His proud career had gone and with it all his ambition. The padre reasoned with him and gradually restored him to calmness. He even obtained some music manuscript paper for Ivor so that he could compose if he felt like it.

For the first time in his life Ivor did not want to write music. Instead, he jotted down on the bar-lines his desperate reflections. He acknowledged that other people were suffering agonies far worse than his and he knew that his own sentence was very short compared with some. Yet why should he, who had but transgressed a minor regulation, be closeted with and treated the same as 'the most habitual robbery with violence, sex outrage, sub-human creatures'? A more profound and disappointing thought struck him. 'I have always been surrounded by people – never alone – had an idea that if I was alone I should "find myself" – discover some rare new philosophy, some staggering new revelation – find a new depth of soul – but no – not at all. I have learned nothing. I'm just the same – only very angry and resentful. Perhaps – and it is possible that when I get home, my having suffered a lot and having been so terribly lonely, *will* do something for me but I very much doubt it . . . Oh, Christ Jesus help me to get through this and come out *sane* – I think the root of insanity is sheer utter futile black boredom . . .'

The order of release came on 12 June. He emerged soon after midnight to avoid the crowds that would otherwise have gathered outside the prison gates. From Wormwood Scrubs he was driven swiftly to Redroofs. Eddie hastened down and was relieved to see that, physically, he was not much different though very thin as he had eaten nothing but sugarless porridge and drunk only cocoa during his imprisonment. Following his first night of liberty he woke up at half-past six, the prison time, and suddenly realised that he was free. He could, if he wanted, go out through the door, open a window, stroll around the house. He got out of bed and wandered down to the pantry. On a shelf stood a bowl of his favourite food. He picked it up and devoured the cold rice pudding with greedy relish.

He told Eddie of the padre who had done so much to help him through the ordeal. Despite the black comments he wrote in his prison diary he thought he had learned something after all: he must not take things for granted, he must value the smallest pleasures of life. A very bad Salvation Army band that played at Wormwood Scrubs had seemed to him as sweet and musicianly as the New York Symphony

Orchestra conducted by Toscanini. He believed, too, that he was cured of smoking since he had done without cigarettes throughout the whole period. (Very soon, though, he was back on his usual sixty Abdullahs a day.) Also he wanted to do something for the people left behind. A large cheque went to the prisoners' welfare fund and he gave a piano to both Wormwood Scrubs and Holloway. Each week he sent complimentary tickets for *The Dancing Years* to warders and others, and every month he organised a concert party for the entertainment of his one-time fellow prisoners, though he did not, excusably, choose to return there himself.

Summer came to Redroofs. While the lilac bloomed and the trees put on new greenery Ivor convalesced and read the thousands of letters people had written him about the prison case. They were from every level of society. Many of his correspondents had never seen him but admired his music and wrote out of gratitude. Others spoke movingly of having undergone the same experience as he had. Some were funny enough to make him laugh aloud and some touched him very deeply. He did not often refer to the events of the past few months and when he did it was usually in a tone of sardonic humour. As he drove in the car with Heather Thatcher one day she remarked: 'Ivor, the Rolls looks marvellous. Is it a new one?' 'No,' he replied, 'I've just had the arrows painted out.'

There was a new, strange expression in his eyes, and the shadows beneath them turned darker and deeper. He never regained the weight he lost in prison and when he sunbathed his body looked thin and lanky. Sometimes a fit of irritability would seize him. He did not laugh as much as he used to, although the bitterness he felt was steadfastly repressed and only disclosed in rare flashes. It must have been aggravated some months later when a very well-known dance-band leader was charged with a similar offence against the petrol regulations and escaped on payment of a trifling fine. Winston Churchill himself told Eddie Marsh that he thought Ivor had been treated with undue harshness and that the prison sentence was ridiculous.

Ironically enough the year of Ivor's imprisonment in 1944 was also the year when his earnings reached their highest peak ever, a total of more than thirty-six thousand pounds. His reputation and his enthusiastic following increased rather than declined, since most people shared Churchill's opinion and believed him to have been the target of judicial vindictiveness. He began to recover his poise and to think once more of facing an audience. A week later he felt well enough to go back to *The Dancing Years*. The evening of the 20th was hot and sunny, for during the war the hours were governed by double summertime and the curtain rose in what was really late afternoon. Ivor loped from The Flat and along Maiden Lane to the stage door of the Adelphi. Several passers-by wished him luck and he replied with a nervous smile. The house was packed and suspenseful. The orchestra swung into the overture and the curtain went up on the opening scene of dawn over a Viennese garden. A night watchman's voice echoed, his lantern glinted and the light slowly came up. An air-raid warning was in progress and a flying bomb could be heard exploding in the distance. The audience ignored it and concentrated on the girlish figure of Roma Beaumont skipping into the limelight. Ivor was not in the habit of writing long build-up scenes for himself and his first entrance had an almost casual, nonchalant air. Instantly a vast wave of applause crashed out. Cheers and clapping arose from all parts of the house and a thundering welcome greeted the slight and apprehensive figure at centre stage. He stood there, his arms hanging at his sides, while the roar of admiration surged about him. At that moment, with perfect timing, the sound of the 'All Clear' was heard outside. The stage manager consulted his stopwatch and found that the reception lasted for two minutes and forty-nine seconds precisely.

The play continued in an atmosphere of euphoria. At the concluding Nazi scene, an episode which under the circumstances was peculiarly difficult to play, Ivor acted with immaculate dignity. Afterwards he ushered the principals forward to take their curtain calls. When his turn came the applause grew to a crescendo again and some of the spectators began singing 'For He's A Jolly Good Fellow'. He stepped to the footlights and began speaking. 'This has been the most exciting and wonderful thing that has ever happened to me,' he said. 'I've always known your kindness to me as a player, but tonight I feel it's kindness to me as a person. If I've been in any way enriched by the experiences of these last weeks, I shall try to hand it on to you.'

Back in his dressing-room he could hear the cheers going on long after the National Anthem had been played and the show formally brought to an end. The company held a little party in the bar with drinks and toasts and jokes. The padre from Wormwood Scrubs was there with his wife and so were all of Ivor's closest friends. Ivor told Eddie Marsh that his immediate plan was to act in six performances of *The Dancing Years* from Wednesday onwards each week, staying in London at the Savoy because of the flying bombs and allowing himself the remainder of the time at Redroofs. He was, thought

Eddie, 'really quite his old self, and full of gaiety'. Speaking of the reception that had been given him he remarked to Eddie that while it was going on he had thought to himself: 'Now, you know, I haven't come back from Normandy with a V.C. I've merely been doing a spot of time.'

3

HUNTERSMOON

'We of the theatre are artists. We write and act to please the public, to "fill the plush", to convey our emotions across the footlights and share our rhapsodies with the audience. No matter how good a play or an operetta may seem to be, if it fails to draw an audience then, to my mind, it ceases to exist, to have any useful purpose.'

Ivor Novello

AT THE outbreak of war in 1939 an official body was set up to provide entertainment for the armed forces. It was baptised 'The Entertainments National Service Association', known for short as ENSA, and from its headquarters in Drury Lane Theatre, which had been taken over for the purpose, there set off many concert parties with the brave intent of diverting troops at home and on the war fronts abroad. ENSA's activities quickly grew and soon it was providing recitals, concerts, film shows and companies touring variety, revues, dramas and musicals, all with fit-up equipment that enabled them to play one-night stands in every sort of building from mission halls to gun emplacements. The quality of the entertainment, it must be admitted, varied considerably, and a cynical wag, reported to be Tommy Trinder, claimed that the initials ENSA stood in reality for 'Every Night Something Awful'.

Ivor had already done a lot of troop entertainments and after the run of *The Dancing Years* ended he decided, at the suggestion of Basil Dean, his director on *The Constant Nymph* and now head of ENSA, to tour the Invasion front in France. His choice of play fell on *Love From A Stranger*, a thriller adapted from an Agatha Christie novel by the actor Frank Vosper. The leading character, a murderous madman, was the sort of rôle Vosper played with eerie brilliance, for he had the gift, like Ralph Richardson, of hinting with uncrushable blandness at depths of villainy. Ivor took this part and cast Diana Wynyard as the woman he marries and intends to kill for her money. He also included in the company Margaret Rutherford whom, earlier that year, he engaged to follow Sybil Thorndike as the White Queen for a revival of *Alice In Wonderland*. A good sport like Dame Sybil, she flew through the air with comparable majesty. She had just completed a long run as Madame Arcati, the medium in Noël Coward's *Blithe Spirit*, a rôle which confirmed her reputation on the West End stage. Madame Arcati, it will be remembered, was partly inspired by Clemence Dane, a lady whose penchant for making gaffes which delighted her ribald friends was shared by Miss Rutherford. Having received the signal honour of an invitation to a party at The Flat, the creator of Madame Arcati duly ascended in the terrible lift and was met by Ivor who threw open the door to reveal his theatrical friends assembled in the glamorous décor. 'Oh, Ivor!' she declared, her famous jowls a-quiver with emotion, 'it's fairyland!'

Attired in special-issue Army uniforms – Ivor and Bobbie Andrews, who was also in the cast, wore peaked hats at a daring angle and Margaret Rutherford sported a floppy beret – the *Love From A Stranger* company embarked for the French coast early in July. The day was uncomfortably hot, the sea behaved badly, yet by afternoon they were giving their first performance on a tented stage in the middle of a giant field. At either side were canvas dressing-rooms, while in front stretched an audience of some two thousand weary soldiers, not all of whom could have heard what was being said on stage. Flies and midges danced in the merciless sunshine and perched on Diana Wynyard's nose at the play's dramatic moments. Overhead aeroplanes roared and spluttered as they came and went on bombing sorties. A Mustang dived low at the audience to make sure they were not Germans. A Spitfire launched into a noisy victory roll. In the tenderest, most intimate passages the actors found themselves shrieking at the top of their voices. Between the acts Ivor rested on an upturned box. 'I can only suppose,' he smiled wanly, 'that all these bloody aeroplanes were sent here specially by Lilian Braithwaite.'

From there they travelled to the pretty little theatre in Bayeux and played for a fortnight at a rate of three and sometimes four shows a day. *Love From A Stranger*, a supposedly chilling melodrama, is hard to do under the best circumstances, and putting it over at ten o'clock in the morning to an audience of soldiers just returned from the front line was an impossible task. Some, indeed rows of them, fell asleep directly the curtain rose. They woke up at the end when Ivor stepped over to the piano and said: 'I wrote a song which your fathers seemed to like very much. It went like this.' Whereupon he banged out 'Keep The Home Fires Burning' and they all, even the weariest, joined in the chorus. After which he would announce: 'And now I've

written a new one. It's called "When You Come Home Again". It's
never been played before in public; let's try it out on you.' Although
they did not know the verses they hummed the tune, for it had an
atmosphere, an irresistible lilt that captivated at first hearing. Later it
was to emerge as 'We'll Gather Lilacs'.

The ENSA tour went on into the autumn of 1944. It played in
barns, tents, canteens, cinemas, sheds and even, as at Bayeux, in
theatres. On pianos that were out of tune, with keys that stuck and
often were found to be missing at the crucial point of a melody, Ivor
played 'Keep The Home Fires Burning' and other songs with every
appearance of zest and enjoyment. Exhausting though it was, entertaining the troops gave him a welcome break from interminable repe-
titions of *The Dancing Years* – and from memories of Wormwood
Scrubs.

After eight weeks of playing towns and villages in Normandy and
Belgium the *Love From A Stranger* company ended its journey with
a farewell performance at Brussels. Tom Arnold had arranged yet
another provincial tour of *The Dancing Years* and Ivor went back
to work in England. Conditions were not quite as bad as at the
height of the war, but even so fortitude was needed. The scenery,
direct from Drury Lane Theatre, went by train and was frequently
mislaid. At Morecambe the greater part of it was overlooked at the
station and performances could not begin until Tuesday, when,
with the aid of RAF personnel as amateur stage-hands, it was shuf-
fled into place. A dance-hall occupied the floor above and during
the interval revellers tramped down to see what was going on
below. They saw Ivor striking romantic attitudes in the third act
and, with a rude expletive, trooped out again to dance the Hokey-
Cokey upstairs. Scenes were cut because back-drops would not fit
the stage. People caught colds in draughty halls. Ivor went down
with a particularly vile one and Barry Sinclair was drafted in to take
his rôle. He did so with no little success and, returning late at night,
proudly told Ivor about the full houses he was drawing. 'Shut up,'
Ivor rejoined, 'I don't want to hear about that. Now I'll read you
what I've written this afternoon.'

He spent all his time in bed scribbling a new play. 'I'm stuck for a
line – for Zena,' he would suddenly remark. 'She's just arrived at the
house by train.' Barry Sinclair would suggest a speech or a cue and
Ivor gratefully wrote it in. By the time they gave the final performance
of *The Dancing Years* at the Blackpool Opera House in the early
months of 1945 he had completed *Perchance To Dream*.

His first draft had as setting an old English country house called 'Huntersmoon' and covered the years from 1818 to the present time. For himself he visualised three different rôles: in the first generation he was a Regency buck who operates as a highwayman to pay off his debts, in the second he reappeared as a Victorian composer who loses the woman he loves, and in the third he acted their descendant and, this time, won the hand of the girl who represents the love he had lost in earlier generations. As a climax the ghosts of those who peopled Huntersmoon over the years are evoked and their past unhappiness is blotted out by the romance of their modern equivalents so that they at last can sleep, perchance to dream. The quotation from *Hamlet* was an example of Ivor's flair for titles, and the more he thought about the idea the more his enthusiasm grew. He outlined it to James Agate over dinner one evening at the Café Royal. Agate cynically replied that audiences wouldn't be interested. 'They won't like it,' he grunted. 'You'll find that even a first-class cast, charming music and a good plot won't save the show. What the modern generation apparently wants is plenty of hot music and transatlantic rhythm.'

Once Ivor had made up his mind to do something he was rarely swayed by other people's opinions, although Agate's blunt judgement damped his enthusiasm. Soon afterwards he was in Brighton, a favourite town of his, and found himself admiring once again the Royal Pavilion's flamboyant design, its turrets and spires and domes that stood out in unexpected silhouette by the waves. The Regency had always been the age he preferred and he saw, in his mind's eye, the first act of *Perchance To Dream* with the men in cravats and ruffled shirts, the women in leg-of-mutton sleeves and bonnets. A soldier and his girlfriend were looking around the State Apartments. 'They don't build wonderful places like this nowadays, do they?' observed the soldier. Ivor heard the remark and decided instantly to go ahead with his Regency play in spite of the scepticism Agate had expressed.

Perchance To Dream, according to Samuel French's businesslike catalogue of musical plays, contains 'a fair sprinkling of lushly harmonised numbers in, perhaps, the most romantic and musical' of Ivor's works. It does not rely, as do some of his earlier plays, on spectacular stagecraft and exciting incidents but depends, instead, on the charm of a well-written score and the nostalgic appeal of Regency and Victorian settings. Soon after the opening chorus and as early as the number which almost immediately follows it, Ivor attacks the audience with 'Love Is My Reason', a beguiling slow waltz given to Lydia, the Drury Lane actress who is Sir Graham Rodney's lover. The entrance of Lady Charlotte, his rich aunt played by Margaret Rutherford, prepares for the quintet 'A Lady Went To Market Fair', which is uneasily close to Sullivan's 'No Possible Doubt Whatever', both in tempo and figuration, although the part-writing is skilful enough. Ivor recovers himself with the next number, 'The Night When I Curtsied To The King', a deft pastiche of folk-song in the style of Edward German, prettily harmonised and ingenuously charming. When Sir Graham as an amateur highwayman robs a coach and finds it contains only Lady Fayre and her ward Melinda, he promptly falls in love with the latter and provides an excuse for 'Highwayman Love', a robust melody perfectly tailored for Olive Gilbert. The Regency period ends with a sung ballet portraying the seasons: Summer is a brisk waltz, Autumn a languid andante, Winter a sparkling scherzo and Spring a bustling allegro.

The Victorian second act opens with 'A Woman's Heart', slow, hesitating and cleverly timed to express emotional indecision. Then comes the big number, 'We'll Gather Lilacs', which in the original context was designed as a Victorian ballad for two women's voices. There are several stories of how Ivor came to write this, one of his most famous songs. Alec Robertson contended that the actor Alfred Lunt spoke to Ivor on a visit to America of his nostalgia for the lilac trees at Redroofs. Ivor is supposed to have said, 'I've made up a tune about it,' and forthwith produced the melody. Since, however, he did not go to America in the half-dozen or so years before *Perchance To Dream*, the account is unlikely. Another version has it that one day, seeing Lynn Fontanne, Lunt's wife, in a white dress beside a lilac tree at Redroofs, he was impelled to write the tune.

Whatever its origins, 'We'll Gather Lilacs' became almost as popular as 'Keep The Home Fires Burning'. The repeated note of the refrain, as inspired in its simplicity as Sullivan's 'Lost Chord', and the warmth of its chordal development ensured that it was played everywhere in Britain during the years following the war and for a long time after. No less apt in period feeling is the 'Victorian Wedding' music which contains a pert bridesmaid's dance, a polka that might have come out of any Dickensian revel, and, as climax, one of those expansive waltzes, 'My Heart's Afire', which by the sturdy nature of its harmonies declares confidently that all is for the best in the best possible of worlds. As a change from polkas and mazurkas Ivor then inserted a special number called 'The Glo-Glo', delightfully Vic-

torian in its lyric but, as for the musical content, a return to the
Edwardian dances of his youth. Another new item, an 'Elopement'
duet, artfully utilises folk-song elements before the concluding scene
and its ghostly harmonic ninths which accompany the returning
spirits who occupied 'Huntersmoon' in Regency and Victorian
times.

As usual many friends adorned the cast. Bobbie Andrews was
Sir Graham's wicked cousin during Regency times and, in the last
act, a modern kinsman, sympathetic on this occasion and happily
united with a lady called Iris (Muriel Barron) who uncannily
resembles the Lydia of Act One. Olive Gilbert deployed her con-
tralto tones as a Regency actress and a Victorian mother while
Roma Beaumont, successively incarnated as Melinda, Melanie and
Melody, brought piquancy to the rôle of the heroine. As for Ivor,
well, he gave his fans the Ivor they wanted, an Ivor who, regardless
of the unbecoming red wig he donned in the first act, displayed his
lovely profile in a series of well-contrived romantic tableaux.
Rehearsals, as always, evolved in chaos and went on long into the
evening. Ivor, following his custom, had written too much and was
obliged to cut ruthlessly. The plot, as will be gathered, spun
complications which demanded perpetual vigilance from spectators
if the intricacies of the story were to be appreciated. Eddie Marsh,
ever helpful, devised a genealogical tree laid out to explain the
ancestry of Sir Graham Rodney. It was painted on a large drop
cloth for the benefit of those anxious to learn, although in the
excitement of a Novello first night one doubts if Eddie's thoughtful
gesture received the attention it deserved.

Since Christopher Hassall was still in the army Ivor himself wrote
the lyrics of *Perchance To Dream*. If they lack the touches of humour
Chris might have added they are, in general, apt and sympathetic to
the voice, although a phrase like 'In search of sunshine' may trip the
unwary singer. Harry Acres did the orchestration and wrapped Ivor's
melodies in the famous 'Novello sound' which filled the Hippodrome with its ripe sonorities at the first night in April, 1945.
Nothing, it seemed, had changed: the death of Mam, the prison interlude, might never have happened, and Ivor was back again on his
pedestal, the idolised hero of curtain after curtain, the object of
breathless adoration. Did Miss Constable, one wonders, ever see
Perchance To Dream?

There was not an empty seat to be found at any performance of the
new play which continued for over two years and enjoyed the longest

unbroken run of any Novello show. It reached a total of one thousand and twenty performances and then was only taken off because Ivor decided to tour it in South Africa. Throughout the difficult post-war days theatre-goers flocked to it. They came back again and again because they were tired by what they had gone through since 1939 and sought escape from austerity in the warmth and glamour Ivor knew so well how to provide. A special performance was given on behalf of the King George Pension Fund for actors, a charity supported by Ivor, and Queen Mary attended. During the interval she sent for him and gave him an audience in the royal box. The gesture meant a great deal to him.

At the first night, wrote James Agate, 'the curtain, when it went up, took with it the entire audience, which remained in its seventh heaven until, after three hours and a half, the curtain descended and automatically brought the audience down with it. The actor's nonsense had obviously suited their nonsense.' There were 'aeons of ballet', he commented, and 'a very, very great deal of lush, romantic music, scored principally for harp after the manner of that popular composer Herr Mittel Europa', although he praised Olive Gilbert's 'admirable singing' and 'Miss Rutherford's magnificent determination to stand no nonsense and deliver none'. *The Times* observed acidly that 'all the songs gain much from the rapture with which Mr Novello listens to them . . .' Confronted with such an obviously popular triumph there was little for a resigned critic to say.

Now that *Perchance To Dream* was launched Ivor busied himself with other things. Back in 1926 he had conceived the ambition of owning one hundred thousand pounds in Consols and, throughout the years, had bought up gilt-edged securities at carefully chosen moments. In 1945 he at last achieved his aim with an accumulation representing the face value he aimed at. He sold out and realised over eighty-eight thousand pounds. Some of the money he put into a revival of Somerset Maugham's play *Our Betters* which he produced. He also gave advice and used his influence to help the young Peter Daubeny on his way. Daubeny came of an old family descended from a long line of military men, a circumstance which caused his father to view with misgiving his youthful theatrical ambitions. In spite of parental forebodings he trained as an actor at the Liverpool Repertory Theatre until the war and family tradition ensnared him in the Coldstream Guards. At Salerno he was blown up by a mortar bomb and so badly wounded that his left arm had to be amputated. While he lay in the hospital ward he realised that if, as an actor, his career was ended, as a theatrical manager he still had a future.

Ivor had already met him in Liverpool and kept up their friendship throughout the war. Just before Daubeny was invalided out they had dinner at the Savoy Grill and discussed his plan for management. Ivor promised that he would write a play for him. He added: 'From now on you can trust very few. The theatre is the most exciting profession in the world. It is also a very dangerous and treacherous one. Never mind what people think of you. Follow your own judgement and no one else's. And if ever in trouble over anything, come to me. I will never let you down.' Soon afterwards he helped Daubeny seize his first chance in presenting a new play about the Prince Regent and Mrs Fitzherbert. Mary Ellis acted the latter rôle with moving tenderness, the décor, in which Somerset Maugham's ex-wife Syrie had a hand, glittered with elegance, and the critics were favourable. The piece ran for just under a month.

Two years later came a telephone call from Ivor inviting Daubeny to Redroofs for 'a great surprise'. Ivor, lolling in his vast bed, presented him with a play he had just written and which he intended for the Daubeny management. Gratified, overjoyed, the young impresario caught his train back to London and began reading the manuscript. It was called *We Proudly Present* and involved the struggles of two amateurs freshly demobilised who take over a run-down theatre after the war and hope to revive it with a new play. As in *Party, Proscenium* and *The Sunshine Sisters*, Ivor here invited the audience to peep behind the scenes at the world of theatre that was his life. The young men's secretary Phyl is a retired actress who often clashes with the star they have engaged for the lead, the unbearable Sandra Mars:

Sandra	Oh, Phyl – may I – would you telephone Tennents for me – tell them I've been kept.
Phyl	That's not going to surprise them.
Sandra	[laughing gaily]. Oh, what a comédienne – she always was – all those years ago.

There are many other jokes to be appreciated only by theatre addicts. A typical one runs like this: 'She's as difficult as hell, but who else is there? Everyone's either filming or they've got a moral obligation to Tennents.' Rehearsals are a shambles, the cast throw fits of temperament and the leading man resigns because of Sandra's unpleasantness. She, however, saves the day because she persuades the author to rewrite his highbrow play completely so that it becomes a farce. Ivor allows himself only one reference to the outside world, and that a wry one, when the budding management realise they may have infringed post-war building regulations and neglected to obtain permission for work done on the theatre. The thought of imprisonment looms. 'I couldn't care less,' says one of the characters. 'Prison's wonderful – regular food – solitude – I can't wait.'

By the time he reached Paddington Daubeny's elation had evaporated. *We Proudly Present*, written to the same conventional formula of exposition/problem/dénouement Ivor used in all his other straight plays, had moments of fun and passages of effective dialogue but seemed on the whole flat and parochial. Daubeny compared it with Noël Coward's *Present Laughter*, another play about theatricals, and found it lacking in wit and vision. He could not, alas, refuse it, for Ivor had in his generosity thought to do him a good turn and really believed that the new play would be an enormous success. With a heavy heart he engaged Phyllis Monkman as 'Phyl', a part Ivor had written for her specifically, and Peter Graves and Tony Forwood as the two young men. In the rôle of Franzi Mahler, a flamboyant Viennese star, he cast Irene Handl, usually an exponent of comic cockney maids though here, for once, reverting to her true origins since her family was of Austrian descent. Two other reliable West End figures, Mary Jerrold and Ena Burrill, helped bring the play to life at rehearsals under Max Adrian's witty direction, and the atmosphere became optimistic. Only one other person shared Daubeny's low opinion of *We Proudly Present*. Noël Coward wagged a finger at him and snapped: 'I should not have minded losing my arm, but I should mind, desperately, losing my integrity.'

Naturally Ivor believed that his play would be a great hit and rejoiced in advance on Daubeny's behalf. At the same time he showed modesty and was prepared to rewrite scenes that were giving trouble. 'Let's try it and see how it goes' was his cheerful response to any suggestions for improvement or alteration. On one point, however, he was obdurate. Later in the run Tony Forwood, who played one of the theatrical managers, had to leave and Daubeny took over his part, a circumstance which brought helpful publicity from newspapers amused by the sight of an impresario caricaturing himself. During an episode with Ena Burrill Daubeny was suddenly overtaken by a fit of uncontrollable laughter which spread to others on stage. Most actors have experienced this phenomenon which the French call *fou-rire*, a spasm of giggles caused by some trifling incident or remark or even a passing thought. For no valid reason a chuckle is born and develops into full-throated laughter which the unfortunate victim is powerless to stop. After the matinée Daubeny walked in Hyde Park desperately trying to quell an emotion that threatened to become hysteria. He could not help himself and at the evening performance the same thing happened. Ivor got to hear of it and was extremely angry. He had, a long time ago when very young and inexperienced, broken into laughter on stage – but only once, and since then had never allowed himself to connive at something which he regarded as the worst possible sin, that of treating the public with contempt. At ten o'clock in the morning he called a special rehearsal. Stony, grim-faced, he announced: 'You've failed me disgracefully. I'm bitterly disappointed in you. You have let the public down badly. We will go through the play from beginning to end with a fresh and sharply focused vision.' They did, and that evening the episode was played in full seriousness. Ivor smiled again.

Despite earlier fears *We Proudly Present* did quite well and after a five-month London run went on a successful tour. Ivor's gesture had helped Peter Daubeny to found the organisation which, a few years later, was to present the annual World Theatre Seasons featuring in London each spring the best of the world's great theatrical companies. *We Proudly Present* also marked a small milestone in that it was among the last plays to be seen by James Agate at the end of a long career as the outstanding drama critic of his time. Suffering from dropsy, a weak heart and a racking cough, he went to the first night and sat in a box 'whimpering with pain'. He liked what he saw and enjoyed this 'witty, malicious peep behind repertory scenes' which enabled him to quote, apropos of the outrageous leading lady, one of his favourite passages describing Sarah Bernhardt, for him the greatest actress of all. Especially did he enjoy the Viennese star who, in reply to the director's protest that his play is not a musical, snaps: 'But in the second act there should be a drawing-room mit piano. Vell, at dat piano I sink five sonks. It is quite simple.' The women, he concluded, had the best of it: 'I stopped counting the number of times that Miss Irene Handl snatched the play from Miss Monkman, Miss Monkman from Miss Burrill, and Miss Burrill from Miss Monkman.' He enjoyed the evening far more than any of Ivor's musical plays. In any case he had already given his final verdict several years back at

C. B. Cochran's Albert Hall production featuring music-hall songs: 'Ivor, who was fifty last January, didn't look a day over thirty-five; his charm is as amazing as ever. I shall always say that there are more brains and more sheer acting capacity in this young man than anyone has ever supposed.' A month after *We Proudly Present* Agate was dead.

Part Six

AN ABDICATION

'Ivor Novello is a master of the shameless cliché, and if I were Sarah Bernhardt I would ask him to write all my plays for me . . . I don't say that Massenet and Puccini didn't do it better. The point is Mr Novello does it, does it very well, and keeps alive a whole part of the theatre which is, to my vulgar mind, very valuable and important and enjoyable. He also does what few poets seem to be able to do nowadays. He provides real poetry for the masses.'

Philip Hope-Wallace

1

THE MIXTURE AS BEFORE BUT DIFFERENT

'We've had so much austerity, we haven't seen any beautiful things. I
think I'm going to do the last of Ruritania, and we can have the lot,
Kings and Queens, Princes and Princesses, church music, everything. I
shall naturally write a lovely part for myself – for my old age.'

Ivor to Vanessa Lee

IN 1947 *The Dancing Years* went off anew on one of its endless provincial tours and returned to London at the Casino for another long
run while Ivor, at the Hippodrome not far away, was still appearing
in *Perchance To Dream*. Although the latter was still drawing full
houses he decided to take the production with him for a ten-week
season in South Africa. The play had many memories, not least of the
evening when news arrived that the war had ended in victory and the
whole house stood and jubilated wildly for half an hour. Ivor longed
for the sun. Apart from his ENSA travels in France and Belgium
he had not been out of England for years, and now the South African
invitation meant that he could again satisfy his wanderlust.

With the exception of Zena Dare in place of Margaret Rutherford,
the company he led was the same as that of the London production.
The only other significant change involved his secretary. Lloydie
Williams, the faithful companion who administered his affairs and
shielded him from the importunate, had been disabled by a stroke.
He lived, just, at Redroofs and was able to get about in a wheelchair.
His days passed in sitting and listening to the conversation,
although he still had enough strength to use his hand for smoking a
cigarette. Lloydie was a friend rather than an employee and Ivor did
everything possible to ease his last years before he slipped
thankfully into death. His place was filled by Gordon Duttson, a
promising young actor from the cast of *Perchance To Dream*. At
first he was reluctant to take on the job but Ivor and Bobbie spoke
persuasively. Soon afterwards Eddie Marsh came to dinner and
Gordon was profuse with his 'Sir Edwards'. Eddie glanced at him
and, in his fluting voice, remarked: 'Would you do me a favour?' The

new secretary nodded and wondered what was to come. 'Please don't call me Sir Edward,' continued Marsh. 'It makes me feel so old. Please call me Eddie.'

Perchance To Dream had its Johannesburg première in December, 1947, and met with a perfect reception. It went on to Cape Town and won Ivor acclaim as warm as anything he experienced at home. There were sights to be seen, Table Mountain to be explored and, above all, hot and perpetual sunshine to be absorbed in long lazy siestas between performances. The trip, declared Ivor, was the most consistently happy period of his life. From South Africa he flew to Jamaica and bought a house at Montego Bay which he regarded as a haven from English winters. Here a verandah looked out over trees and lawns where he sunbathed in a climate that reminded him of California and restored energy sapped by a recent illness on tour. While away from England he also visited New York and was asked to lunch by Greta Garbo. With Gordon, Bobbie and Olive Gilbert he went to meet her. It was a rainy day, and as they approached the modest restaurant they saw, waiting outside for them, a figure in shiny fisherman's hat and macintosh looking like any practical, ordinary woman. Afterwards Ivor had arranged a showing of his early silent film *The White Rose*, now more than a quarter of a century old with himself looking correspondingly young. When the film was over he asked her eagerly: 'What do you think of me?' 'Verree byootifull!' she purred.

Not all his spare moments on the South African tour were devoted to sun-worship. As he once said: 'While I am playing in a production it absorbs my entire energies, mental and physical. Then, towards the end of its run – an end, by the way, dictated by my own restlessness, and not lack of public support – I get the desire to work on something else.' He had reached this stage with *Perchance To Dream*. At the Carleton Hotel in Johannesburg the outline of a story began to take shape in his mind. A piano was brought up to his suite and he tried out vague melodies, half-formed tunes, little motifs that seemed to come from nowhere but were demanding expression. Out of the confusion of inchoate melodic lines and jumbled chords definite themes were emerging. He had them recorded, played them back and found, here and there, phrases that he could elaborate and polish into something worthwhile at the keyboard. Then he played them over to his friends and waited for their verdict. Sometimes he agreed with their judgement. Sometimes nothing they said would change his opinion. Most often he was right.

Whole scenes came into existence like this. It was impossible for him exactly to say why one seemed 'right' and why another did not. His decisions were purely intuitive, and although no one is able to judge what will succeed on stage until an audience is actually present, instinct and experience can serve as a good rule-of-thumb guide. In his suite at the Carleton his first idea had been to write something about the Welsh Eisteddfod, a topic, given his background, which was entirely suitable and characteristic. He went so far with it and then found he could not carry on. Yet although he had reached a dead end his subconscious mind was still working and turned him in the direction of a Ruritanian romance which, as it unfolded, he decided to call *The Legend of The Snow Princess*. After a while his inspiration altered course and flowered into *King's Rhapsody*.

He was now fifty-six years old and the facts of life were such that he could no longer hope to present himself, even with the aid of his durable good looks, as the youthful hero he played in *Glamorous Night* or *The Dancing Years*. Why should he not face reality and act the part of a middle-aged man? It was the sort of rôle Maurice Chevalier had been filling with great success once his early spark was gone, and the combination of maturity and worldly wisdom had proved even more irresistible. Thus, in what Ivor decided would be his last excursion to Ruritania, he presented himself as Nikki, a prince who has been in exile for some twenty years on account, it is said, of a scandalous love affair. The old king of Murania dies and Nikki is recalled to succeed him. The king of Norseland, a friendly power, hopes to arrange for political reasons a marriage between his daughter Princess Cristiane and Nikki. He breaks the news on her eighteenth birthday and waits, a little apprehensively, for her reaction. It is, to his relief, very favourable since over the years she has nourished a schoolgirl passion for Nikki and pasted into her scrapbook every photograph and press cutting she could find about him.

The scene moves to Paris where the Queen Mother of Murania tells Nikki of his father's death and urges return to his native country and the throne. He will also have, she adds, the perfect Queen in Princess Cristiane. Her arguments do not convince him. He has lived so long in Paris that he looks on it as his natural home, and, moreover, he does not wish to end his association with the actress Marta Karillos. Finally the Queen Mother wins him over, although he afterwards confides in Marta that, despite being obliged to marry

Cristiane and produce an heir, she, Marta, will always remain his true love. The throne of Murania is duly taken up by Nikki who, however, is not so keen to go through with his marriage to Cristiane. She adores him and is saddened by his obvious avoidance of her. Her distress grows when she learns that the political crisis which prevents him meeting her is only an excuse for him to go on seeing Maria Karillos who has travelled in his company to Murania. 'I'm beaten before I start,' laments Cristiane. Alone in her boudoir she sits at the piano and sings. Nikki appears while she does so and listens to her, fascinated. He has been drinking and does not recognise her. She passes herself off as the confidential maid Astrid to whom, encouraged by another bottle of Imperial Tokay, Nikki complains about his forthcoming arranged marriage and speaks bitterly of Cristiane. Why so bitter? she asks. He answers that a condition of the marriage is that he should expel Marta from the country. Gradually he softens, the conversation takes an intimate turn and she falls into his embrace. Outside a gypsy quartet serenades the Princess. A hand appears at her window and draws the curtains.

At a palace ball Marta Karillos outrages the Queen Mother by making a glamorous entrance. Nikki denies inviting her. When Cristiane enters he recognises her as 'Astrid' to whom last night he had made love. She thoroughly enjoys his furious bewilderment, especially as Marta's invitation is in fact her own cunning idea, and asks Nikki to introduce her. 'I am sure Madame Karillos could teach me so much,' she says after a brief chat about music. 'I think, your Royal Highness,' retorts Marta, 'that I can teach you nothing.'

Some months later a salute is fired to mark the birth of Cristiane's child. Nikki is with Marta in her villa that night and they count the number of rounds. It comes to twenty-one, the figure traditionally used to announce the arrival of a son, and the unwilling father comments sardonically that he cannot rejoice at the advent of a 'small piece of humanity' intended to push him off the throne. When Cristiane insists that Marta must leave the country he declares that if she goes he will go too. She implores him to stay but, having been trapped once by her scheming, he is determined not to be caught out again. 'It was my only way!' she cries passionately, and he realises at last how deep is her love for him. Marta returns from a carriage ride, frightened and half-fainting, to tell how she has been attacked by a gang of peasants. A riotous crowd gathers outside and threatening shouts of 'harlot!' float through the windows. Cristiane pacifies the mob with assurances that Marta is her valued friend and that, if she could do so, she would persuade her to stay in Murania. The rioters arc calmed at her intervention and they disperse. Touched by her loyal stratagem, moved by her obvious feeling for him, Nikki begins to fall in love with her.

Marta goes and leaves Nikki and his queen to settle down in peace. The one-time playboy starts taking a genuine interest in his kingdom and plans to introduce democratic measures. Among them is a bill of rights which Cristiane also favours though the Queen Mother, like many in the government, is firmly opposed to it. Nikki declares that if the Assembly rejects it he will abdicate. This, in fact, is what happens. He draws up the deed of abdication, nominates Cristiane as regent and leaves the country for Paris where he is reunited with Marta. Ten years afterwards his son is crowned in the cathedral of Bledz, capital of Murania. Although, for reasons of state, Nikki is forbidden to be there he attends incognito and watches the ceremony from a shadowed corner. The solemn ritual ends, the grand company departs, and as Cristiane leaves she drops a white rose on the steps of the altar. Nikki walks forward and picks up the rose. At the altar in the deserted cathedral he kneels and prays for the future of the boy king.

Chris Hassall was now demobilised and once again wrote lyrics for Ivor. Together they went over the score, choosing, rejecting, building up or cutting down in the familiar routine that had evolved over a decade of collaboration. They knew each other so well, they shared so quick an instinct for what was appropriate and what was not, that the work got done smoothly and happily. No one, of course, could blame Ivor's lyricist for writing, in the march called 'Take your girl', lines such as the following:

> Johnnie was gay
> On that red letter day,

since it was impossible to foresee the meaning which later generations have given that innnocent little epithet. Less excusable was his rhyming of 'June' with 'honeymoon'. Apart from small blemishes like this the words he produced were clear, singable and often witty, as in the case of 'The Mayor Of Perpignan'. The latter, it will be remembered, had been a failure when used in *Arc De Triomphe*. In *King's Rhapsody*, where it turns up as a political lampoon of Nikki, it became one of the hit numbers. 'There's an attractive song I hear everywhere – even in the street,' Nikki says to Marta when he asks her to sing it for him. 'It sounds like the Mayor of – some, some French name.' Marta is embarrassed and very reluctant since she knows that, like the Mayor of Perpignan, Nikki is much less popular than his queen Cristiane, this being in the days before he starts trying to democratise Murania. Fortunately, after she has sung it, he still does not grasp the satirical reference to himself.

Once Ivor had finished notating the melodic lines of his score the individual numbers, in manuscript and on record, were sent to Leighton Lucas for harmonising. On this occasion preparations were even more hectically rushed than usual and there was no time for Lucas to work on 'The Violin Began To Play' which Ivor, in a few hasty minutes, himself embellished with harmonies. Then he conferred with his orchestrator Harry Acres, topping and tailing, deciding what themes to use as 'melos' interludes and choosing the point when reprises were to be featured. After Harry completed the instrumentation Ivor had members of the Liverpool Philharmonic Orchestra play the whole score through at a separate rehearsal, just to make sure the sound was right.

One of the most successful numbers was 'Some Day My Heart Will Awake'. It is sung by Cristiane, nicknamed the 'Snow Princess' for her apparent coldness, when she is teased by her younger sisters. The opening leap of a fourth perfectly matches the optimism of the words – or should one say that Christopher Hassall's words ideally complement the music? – and the song became immensely popular. Another hit was the lullaby 'Fly Home, Little Heart' which the Countess Vera sings to comfort Cristiane on her arrival in Murania. The verse, gentle and swaying, is followed by a richly chorded melody that sweeps forward in stately progression. The finale of the scene where Nikki makes love to Cristiane believing her to be 'Astrid' is provided in the brightly ringing 'If This Were Love'. Almost immediately this is succeeded by 'The Violin Began To Play', a Hungarian-flavoured aria suggesting gypsy violins and zimbaloms subsequently taken up by the Tzigane serenaders outside the window. The other big production number is the trio 'Fling Wide The Gates Of Paradise', a restless and exuberant melody also featured as a reprise to bring the second act to a close.

Along the way there are many agreeable diversions which, though subordinate to the main numbers, show Ivor in resourceful mood. The 'Birthday Greeting' chorus and dancing lesson in the opening scene are pleasant examples of this, as are the 'National Anthem' of

Murania, a dignified succession of block chords, and a swirling waltz for the ballroom scene. The most substantial of these minor items is 'Muranian Rhapsody', a vocal ballet given by gypsy dancers whom the democratically-minded Nikki has invited to perform before the court, despite the Queen Mother's annoyance at 'peasants' being allowed into the royal home. It is a skilful blend which proves that Ivor knew his Delibes. The unaccompanied setting of the Kyrie eleison in the Coronation scene would not perhaps have won the approval of his old teacher Herbert Brewer, but in its theatrical context it is wholly right, which is all that matters where music for the stage is concerned.

'I really think *King's Rhapsody* is the best thing I have ever done,' Ivor told his friend the author Peter Noble. 'In my opinion it has the best story, best music, and is the best-constructed of all my musical plays. It is the mixture as before, but I think it is what people want. I hope I am not wrong.' True, the play contained elements common to *Glamorous Night*: a Ruritanian setting, a king involved with a Lupescu-type mistress, and, at the end, a scene of renunciation. A new factor was the personality of the hero Nikki, a cynical, middle-aged and worldly-wise charmer whom Ivor skilfully contrived for himself. At the end of the Coronation scene, when the singers have intoned the Kyrie, Cristiane has prayed for the boy king, the country's national anthem has been heard and Nikki stands at the altar, white rose in hand, Ivor created a moment of pure theatre that endures in the memory.

With him in the cast were familiar names. Zena Dare played the acidulous Queen Mother and her sister Phyllis was the beautiful Marta Karillos. Olive Gilbert as Countess Vera enriched the lullaby 'Fly Home, Little Heart', and Bobbie Andrews wore a villainous beard as the Prime Minister. Gordon Duttson, while continuing his secretarial work for Ivor, also acted, and a talented woman by the name of Anne Pinder took a small part as a lady-in-waiting at the Muranian court. Miss Pinder was a musician, artist and actress. In *Perchance To Dream* she played several rôles and accompanied at the piano the 'Victorian' duettists in 'We'll Gather Lilacs', as well as designing, very prettily, the cover of the sheet music which the two ladies were holding. Forty years later, at the age of seventy-six, she was found knifed to death in her Battersea flat. Her corpse bore thirty-five stab wounds, and neither the murderer nor his motive has since been discovered.

A happier destiny awaited the girl whom Ivor chose for the vital

rôle of Cristiane. While the revival of *The Dancing Years* was still
running the leading lady had a bad attack of laryngitis and, although
she could still speak her words, was unable to sing. Her understudy
in the wings sang for her and cleverly synchronised the music. The
understudy's voice, thought Ivor, was extremely good, and he gave
her a major audition. Her name was Ruby Moule and she came from
Streatham. She had made her first appearance as a child in the play
Autumn Crocus and sung in BBC radio programmes. Into a very
short space of time she crammed a wide variety of experience with
ENSA tours, concert parties, revues and pantomimes as principal
boy. Ivor decided to make her the lead in a tour of *The Dancing
Years* but then changed his mind and gave the part to someone else.
Miss Moule, by now hardened to the disappointments of the theatre,
went on steadfastly working.

Suddenly Ivor asked her to play Lydia on the South African tour of
Perchance To Dream. Something, though, must be done about her
name and he suggested she think of a psuedonym. As she later told
Sandy Wilson, Ivor sent for her a few days later and pointed at his
dressing-table mirror. On it were written the names 'Vanessa,
Virginia'. She hesitated. 'Don't you like them?' he asked. 'Yes, very
much.' 'Which would you prefer?' 'Vanessa, because I've read Swift.'
Ivor went on: 'I persuaded Vivien to change her name to Leigh, and it
brought her luck. So I'll give you the same name, but we'll spell it
L-E-E.' She was about to go when he added. 'There's only one other
name that I think would have suited you. Sharon.' Miss Lee thought
to herself: 'This has gone too far. I really must tell him.' She opened
her bag and gave him a piece of paper on which she had written:
'Vanessa, Virginia, Sharon'.

King's Rhapsody with Vanessa Lee as Cristiane opened for a
three-week trial run in Manchester. The August of 1949 was one of
the hottest ever and the company, Ivor included, travelled up in a
railway carriage alive with heat. The warm weather did not deter a
packed house in holiday mood and the overture, heavily applauded,
led to triumph after triumph. 'Win,' said Ivor to his company manager Winifred Newman, 'I think I've got my biggest success ever, but,
oh dear, I do feel so ill.' On 15 September *King's Rhapsody* began its
London run at the Palace Theatre. Vanessa Lee's singing of 'Some
Day My Heart Will Awake' was only one of the successes in a
crowded evening: her playing of the seduction episode confirmed
that she was a good actress into the bargain. The Coronation scene,
with Ivor 'looking half Hamlet, half Antony, and wholly the darling

of the public' as the *Observer* commented, brought a torrent of cheers. At curtain-fall the principals took their bow and were gracefully handed forward by Ivor who, at the end, loped to stage centre and thanked the audience with his boyish grin. 'There is an element of uncertainty in everything but in an Ivor Novello first night,' wearily remarked *Punch* as it chronicled the launch of yet another 'luxury liner' in the theatre. 'All concerned, from the captain-owner to the humblest hand, are cheerfully confident that they are in for years of golden voyagings, and this air of confidence – exuberant and unrestrained – makes an Ivor Novello first night unlike any other.'

The mirror in Ivor's dressing-room showed what the public thought. On it he wrote in greasepaint, each night, the box-office takings. Since that dressing-room was like a railway station with dozens of people coming and going, anyone who wished could see the exact state of business at any given time, a situation which discomfited Tom Arnold, the presenter of *King's Rhapsody,* who preferred not to disclose figures that would interest his competitors. Within twenty-four hours of the first night, advance bookings indicated a minimum run of a year at least and the possibility of several to follow. For Ivor the box-office was the only true guide, not because he was greedy for royalties but because high figures meant success and gave him the pleasure of achievement. All the time in his dressing-room a loudspeaker relayed what was being spoken and sung on stage so that he could check how the performance was going and also enjoy the sound of what he had created. He took an ingenuous delight in work he had written from the heart and with complete sincerity. When the gramophone records of music from *King's Rhapsody* were delivered at Redroofs he played them over and over again until his eyes glistened and tears ran down his cheeks.

At the same time as Ivor was playing London in *King's Rhapsody* no less than four of his other productions were out travelling the land. They were *Glamorous Night, Careless Rapture, The Dancing Years* and *Perchance To Dream.* The four companies appeared at the larger of the two hundred or so theatres throughout the country and, like some long-term investment that pays a regular dividend, contrived to draw good houses wherever they went. To this record (for no one else has ever rivalled it) must be added the frequent billing of his 'straight' plays at repertory theatres up and down Great Britain and the numerous revivals by amateur societies, for, long after a play has quitted the West End, the non-professional rights go on yielding a regular income over the years. All this happened at a period when the new wave of American musicals like *Oklahoma!*, *Carousel* and *South Pacific* were competing heavily with Ivor's brand of entertainment. In his review of *King's Rhapsody* the critic Harold Hobson wrote: 'The music is quite enchanting, and Novello's performance extraordinarily accomplished and beautifully timed. How superbly he manages to bring off the different aspects of the theatre into a single harmonious whole. *South Pacific*, the current hit of the Broadway stage, requires Rodgers, Michener, Logan and Hammerstein to do what Novello achieves single-handed in *King's Rhapsody*; and then, in my opinion, they do not do it so well.' Yet even a *tour de force* like this was not enough to halt the onward march of Rodgers and Hammerstein, and Ivor knew it. When people asked him what he planned to do after *King's Rhapsody* he would say: 'I don't know. But I really can't go on doing this Ruritanian business much longer.'

He thought that *King's Rhapsody* might well be his last musical play. 'Let's face it,' he told a journalist some time after his fifty-sixth birthday in 1949, 'I cherish no illusions about my age. With each new musical I find it increasingly difficult to fit myself into a character who neither sings nor dances. It gets tougher as the years go on.' Towards the end of 1950 he seized the opportunity of composing a musical play for Cicely Courtneidge. Some peculiar fate seems to rule that vintage actresses who began their careers at a very early age should have made their first appearance as Pease-Blossom in *A Midsummer Night's Dream*. Cicely was no exception, though from Shakespeare she moved into Edwardian musical comedy and on to revue and every type of play imaginable, brightening them all with an irrepressible vigour that sparkled for well over half a century and brought her apotheosis as Dame Cicely Courtneidge.

Thirty years ago Ivor had composed 'The Dowager Fairy Queen' for her. Now her current show had ended and she asked him if he had a job for her in *King's Rhapsody* or any of his other productions. 'Oh dear,' he replied. 'I'm disappointed. I hoped you were coming to see me about doing the music for your new show.' Her husband Jack Hulbert had suggested the idea of Cicely as a musical comedy actress who in retirement sets up a drama school. The play was being written by the dramatist Arthur Macrae and the collaborators eagerly accepted Ivor's proposal of a score. A previous engagement led to Macrae dropping out early on and he was replaced by the Scot Alan

Melville, possessor of a malicious wit that could be amusing or, if you were the target, highly unsettling. He had worked on a number of intimate revues, as they were then known, which gave lethal opportunites to the satirical talent of Hermione Gingold, and he was also to write plays noted for their acerbic dialogue.

Melville found Ivor the easiest of collaborators although initially he was daunted by the prospect of following Christopher Hassall. Melville was accustomed to writing the words first and then leaving the composer with the tricky chore of fitting them to the music. Ivor did not object. 'Just let me have your lyrics and I'll see what I can do with them,' he said. Melville soon realised that Ivor knew all about lyrics. 'I'm sorry,' Ivor remarked about one of the numbers, 'you said you wanted a waltz here, and this could never be a waltz.' He looked at it for thirty seconds. 'It could, you know, if you cut out every third line.' Melville fumed. He examined the thing again. Ivor was right and the lyric came out much better.

They worked together at Redroofs on Sunday mornings. Melville was astonished at the speed with which Ivor composed. 'The man oozed tunes; they were packed inside him like clothes in a bulging suitcase at the end of a long holiday,' he said later. What is more they were born almost ready-made and practically note for note the same as in the finished version. One of the big numbers was called 'Vitality' and when it was completed Cicely Courtneidge visited The Flat to hear it. Would she like a cup of tea? Ivor enquired. 'No, no,' she said. 'Let's get down to work.' With Ivor at the piano Melville burbled his way through this exhausting item which lasts twelve minutes in performance and is accompanied by a very strenuous dance routine. 'M'm,' said Miss Courtneidge at the end of it when Melville sank perspiring into an armchair. 'I think I *will* have a cup of tea, dear.'

The new play was, one regrets to say, called *Gay's The Word*. 'Gay' is the name of the actress who leaves the musical comedy stage and sets up a drama school in Folkestone. In the quartet 'Teaching' four of her staff lament that because they themselves were unable to learn they have had to take up teaching pupils who are equally bereft of talent. They also dance a 'Teachers' ballet' which has an innocent charm complemented by the ingénue's aria 'Sweet Thames', an evocation of the river in Edwardian style. The same flavour characterises 'Bees Are Buzzin'', a polka with echoes of Mendelssohn's *Spring Song* and a refrain that haunts the mind persistently enough to stop your falling asleep at night. The score includes several romantic

items, the most attractive being a general satire on the awkwardness
of the typical Englishman in love. There is, in addition, a deal of theatrical 'shop' which both Ivor and Melville, being very much creatures
of their environment, could not resist, as in Gay's 'It's Bound To Be
Right On The Night' about the horror of a pre-London tour and its
last-minute panics:

> You cut, rehearse, rewrite Act Two in toto,
> Build up your beastly part, sit up all night;
> You are interviewed non-stop, complete with photo,
> Feeling eighty-nine but looking madly bright.
> Suppose the worst occurs, the damn thing flops?
> You wonder, will someone buy the props?

The most striking thing about *Gay's The Word* is the manner in
which Ivor laughs at himself and mocks the type of play that made
him famous. The opening chorus declares:

> Ruritania!
> The former delights
> Of Glamorous Nights
> No longer constitute a raving mania
> In Ruritania . . .
> Since Oklahoma
> We've been in a coma
> And no one cares for us.

To make the point quite clear one of the subsequent numbers,
'Guards On Parade', becomes a parody of 'We'll Gather Lilacs' in
march tempo. You feel that Ivor, whose whole career was based on
knowing what the public wanted, had with his unerring flair scented
a change in taste and turned his back with amused resignation on the
formula which had given him so much success.

If, though, *Gay's The Word* jokes about Ivor's Ruritanian past, it
champions with defiant nostalgia an older and more vulnerable
tradition by hymning the great names of the music-hall. When Gay
seeks to inspire her pupils with the quality they need to reach the top
of their profession she tells them:

Vitality
The stars who gained their immortality
Knew with finality the practicality
Of something that's lacking in us.
They all had vitality plus!
Do your remember Gertie Millar, no you wouldn't I'm afraid
Seymour Hicks and Vesta Tilley's swagger cane?
Lily Elsie as the 'Widow'
José Collins as the 'Maid'
Dear old Robey, Billy Merson at the Lane . . .

The list unfolds with Gracie Fields, Hetty King, Phyllis and Zena
Dare, G. H. Elliott and other whose names today would call for
explanatory footnotes, although to someone like Ivor, who had seen
and admired them all, they were living memories. Why, the song
repeats, were they always at the top of the bill? Because they had the
force of personality which modern crooners and other microphone-
addicted performers do not possess. In 'Vitality', which closed the
first half of *Gay's The Word*, Cicely Courtneidge sang and danced
like a bomb exploding. As Alan Melville noted, a London theatre
audience is very quick to make for a drink immediately the interval
arrives. At this point, however, they ignored the attraction of the bar
and stood to cheer and cheer her yet again.

Thorley Walters played the male lead in *Gay's The Word* and was
impressed throughout by Ivor's professionalism and modesty. He
went down to Redroofs for lunch and as they walked in the garden
Ivor took his arm and said: 'I'm going to write a show for Cis and you
and I want to be sure that I get it right for you, especially the comedy.
Will you tell me anything you don't like?' Some months later, when
Gay's The Word had established itself to capacity business, Ivor
supped with him at the Ivy. He was in buoyant mood. 'I'm giving up
acting,' he said. 'I am going to spend the rest of my life writing shows
for Cis and you!'

The new play had a try-out in Manchester where a chaotic dress
rehearsal inspired the deepest pessimism. Few scenes went right,
none of the dance routines worked out properly, and the atmosphere
declined into sombre confusion. Ivor, still playing in *King's Rhapsody*, was obliged to fly up on the morning of the opening and pull it
together. Cuts were made, new business was introduced and current
ideas were replaced with fresh ones. After hours of laborious toil he
flew back to London. That evening he heard on the telephone that

Gay's The Word had been greeted at the end with eight tumultuous curtain calls. It was a triumph he shared with Cicely Courtneidge who, as a burlesque artist, proved herself to be unique.

Gay's The Word launched a ten-week season in Manchester and went on a long tour prior to London. Ivor was pleased but did not seem to show his usual high spirits. Just before the second anniversary of *King's Rhapsody* he had felt very ill and gone into a nursing home for an operation. Immediately the box-office receipts dropped. When he came back they went up again, but although on stage he acted impeccably, in private life he had changed. He looked thin, almost gaunt, and an air of urgency possessed him. Everything he did was hurried through as if he sensed that time was short. At one moment he spoke of retirement. At another he impatiently outlined ideas for his next show to be called *Lily Of The Valley*. The setting was his homeland of Wales and he would play the part of an elderly music teacher who discovers a gifted singer, a rôle intended for Vanessa Lee. With *King's Rhapsody* he had grown gracefully into middle age. *Lily Of The Valley* would enable him to carry on the process, for by the time of production he would be sixty at least. He turned to his make-up mirror and saw the strands of grey in his hair which, for so many in the audience, gave him added attractiveness. Then he put on his dark uniform with its gold epaulettes and red sash for the ballroom scene in *King's Rhapsody* where his entrance always provoked murmurs of admiration. Carefully he attached to it the big paste star that the actor Edmund Kean had once worn and, after him, Henry Irving. It had become a mascot.

By the Christmas of 1950 he was very tired. The ready smile was always there for the crowds who gathered at the stage door, he still entertained generously at Redroofs, his charm remained as warm as ever, but from time to time he would slip away to be on his own. During intervals at the theatre he would mysteriously disappear and then, as abruptly, materialise again. He wanted a rest and decided on a holiday at 'Wyndways', his home in Montego Bay. The party he took with him on the last day of 1950 included Alan Melville, Beatrice Lillie, Bobbie Andrews, Phyllis Monkman and Olive Gilbert. The flight was bumpy. At Nassau the aeroplane was battered by an electric storm and lightning danced on the wing-tips. Two nuns among the passengers thoughtfully crossed themselves. Beatrice Lillie, sitting next to Alan Melville, demanded a large Scotch and was about to drink it when the aeroplane suddenly lurched into a violent drop. The liquid rose through the air and feel neatly on Melville's lap.

'I think,' said she, 'I think I will have another large Scotch, dear.'

At Montego Bay the weather made up for the bad flight. The sky was radiant, the blue sea glittered and Ivor lolled thankfully in the sun. His next-door neighbour was the press magnate Lord Beaverbrook who, through a gap in the bougainvillea hedge separating the two properties, would appear around six o'clock bearing food he thought the company might enjoy for dinner. Wearing his Panama hat he posed for a snapshot, rugged with good health and beaming enjoyment of life. Beside him stood Ivor, many years his junior but with a conventional smile that failed to hide his wan look and tired eyes.

'It's been a wonderful holiday,' Ivor wrote from Jamaica, yet despite the climate in England, the flu epidemic and the meat rationing, 'of course I'm dying to get back to the Theatre.' He returned on Monday, 12 February, to a London wrapped in sleet and snow. Wind gusted round corners and blew the falling flakes into angry whirls. He suspected he had caught a chill and coughed frequently. Beneath the sun-tan his features were drawn and pallid. Press photographers moved in and reporters asked questions. Yes, he had had a marvellous holiday and done a lot of painting. Yes, he hoped to see the London first night of *Gay's The Word* and to take up his rôle in *King's Rhapsody* again next week. At The Flat he collapsed into bed with a temperature of one hundred and two.

Olive Gilbert who lived in an apartment below came up and watched at his bedside. For some years now she had not only sung in his plays but also looked after him as an unofficial housekeeper. In London and at Redroofs she helped to run the home and organise the staff. Such was her devotion to him that she even put up with his regrettable taste for candy-floss. On their last trip to Brighton together he had been unable to resist the lure of a candy-floss stall on the pier and had joined the queue. While crowds of people stared in surprise he walked along the pier eating the sickly stuff, the wisps of fine-spun sugar clinging to his hands and melting on his coat.

He did not want candy-floss now and lay motionless in bed, a slight smile on his face, as Olive summoned doctors and administered medicines. The dress rehearsal for the London opening of *Gay's The Word* was held in his absence, although he dearly wanted to attend it. He insisted on going to the first night regardless of a temperature that was still dangerously high and in the face of concerned protests from Olive and all his friends. It was nearly twenty years, he argued, since he had been to one of his own first nights as a member of the audience, and that was *Fresh Fields* in 1933. He got his way and saw the performance from a box. The audience caught sight of him in his dinner jacket with the dark red carnation in the button-hole and clamoured for a speech. Ivor stood up and waved towards the stage. He pointed at Cicely Courtneidge and the cast and said: 'But don't applaud me – don't look at me. Look at her – applaud her – give it all to her – she's worth it – she deserves it . . .' In all the excitement his old smile came back and his eyes shone with delight.

2

HYMNS NEITHER ANCIENT NOR MODERN

'To which school of British musicians my own humble efforts belong it is difficult for me to say. Viewed dispassionately, I am sort of betwixt and between; if there was a hymn that was neither ancient nor modern, it would be me.'

Ivor Novello

IN 1934, after a decade of theatrical management which began with *The Rat*, Ivor once did a calculation. He found that during those ten years the average run of the plays he had written and presented worked out at 292 performances each. In 1951, had he continued his estimate for the remaining years, he would probably have found that the overall figure was higher still. Of all the rewards success gave him the one he appreciated most was being able to live exactly the sort of life he wanted. It meant that he could stay in bed until midday toying with a prolonged breakfast of coffee and toast and battling with *The Times* crossword. Sometimes he would dictate a play, scene by scene, or sketch out a libretto. After a light lunch he played the piano, went to a film or saw the matinée of a play. A quick nap prepared him for the evening performance to which he drove in the Rolls-Royce.

Whatever he was doing, ideas came to him at any time and in any place. During *Perchance To Dream* one night he sat playing the piano on stage while the lights went down for a brief interlude to show the passage of time. A tune began to form itself. Gordon Duttson came on in his rôle as Tomas to announce the arrival of a lady played by Roma Beaumont. Ivor, preoccupied with notating the melody, murmured: 'Please ask her to wait. I won't be a minute.' Gordon obediently made his exit and joined Roma Beaumont loitering in the wings. The stage manager fretted anxiously. Minutes passed and Ivor played his tune over several times while the audience, unaware that anything unusual was taking place, listened with enjoyment. Ivor finished writing down the notes on a bit of paper and gestured for the action to continue. Much relieved, Gordon ushered in Miss Beaumont and the play went on. The melody born in these unexpected circumstances was 'Some Day My Heart Will Awake.'

The only thing lacking in Ivor's enchanted existence was a family. Childlike himself, he loved children and enjoyed being with them. But children are only one part of family life, and it is doubtful whether, in Ivor's crowded routine, there would have been room for a woman. In any case, as has been said, he could only perform adequately with men. He confided in Peter Noble: 'All I know is that I have suffered deeply from love and had my greatest joy from friendship. One of the things that I enjoy most in life is to look round when I am having a little party in my flat and see that out of the forty people present there are at least thirty whom I have known for more than twenty years.'

Ivor had innumerable friends and they were the substitute for the family which was denied him. His first secretary Lloydie Williams had been with him for thirty years and so had his business manager Fred Allen and his chauffeur Arthur Morgan, while his dresser Bill Wright stayed with him from 1934 until his death. Others who joined him later in his career like Gordon Duttson carried on the tradition. In London and at Redroofs the domestic staff were feudal in their devotion to Ivor. Among them was the cockney chef, a virtuoso of cuisine and a man whose iron self-composure was shaken only once. This happened on a visit by Greta Garbo, herself a gourmet, whom Ivor brought unannounced into the kitchen. The chef, poised over a soup, looked up at the vision approaching him. 'Oh, Gorblimey!' he exclaimed and rushed off to put on a clean uniform.

Ivor had to have people around him. He was rarely alone and preferred to be in the company of those he knew, always providing he was at liberty to vanish whenever he felt like it. His genius for friendship extended beyond the theatre and took in Eddie Marsh, Clemence Dane, Lady Juliet Duff, writers, composers and even drama critics, for he was a charitable man and bore no grudges. He gave people the benefit of the doubt, was always ready to trust them, and only when they betrayed him did he withdraw his confidence. Jealousy was unknown to him and he delighted in the success of friends as wholeheartedly as they themselves did. Despite tales to the contrary he did not see Noël Coward as a rival, and although the latter often criticised his plays in wounding terms Ivor refused to be annoyed.*

* Coward found *Gay's The Word* '. . . stinking with bad taste and the inter-mixed vulgarity of Ivor and Alan Melville. Cicely Courtneidge a miracle of vitality and hard work, but, oh dear, with that horrible stuff to do. It was rapturously received by a packed house.'

Criticism of this sort had no effect on him at all, however harsh, and he simply ignored it. He was supremely self-confident and blessed with an inner certainty that he was right. Again and again his friends, Coward the most vocal among them, would advise him not to carry on with a given project. He would listen to them, smile affably, say 'Thank you so much, duckie, for your wonderful thought,' and continue unperturbed on his way. Very rarely did instinct mislead him. It was different, of course, when rehearsing a new play and his professional colleagues had suggestions to make. He paid careful attention to what they said, cheerfully cut and revised, and had no false pride about changing his work if he thought someone else's ideas would make it more effective. This readiness to listen and learn from others, which he kept all his life, helped him to succeed in the different careers he undertook. Almost by accident he became a film star, an actor in the theatre and a playwright. Yet he never trained for the cinema, nor went to any drama school, and no one taught him how to write plays.

His character was a blend of humility and confidence. To this he added a single-minded determination which sometimes verged on ruthlessness. It came out in professional matters when he arranged for others to take the responsibility of sacking inefficient employees. In private life he showed it when, for example, he pursued Christopher Hassall and disrupted his family. Yet even those who might reasonably have had a grievance were reluctant to speak ill of him. He was so generous with both his money and his time, he was so thoughtful, he was so sympathetic to hard-luck stories. At the worst moment in his life when he served a prison sentence he was comforted by an overwhelming surge of affection that came from his many friends and from hundreds of unknown admirers. There was little else to sustain him, for, unlike his Welsh ancestors, he had no religion, that 'vast moth-eaten musical brocade' as Philip Larkin called it. The experience may have helped him artistically to deepen the mature portrait he drew of Nikki in *King's Rhapsody*, but, physically and temperamentally, it broke something within him and shortened his life.

His plays were written to give immediate pleasure and display the talents of gifted actors and actresses. He sought no more than to please and did so to such effect that he earned wealth and celebrity. It can be argued that Shakespeare, Molière and Dickens were best-sellers in their time and ever heedful of the box-office. They, however, offered something else beside pleasure for the groundlings.

Anthony Burgess has remarked that a novel – and for 'novel' we may also read 'play' – is a presentation of people in action. 'The difference between the so-called art novel and the popular variety,' he goes on, 'is perhaps that in the first the human beings are more important than the action and in the second it is the other way about.' Ivor's plays contain a great deal of action and many opportunities for the particular gifts of particular players, but little in the way of human beings or subtle character-drawing. He knew the quality of the goods he was delivering and made no claim for them apart from their ability to 'fill the plush'. It is unlikely that they will ever be revived since they cater exclusively for tastes and attitudes that have long since vanished with the years. While they are efficient pieces of dramatic construction their dialogue is out of date and not even 'period' enough to merit a second glance. Perhaps, in another century, they will some of them be reprinted as curious examples of long-dead theatre, much as today obscure Jacobean comedies are reissued with voluminous notes to elucidate the many topical references.

The musical plays are different. That an audience still exists for them is proved by the many amateur revivals and by the royalties which continue to flow into the estate. Here a practical difficulty supervenes: in Ivor's day it was possible to mount productions which, besides involving spectacular scene changes, could also afford to employ over a hundred singers, actors and actresses, dancers, orchestral players and stage personnel. In these days the expense would be enormous and would amount, after initial costs had been recovered, to something like a hundred thousand pounds a week. The male lead, too, was written by Ivor with himself in mind and relies heavily on the magic which only he could create with his inimitable look and manner. On the other hand the vocal parts are laid out effectively enough to be within the range of competent singers, always remembering that Ivor's unique style of writing demands a semi-operatic approach. He catered, moreover, for a human need which is filled in modern times by high-life soap operas with plots more incredible and audiences far vaster than anything he could ever have conceived. Even the Ruritanian settings involving kings and queens and princes would not seem misplaced today in a country where the royal family is the subject of perpetual attention stimulated by millions of words in the press and endless appearances on television screens.

The music, essentially theatrical, endures. The melodies wear greasepaint and breathe an atmosphere of stage lighting and red curtains. They come from a realm of illusion which Ivor believed in so implicitly that multitudes were persuaded to join him there. Life is hard, they seem to say, and often unpleasant, so why not indulge yourself? All art is, in a way, escapist, Ivor's more than most, and the tunes invite you with an engaging air to relax and let yourself be swept away in a heedless flow of pretty sound. His musical ancestry is clear. On occasion there is a trace of Stanford and the other Victorians whose choral works he sang as a boy in Magdalen Choir. 'Some Day My Heart Will Awake' recalls the andante of Saint-Saëns's third piano concerto. From time to time Mendelssohn creeps through and even a touch of Fauré may be heard. Although the music he loved best was Wagner's, Richard Strauss's, Ravel's and Debussy's, the composer who really shaped his own stage technique was Puccini of the vivid sweep and unashamed, outright appeal to emotion. Mozart was too stylised, too classically restrained for him. He needed the Romantics and their passion. A significant name on the list of favourite musicians he once drew up was that of Erich Korngold, composer of many Technicolored Hollywood film scores but also of operas and orchestral works that lately have been the object of serious critical attention.

His impressionable years were spent watching and listening to the Edwardian musical comedies popular in his youth. Repeated visits to the theatre and study of the vocal score had made him familiar with every note of Lehár's *The Merry Widow* and given him a lifelong penchant for waltzes. At each opportunity he put them into his own scores and wrote many of his songs in 3/4 tempo. Like Noël Coward he was raised on the music of Sullivan whom he venerated. Another of his idols was Lionel Monckton, perhaps the finest of Edwardian stage composers and one whose accomplished melodies, 'Arcady Is Ever Young', for example, and 'Come To The Ball', provided him with a model. Ivor was a very English composer and absorbed from Edward German's *Merrie England* and *Tom Jones* that strain of yeoman-like rusticity found in his patriotic song 'Rose Of England' and the folkloric elements of *Perchance To Dream*. The music of Elgar appealed to him also, and 'Keep The Home Fires Burning' shares with 'Land Of Hope And Glory' a sense of defiant pageantry. All these influences were absorbed and gave rise in due course to his own very individual type of musical play. A blend of opera, operetta and musical comedy, it was all these things and something else besides which, like love, is easy to recognise but hard to define: 'A musical romance devised, written

and composed by Ivor Novello', as the legend described it on the
title page of his scores.

His good fortune was bound to encourage envy. He once, mildly
and with truth, protested: 'I know certain people say: "Oh, Novello
just churns the stuff out; it's easy!" Is it? If it were, in fact, so simple,
they would do it themselves – and I know that for many of them it is
not for want of trying. But it isn't at all easy, not even for me. In the
past decade I have written four musicals, which must certainly take
them out of the category of pot boilers. And I wrote these four
because I had to. Because the music was bubbling inside me, waiting
to come out.' Ivor was not an intellectual. His reading was confined
to novels which he devoured voraciously, and, apart from an unexpected liking for the music of Bliss, Walton, Bax and even Schoenberg in addition to the composers one more easily associates with
him, his tastes were very much the same as those of the ordinary man.
This explains why he was able to give the general public what it
wanted. The music he wrote for them was the music he enjoyed
himself, and the plots he made evolved in a romantic world that
corresponded with their dreams. Highbrows mistrusted his ability to
move the public's heart and they never forgave him.

As an actor Ivor did very well in his own plays where he could
tailor rôles to his personal measure. Then *The Happy Hypocrite*
and *Henry V* showed that he could do much more than the light,
playful sort of thing which his admirers wanted of him, and convinced the critics that his potentiality was greater than they had
supposed. The box-office thought otherwise and soon he was back
within the golden cage of his own devising. Even there, however, he
continued to surprise those who tended to undervalue him. The
film critic C. A. Lejeune was among them, and after seeing him act
she broadcast her impressions on the radio. 'I'm one of those
women who has spent my life trying not to see Ivor Novello,' she
said. 'I thought perhaps it was more interesting not to see him.
However, I was dragged into it at last, and I sat in what I consider as
a very difficult seat to see from, and from that point, when I was
nearly touching the roof of the theatre, because there were so many
people there, I found that he came through as the most tremendous
stage personality, a really great theatrical technician, the like of
which I have not seen for a very long time. And I was most struck by
his really good hard theatre-sense, by his beautiful timing, his gestures, all of which were exactly right for the stage. And, above all, I
think, by the way that that voice, so exactly pitched to carry to the

very top of the theatre, every word clear – my goodness! – is very uncommon these days.'

She had seen him in *King's Rhapsody* where he displayed an actor's craft refined by the experience of a lifetime and by perpetually watching, listening and learning from others. He was fit enough, or so he thought, to return on 26 February, 1951, after a brief and reluctant stay in bed which he left, at one point, to witness Peter Daubeny's new production of *The Gay Invalid*, an adaptation from Molière starring the octogenarian A. E. Matthews who constantly forgot his lines but always made up for it with impromptu business and spontaneous dialogue which often was better than the original. Ivor sat in a box with Phyllis Monkman and told Daubeny that it was a play he would have been delighted to put on himself. A malaise passed over him and he needed a sip of brandy to recover, but he stayed for the rest of the play with obvious enjoyment. Later on in the run, when takings began to fall off and Daubeny feared he would have to shut down, Ivor proposed, with typical generosity, to put in extra capital.

Immediately he reappeared in *King's Rhapsody* the box-office perked up after the lull caused by his absence and houses filled again. The production had been completely redressed and glittered with a new splendour. The occasion of his return was like a first night with Ivor making a speech at the end and the audience giving him an ecstatic welcome. He felt, he said afterwards, like the prodigal son back among the fatted calves. The sentiment was touching even though the expression of it might have been unfortunate.

He acted the rest of the week in *King's Rhapsody* and, after the Saturday evening performance, drove to Redroofs where his guests included Lady Juliet Duff and Alan Melville. Most of the weekend he stayed in bed playing Canasta, a game for which he had lately developed an obsession. Alan Melville, summoned from downstairs, came up and sat expectantly on the end of his bed. Ivor mentioned *Gay's The Word* and said: 'We're going to do another one. I'm coming out of *King's Rhapsody* and we're going back to Montego Bay, just the pair of us.' He had, he went on, already thought of the title, which was to be *Lily Of The Valley* and he outlined the plot with the Welsh setting he had been working on before *King's Rhapsody* intervened. That Sunday morning Lady Juliet got out her Brownie camera and dragooned Ivor and friends into posing for her. She took such a long time fiddling with the machine that Ivor grew impatient and muttered: 'Oh, come on, dear, for God's sake: you're as slow as Wolfit.' This, the last photograph to be taken, shows him wrapped up against the cold wind, his smile broad, the cheeks cavernous.

On Monday, 5 March, he went back to London in the Rolls. As he made-up for the evening performance he told his dresser Bill Wright of the pains in his arms and chest that had worried him over the weekend. They were gone now, he added. 'I suppose it's rheumatism,' he said. 'Well, we all get it, you know, as we go along,' Bill replied. Others had noticed recently how Ivor would one day look very ill and, the next, would appear to be radiant. It is a symptom of heart trouble that the victim should seem to bloom suddenly like a flower and then, as suddenly, be cut down.

After the show he returned to The Flat for supper with Tom Arnold. He fumbled when trying to open a bottle of champagne. 'Are you all right, Ivor?' Arnold asked. 'I've got some pain, but I'll be all right,' Ivor replied. He was persuaded into bed and Arnold left, knowing that Bobbie Andrews and Olive Gilbert would soon be returning. When they came back Olive descended to her flat underneath and left Bobbie with Ivor. Bobbie looked around, saw the remains of the oyster supper and also the havoc Ivor caused when wrestling with the bottle of champagne: in the end he had smashed it with a hammer and the contents exploded all over the room.

Olive was in bed by a quarter past one. Her telephone rang and she heard Bobbie telling her that Ivor was very ill. She flew upstairs and saw Ivor, ashen-faced, in bed. She propped him up, finding him cold to the touch, and sent for the doctor. The smelling salts she gave him were too weak and she tried out some extra strong ones. Still he could not smell them. The pain, he whispered, had gone for the time being. The doctor arrived, and while he examined him Olive stood by the door. Ivor spoke to him of an earlier attack and of how he had mentioned it to no one since it passed off. 'I'm afraid I've had it,' he muttered. A little while afterwards Olive heard a long sigh. Ivor died, of a coronary thrombosis, at about a quarter past two in the morning of Tuesday, 6 March. He was just fifty-eight years old.

No one could believe the news. To Eddie Marsh it came as an unforgivable stroke of fate. He was seventy-nine and in frail health. Early in the morning his telephone was out of order, and Christopher Hassall, anxious to spare him the shock of hearing about Ivor's death on the radio, called to tell him. He knew that what he had to say, however gently he phrased it, would shorten Eddie's own life. The words were spoken. In silence Eddie bowed his head very low and clenched his fists with impotent rage – rage that he himself should be still alive after so many years while others more useful and gifted should be cut down in their prime: first Rupert Brooke, now Ivor.... Disgust overwhelmed him but he repressed his tears with grim self-control. 'This is one of the worst blows that could have befallen me,' he wrote to a friend.

The funeral arrangements were made by Harrods. It so happened that Alan Melville was moving house to Brighton at the time and his London flat stood empty except for packing-cases. He felt, nonetheless, that he should do his best to cheer up Ivor's entourage and he invited them round for drinks. His move had also been entrusted to Harrods, and at that moment Ivor's body was being collected for transfer to the firm's mortuary. After four or five large gins hospitably dispensed by Melville, Bobbie Andrews with hysterical tears rolling down his cheeks giggled: 'Wouldn't it be dreadful if they got muddled, and Alan's furniture went to Harrods and Ivor got carried down to Brighton!'

Solicitors were consulted and funeral invitations were sent out. The actress Ivy St Helier telephoned Bobbie in her distress. 'Bobbie darling, I'm *so* upset. I know if I go I'm sure to break down – what *should* I do?' she lamented. It would be too awful if she created a scene, but she couldn't stop crying, she explained. What *should* she do? Bobbie heard her out with sympathetic patience until finally, at the end of his tether, he snapped: 'Ivy darling, only you can decide. Ivor wouldn't be going himself unless he had to.'

The funeral took place on a March day of blustering winds and icy blue sky. It was like a state occasion with immense crowds lining the streets on the way to Golders Green crematorium. The ceremony was broadcast on the radio. Many more thousands gathered outside the red brick building to see the hearse laden with a big cross of white lilac, red roses and violets as it drove slowly through the multitude. Behind it followed the red Rolls with Morgan at the wheel and then other cars bearing immediate mourners like Olive Gilbert, Peter Graves, Tom Arnold, Phyllis Monkman, Ivor's accountant Fred Allen, his house-keeper from The Flat, his staff at Redroofs, and his dresser Bill Wright. Through the open door of the chapel came the notes of 'We'll Gather Lilacs' to be heard by a vast gathering that stretched as far as could be seen into the distance. Despite the many famous names there, what made the event so impressive was the huge number of ordinary people who had interrupted their daily routine to honour the man whose personality and music had given them so much pleasure.

A year later Eddie Marsh returned to Golders Green and unveiled a bust of Ivor. He took as the theme of his address a couplet from a translation he had once made of La Fontaine:

> Some few there be, spoilt darlings of high Heaven,
> To whom the magic grace of charm is given.

He dwelt on Ivor's 'brilliant gifts' and spoke nostalgically of 'his gallant spirit, and the fun it was to be with him'. He was there, he said, by right of his 'thirty-six years of affection'. Then the old man folded his notes and was driven back to the small and lonely flat where he now lived in Walton Street. In the course of his long and very distinguished life he had known and worked with many talented people. None of them had entranced him so much as Ivor, and none of them had he loved with so deep, so abiding a fondness. Existence meant little to him without Ivor's bright presence, and he welcomed the prospect of his own death.

3

ENVOI

IVOR'S ESTATE was valued for probate at £146,245 2s. 4d., an amount which may, even in 1951, have appeared unexpectedly small until it is remembered that over a long period he had been buying annuities for himself and so investing many thousands which, on his early death, reverted to the insurance companies.* The will, drawn up and signed just a year before he died, testifies at once to his businesslike approach and his generosity. Twenty thousand pounds were bequeathed to his oldest friend Bobbie Andrews and other cash legacies went to Olive Gilbert, Phyllis Monkman, Peter Graves and Henry Kendall. His domestic staff were remembered with various sums of money and annuities as were pensioners whom he supported during his lifetime. Olive Gilbert received his collection of jade, amber and rose quartz while Bobbie inherited most of his pictures, jewellery and *objets d'art*. Bobbie was also left Redroofs on trust together with the furniture. The Flat, having only been rented, was given up. The house in Montego Bay, acquired with profits from selling the Consols bought out of money made long ago on *The Rat*, was to be sold and the revenue put in the hands of trustees appointed to run the estate. In a codicil added a few months before Ivor died the copyright and royalties on *The Dancing Years* were left on trust to Tom Arnold for the benefit of his son who was also Ivor's godson.

* The equivalent figure in today's inflated currency would be £731,225.

All private debts owing to him were cancelled and the friends and colleagues to whom he had lent money to help with mortgages and other commitments were excused repayment from the day of his death. When he made his first big earnings with *The Rat* he had given as a reason for investing them the wish not to be forced in old age into reliance on the King George V Pension Fund for Actors and Actresses. By a pleasant circumstance he was able, in his will, to leave the Fund a bequest of four thousand pounds. He also bequeathed large amounts to the Actors' Orphanage, the Actors' Benevolent Fund and the Theatrical Ladies' Guild. The Royal Academy of Dramatic Art in Gower Street was allotted four thousand pounds to establish an Ivor Novello Scholarship which, between 1952 and 1964, benefited nine student actors and actresses. It has continued to help young people even though, in 1965, all scholarship resources at the Academy were pooled because of the rise in tuition costs.*

During the years since 1951 Ivor Novello Charities Ltd., the company set up to administer his estate, has distributed over half a million pounds among deserving causes. Royalties on his work continue to flow in and, during the last financial year, amounted to over eighteen thousand pounds. If Ivor had never written another word or a note of music, he would still have been able, in his very old age, to live with a reasonable measure of comfort.

He left behind him only one unfinished musical play. This had been the subject of his last conversation with Alan Melville and was tentatively called *Lily Of The Valley*. Renamed *Valley Of Song* and described as a 'musical romance in three acts', it was completed in the event by Christopher Hassall with music adapted and arranged by Ronald Hanmer who also composed additional material. The action opens in Wales immediately before the 1914–18 war and moves to Venice, the raison d'être of a 'Carnival' ballet, after which it returns to the Welsh valleys once again. The first wartime Christmas is saluted with an affecting little carol, 'Bundle In The Hay', and a period touch is added by the insertion of 'Keep The Home Fires Burning' into one of the choruses. The heroine is Lily, a daughter of the valley blessed with looks and a beautiful voice. Her heart is won and broken by the handsome but unscrupulous Ricardo, although she at last finds true love with the earnest young David, conductor of the local choir. 'I Know A Valley', the duet given to Lily and David,

* In 1952 Lord Lurgan also founded at RADA the Ivor Novello Memorial Prize for Grace and Charm in Movement.

has the sound of vintage Novello, and the barcarolle 'Look In My Heart', though the work of Ronald Hanmer, is authentic enough to figure in the original canon. There is no part for a middle-aged Ivor in the play, and one must assume that he either decided not to appear or was prevented by death from elaborating his rôle.

His friends gradually died off. Eddie Marsh did not long survive him. In 1952 Eddie was present at the unveiling of Ivor's bust in the Drury Lane Theatre Royal. The bust had been sculpted by Clemence Dane and stood for years on a writing-desk in The Flat. Its presence at Drury Lane bore witness to the man who did more than anyone to ensure the old theatre's survival. Of all his protégés Ivor was the one to profit most from Eddie's affection and guidance. Every Saturday morning since the war Eddie had called at The Flat. Now he stayed at home, usually wearing a maroon dressing-gown over his pyjamas with a silk scarf at the neck secured by an opal-headed pin. His only regular date was tea on Tuesdays with Christopher Hassall who never failed to join him. One day he went down to Redroofs on his last visit there and inventoried the pictures. He returned in a car full of canvases he had lent Ivor, among them a Paul Nash which he restored to a prominent place on the wall of his sitting-room. Early in 1953 he found enough energy to 'diabolise' the proofs of Winston Churchill's latest book, *A History of the English-Speaking Peoples*.

On 12 January the octogenarian dozed in bed while his cat slept peacefully on his feet and wisps of fog curled in through a badly shut window. He fell into a coma and his doctor was summoned. Was it, Eddie enquired, reviving for a moment and noting the doctor's grave expression, 'serious'? He made his last coherent remark: 'Well, I can take it.' At three next morning he died. Winston Churchill wrote: 'The death of Eddie Marsh is a loss to the nation, and a keen personal grief to me. Since we began working together at the Colonial Office in 1905 we have always been the closest friends. Apart from his distin-guished career as a Civil Servant he was a master of literature and scholarship and a deeply instructed champion of the arts. All his long life was serene, and he left this world, I trust, without a pang, and I am sure without a fear.'

No one regretted him more deeply than Christopher Hassall. Eddie had encouraged and truly believed in him as a poet. After Eddie's death there were not many others to champion his verse, even though in 1939 he had been awarded the Hawthornden Prize for one of his poetic volumes. He wrote dramas such as *The Player King*, a piece based on an obscure historical episode in the Wars of the Roses which mingled, uneasily, contemporary slang with blank verse at a time when Christopher Fry was applying the same method more successfully. He was happier writing the libretto of William Walton's opera *Troilus and Cressida* which the critic Ernest Newman praised as 'the best poetic text since Hofmannsthal'. His more substantial achievements include a solid biography of his old patron Eddie, a work written with love and scholarship, and thoughtful lives of Rupert Brooke and of the talented but short-lived actor Stephen Haggard. Like Arthur Sullivan, who is fated to be remembered not for his serious and more ambitious work but for his operettas, Hassall's reputation is sustained by the lyrics he wrote to Ivor's music rather than by the poetry on which his hopes rested. In later years his lithe figure grew somewhat corpulent. While hastening from the Savile Club one day in 1963 to catch a train he suffered a heart attack and died almost immediately at the age of fifty-one, seven years younger than Ivor had been at his death.

Bobbie Andrews lived on at Redroofs. The house stood silent among the Berkshire fields. Here once had come Greta Garbo and Cary Grant, Tyrone Power and the Lunts, Binkie Beaumont and all the leading figures of the West End stage. Here plays had been written and music composed at a grand piano that no longer responded to the touch of its owner's fingers. The gramophone which for hours at a time had played the music of Wagner and Strauss and Schoenberg and Ivor Novello was rarely heard. Dust gathered on a visitors' book in which John Gielgud, Ronald Colman and Noël Coward had signed their names. Rooms that once had overheard lively arguments carried on between Mam's booming tone and Ivor's light tenor were full of memories and nothing else. It became increasingly expensive to keep up Redroofs, despite the provision made for a reserve fund by Ivor's will. The fabric was old and in constant need of repair, the grounds were extensive and called for perpetual maintenance, and there was always something going wrong with the six cottages scattered around the main building. The property was sold and used as a convalescent home for actors and actresses. After a while it came on the market again and was converted into three flats by the purchaser. Since then it has changed hands once more and is now the Redroofs Theatre School offering a full-time three-year diploma course in acting, singing and dance as well as a casting agency for those who prove suitable. Ivor would have liked that.

The years went by and Bobbie remained irrepressible. One day in the Charing Cross Road he glimpsed Donald Sinden and trotted across to greet him. 'Donald, my dear,' he said, 'I hardly recognised you – you're looking so young and beautiful – for a moment I thought you were Bobbie Andrews.'

Some time after Ivor's death Barry Sinclair, who had been associated with him in many of his productions, played the leading rôle in a show called *The World And Music Of Ivor Novello*. It went on tour and had arrived at the Golders Green Hippodrome when Sinclair's dressing-room was invaded by Bobbie, Olive Gilbert and Fred Allen, Ivor's business manager. Donald Sinden, invaluable teller of tales, reports that all four crossed the road to an Express Dairy and reminisced over tea about the past. Sinclair was touched that they should have taken the trouble to come and see his performance. 'No, I must tell you what happened,' said Bobbie. That day he and Olive had taken up a long-standing invitation to lunch at Fred's Highgate home. 'What shall we do next?' enquired Fred after lunch. 'Let's go down to the crematorium and look at Ivor's lilac tree,' suggested Olive. So down they went and pored over the lilac tree. 'What shall we do now?' Olive asked. 'Let's go and look at Keneth Kent's urn,' Fred proposed, mentioning the name of an actor who had been Ivor's friend and who was also cremated at Golders Green. They went and looked at Keneth Kent's urn. 'What shall we do now?' Fred then enquired. 'We might as well go and look at Barry's matinée,' answered Bobbie. 'And that,' he concluded his explanation to Barry, 'is why we're here.'

In the early nineteen-seventies the composer Sandy Wilson, who wrote *The Boy Friend*, one of the most successful musicals ever produced, and others as witty as they are stylish, was engaged on preparing his book about Ivor. While researching it he went to see Bobbie who was then mortally ill. At the end of their talk together Bobbie said expansively: 'Ivor adored *The Boy Friend*!' A failing memory, or a clouded mind, or simply the desire to please made him overlook the circumstance that Ivor had died three years before *The Boy Friend* was heard in public.

The number of people who knew Ivor well continues to diminish but his memory is preserved. St Paul's, Covent Garden, known as 'The Actors' Church', contains a panel which commemorates him with a quotation from Shakespeare: 'The dearest friend, the kindest man, the best condition'd and unwearied spirit, in doing courtesies.' The other St Paul's, Wren's cathedral, has a memorial unveiled in 1972 which carries, beneath a stone sculpture of the famous profile, the austere legend 'Ivor Novello, Composer, 1893–1951'. Two months after this memorial was inaugurated to mark the twenty-first anniversary of his death there was a Gala performance of his work at Drury Lane where, in the Circle Rotunda, Clemence Dane's bronze head of the composer may still be seen. The Flat is not forgotten, either. A GLC blue plaque on the wall of the Strand Theatre at 11, Aldwych, records that Ivor 'lived and died in a flat on the top floor of this building.'

'I should like,' Ivor once told an interviewer, 'to make an enchanting curtain speech at the end of a wildly successful first night, and – to the sound of cheers and applause – drop gracefully dead. If possible, *before* the curtain falls.' Although a charmed life had granted nearly all his dreams this was one of the few that just, but only just, escaped him.

LIST OF WORKS

LIST OF WORKS
BY AND/OR FEATURING
IVOR NOVELLO

THE FOLLOWING list is based, by kind permission of Mr Sandy Wilson, on the one he gives in his book *Ivor*, Michael Joseph, 1975. The latter comprises full details of all the songs written by Ivor Novello together with complete cast lists and rôles played in all the productions with which he was associated in any capacity, American productions, individual numbers contributed to revues as well as his own musical plays (printed or not), every film both silent and sound, and the names of his collaborators. It also includes a Discography compiled by Mr Adrian Edwards which notes all gramophone records originally involving Novello and/or his fellow artists from early acoustic recordings to modern long-playing discs. The reader who seeks further information will find it in the Wilson/Edwards bibliography, which, an achievement in its own right, is also a homage to Ivor Novello's prolific inspiration.

Songs

Between 1910 and 1951 Ivor wrote some fifty drawing-room songs and two song-cycles to words by various authors. The most famous is 'Keep The Home Fires Burning' (words by Lena Guilbert Ford) in 1914, closely followed by 'And Her Mother Came Too' (words by Dion Titheradge), first sung by Jack Buchanan in the Charlot revue *A To Z*, 1921.

Musical comedies and revues

1916

Theodore And Co, a Musical Comedy
Gaiety, 14 September.
Book by H. M. Harwood and George Grossmith, from the French of
    P. Gavault.
Music by Jerome Kern and Ivor Novello.
Additional music by Philip Braham, Melville Gideon and Paul A.
    Rubens.
Lyrics by Adrian Ross and Clifford Grey.
Cast: George Grossmith, Leslie Henson, Peggy Kurton, Adrah Fair,
    Davy Burnaby.
13 numbers by Novello.

See-Saw, a Revue
Comedy, 14 December.
Book by Arthur E. Eliot, Herbert Sargent and Arthur Weigall.
Lyrics by A. B. Mills, Arthur Weigall and others.
Music by Philip Braham, Ivor Novello, Harold Montague and others.
Cast: Ruby Miller, Phyllis Monkman, Winnie Melville.
4 numbers by Novello.

1917

Arlette, a Musical Comedy
Shaftesbury, 6 September.
Book by Claude Ronald and L. Buvet, tr. by José Levy.
Adaptation by Austen Hurgon and George Arthurs.
Lyrics by Adrian Ross and Clifford Grey.
Music by Jane Vieu, Guy le Feuvre and Ivor Novello.
Cast: Winifred Barnes, Joseph Coyne, Stanley Lupino.
7 numbers by Novello.

1918

Tabs, a Revue
Vaudeville, 15 May.

Book and Lyrics by Ronald Jeans.
Additional lyrics by Douglas Furber, Adrian Ross, Walter
    Donaldson, Hugh E. Wright.
Music by Ivor Novello.
Additional music by Guy le Feuvre, Bob Adams, Muriel Lillie,
    Herman Darewski, Walter Donaldson, Pat Thayer.
Cast: Beatrice Lillie, Odette Myrtil, Ethel Baird.
10 numbers by Novello.

1919

Who's Hooper?, a Musical Comedy
Adelphi, 13 September
Book by Fred Thompson, based on *In Chancery* by A. W. Pinero.
Lyrics by Clifford Grey.
Music by Howard Talbot and Ivor Novello.
Cast: W. H. Berry, Robert Michaelis, Marjorie Gordon.
11 numbers by Novello.

1920

A Southern Maid, an Operetta
Daly's, 15 May.
Book by Dion Clayton Calthrop and Harry Graham.
Lyrics by Harry Graham.
Additional lyrics by Adrian Ross and Douglas Furber.
Music by Harold Fraser-Simpson.
Additional music by Ivor Novello.
Cast: José Collins, Bertram Wallis, Jessie Fraser.
2 numbers by Novello.

1921

The Golden Moth, a Musical Play
Adelphi, 5 October.

Book by Fred Thompson and P. G. Wodehouse.
Lyrics by P. G. Wodehouse and Adrian Ross.
Music by Ivor Novello.
Cast: W. H. Berry, Robert Michaelis, Thorpe Bates.
15 numbers.

A To Z, a Revue
Prince of Wales, 21 October.
Book by Ronald Jeans, Dion Titheradge and Helen Trix.
Lyrics by Ronald Jeans, Dion Titheradge, Collie Knox.
Music by Ivor Novello, Philip Braham.
Cast: Jack Buchanan, Gertrude Lawrence, the Trix Sisters, Teddie
    Gerard, Marcel de Haes.
14 numbers by Novello.

1924

Puppets, a Revue
Vaudeville, 2 January.
Book and Lyrics by Dion Titheradge.
Additional material by Ronald Jeans and others.
Music by Ivor Novello.
Cast: Stanley Lupino, Binnie Hale, Arthur Chesney.
9 numbers.

Our Nell, a Musical Play
Gaiety, 16 April.
Book by Louis N. Parker and Reginald Arkell.
Lyrics by Harry Graham and Reginald Arkell.
Music by H. Fraser-Simpson and Ivor Novello.
Cast: José Collins, Arthur Wontner, Robert Michaelis.
3 numbers by Novello.

1929

The House That Jack Built, a Revue
Adelphi, 8 November.

Book by Ronald Jeans and Douglas Furber.
Lyrics by Donovan Parsons and Douglas Furber.
Music by Ivor Novello, Vivian Ellis, Arthur Shwartz, Sydney Baynes.
Cast: Jack Hulbert, Cicely Courtneidge, Helen Burnell.
8 numbers by Novello.

Films

The Call Of The Blood (*L'Appel Du Sang*)
Mercanton/Stoll 1920.
Dir: Louis Mercanton.
Script: Louis Mercanton, from the novel by Robert Hichens.
Cast: Ivor Novello, Phyllis Neilson Terry, Desdemona Mazza, Le
    Bargy.

Miarka: Daughter Of The Bear (*Miarka, Fille De L'Ourse*)
Mercanton 1920.
Dir: Louis Mercanton.
Scr: Louis Richepin, from his own novel.
Cast: Ivor Novello, Réjane, Desdemona Mazza, Charles Vanel, Louis
    Richepin.

Carnival
Alliance 1921.
Dir: Harley Knoles.
Scr: Adrian Johnson and Rosina Henley, from the play by Matheson
    Lang and H. C. M. Hardinge.
Cast: Matheson Lang, Hilda Bayley, Ivor Novello.

The Bohemian Girl
Alliance 1922.
Dir: Harley Knoles.
Scr: Harley Knoles and Rosina Henley, based on Balfe's opera.
Cast: Gladys Cooper, Ivor Novello, Constance Collier, Ellen Terry,
    C. Aubrey Smith, Henry Vibart, Gibb McLaughlin.

The Man Without Desire (The Man Without A Soul)
Atlas Biocraft 1923.
Dir: Adrian Brunel.
Scr: Frank Powell, from a story by Monckton Hoffe.
Cast: Ivor Novello, Nina Vanna, Sergio Mario.

The White Rose
Ideal/United Artists 1923.
Dir: D. W. Griffith.
Scr: Irene Sinclair (D. W. Griffith).
Cast: Mae Marsh, Ivor Novello.

Bonnie Prince Charlie
Gaumont 1923.
Dir: G. C. Calvert.
Scr: Alicia Ramsay.
Cast: Ivor Novello, Gladys Cooper.

The Rat
Gainsborough 1925.
Dir: Graham Cutts.
Scr: Graham Cutts, from the play by 'David L'Estrange'.
Cast: Ivor Novello, Mae Marsh, Isabel Jeans.

The Triumph Of The Rat
Gainsborough 1926.
Dir: Graham Cutts.
Scr: Graham Cutts and Reginald Fogwell.
Cast: Ivor Novello, Isabel Jeans, Nina Vanna.

The Lodger
Gainsborough 1926.
Dir: Alfred Hitchcock.
Scr: Alfred Hitchcock and Eliot Stannard, from the novel by Marie
    Belloc Lowndes and the play *Who Is He?* by H. A. Vachell,
    based on the same.
Cast: Ivor Novello, June.

Downhill
Gainsborough 1927.
Dir: Alfred Hitchcock.
Scr: Eliot Stannard, from the play by 'David L'Estrange'.
Cast: Ivor Novello, Isabel Jeans, Robert Irvine, Lilian Braithwaite.

The Vortex
Gainsborough 1928.
Dir: Adrian Brunel.
Scr: Eliot Stannard, from the play by Noël Coward.
Cast: Ivor Novello, Willette Kershaw, Frances Doble.

The Constant Nymph
Gainsborough 1928.
Dir: Adrian Brunel (supervised by Basil Dean).
Scr: Alma Reville, based on the play by Margaret Kennedy and Basil
     Dean, adapted from Miss Kennedy's novel.
Cast: Ivor Novello, Mabel Poulton, Frances Doble, J. H. Roberts,
     Tony de Lungo, Mary Clare, Benita Hume, Elsa Lanchester.

The Gallant Hussar
Gainsborough 1928.
Dir: Geza von Bolvary.
Cast: Ivor Novello, Evelyn Holt.

South Sea Bubble
Gainsborough 1928.
Dir: T. Hayes Hunter.
Scr: Alma Reville and Angus McPhail, from the novel by Roland
     Pertwee.
Cast: Ivor Novello, Benita Hume, Annette Benson, S. J. Warmington.

The Return Of The Rat
Gainsborough 1928.
Dir: Graham Cutts.
Scr: Graham Cutts and Angus McPhail.
Cast: Ivor Novello, Isabel Jeans, Mabel Poulton, Gordon Harker.

Symphony In Two Flats
Gainsborough 1930.
Dir: Gareth Gundry.
Scr: Gareth Gundry, from the play by Ivor Novello.
Cast: Ivor Novello, Benita Hume, Jacqueline Logan, Cyril Ritchard,
    Minnie Rayner, Maidie Andrews.

Once A Lady
Paramount (USA) 1931.
Dir: Guthrie McLintic.
Scr: Zoe Atkins and Samuel Hoffenstein, from the play *The Second
    Life* by Rudolf Bernauer and Rudolph Osterreicher.
Cast: Ruth Chatterton, Ivor Novello.

The Lodger
Twickenham 1932.
Dir: Maurice Elvey.
Scr: H. Fowler Mear, from the novel by Marie Belloc Lowndes.
Cast: Ivor Novello, Elizabeth Allan, Jack Hawkins, A. W. Baskcomb,
    Barbara Everest.

I Lived With You
Twickenham 1933.
Dir: Maurice Elvey.
Scr: George A. Cooper and H. Fowler Mear, from the play by Ivor
    Novello.
Cast: Ivor Novello, Ursula Jeans, Eliot Makeham, Minnie Rayner,
    Cicely Oates, Ida Lupino, Jack Hawkins.

Sleeping Car
Gaumont 1933.
Dir: Anatole Litvak.
Cast: Ivor Novello, Madeleine Carroll, Kay Hammond, Laddie Cliff,
    Stanley Holloway.

Autumn Crocus
Associated Talking Pictures 1934.
Dir: Basil Dean.
Scr: Dorothy Farnum, from the play by Dodie Smith.
Cast: Ivor Novello, Fay Compton, Esme Church, Frederick Ranalow, Jack Hawkins.

The Rat (Sound re-make)
RKO Radio 1938.
Dir: Jack Raymond.
Scr: Hans Gulder Rameau.
Cast: Anton Walbrook, Ruth Chatterton, Rene Ray, Mary Clare, Beatrix Lehmann, Felix Aylmer.

Films of the Musicals

Glamorous Night
Associated British 1937.
Dir: Brian Desmond Hurst.
Scr: Dudley Leslie, Hugh Brodie.
Cast: Mary Ellis, Barry McKay, Otto Kruger, Victor Jory, Maire O'Neil, Trefor Jones, Olive Gilbert, Finlay Currie.

The Dancing Years
Associated British 1950.
Dir: Harold French.
Scr: Warwick Ward and Jack Whittingham.
Cast: Dennis Price, Gisèle Préville, Patricia Dainton, Anthony Nicholls, Gray Blake, Muriel George, Olive Gilbert.

King's Rhapsody
British Lion 1955.
Dir: Herbert Wilcox.
Scr: Pamela Bower and Christopher Hassall, with additional dialogue by A. P. Herbert.

Cast: Errol Flynn, Anna Neagle, Patrice Wymore, Martita Hunt,
     Finlay Currie, Francis de Wolfe, Joan Benham, Reginald Tate,
     Miles Malleson, Lionel Blair.

Plays

Deburau
by Sacha Guitry, tr. Harley Granville-Barker.
Ambassadors, 23 November 1921.
Dir: Harley Granville-Barker.
Cast: Robert Loraine, Madge Titheradge, Leslie Banks, Jeanne de
     Casalis, Bruce Winston, Bobbie Andrews and Ivor Novello (A
     Young Man).

The Yellow Jacket
by George C. Hazelton and Benrimo.
Kingsway, 7 March 1922.
Cast: Ivor Novello, Holman Clark, John Tresakar, Jevan
     Brandon-Thomas.

Spanish Lovers
by J. Feliu Y Cordona.
Adapted from the French of Carlos de Battle and Antonin Lavergne
     by Christopher St John.
Kingsway, 21 June 1922.
Cast: Ivor Novello, Doris Lloyd, Malcolm Morley.

Enter Kiki
by André Picard, adapt. Sidney Blow and Douglas Hoare.
Playhouse, 2 August 1923.
Cast: Gladys Cooper, Ivor Novello.

The Rat
by 'David L'Estrange' (Ivor Novello & Constance Collier).
Prince of Wales, 9 June 1924.

Dir: Constance Collier.
Incidental Music by Ivor Novello.
Cast: Ivor Novello, Isabel Jeans, Dorothy Batley, Jean
    Webster-Brough.

Old Heidelberg
by Wilhelm Meyer-Forster, adapt. Rudolph Bleichmann.
Garrick, 2 February 1925.
Dir: Ernest Benham.
Cast: Ivor Novello, Dorothy Batley, Ernest Benham.

Iris
by A. W. Pinero.
Adelphi, 3 March 1925.
Cast: Gladys Cooper, Ivor Novello, Henry Ainley.

The Firebrand
by Edwin Justus Mayer.
Wyndham's, 8 February 1926.
Dir: Lawrence Schwab.
Cast: Ivor Novello, Ursula Jeans, Constance Collier, Hugh
    Wakefield, D. A. Clarke-Smith.

Downhill
by 'David L'Estrange' (Ivor Novello & Constance Collier).
Queen's, 16 June 1926.
Dir: Constance Collier.
Cast: Ivor Novello, Phyllis Monkman, Glen Byam Shaw, Frances
    Doble, D. A. Clarke-Smith.

Liliom
by Ferenc Molnar.
Duke of York's, 23 December 1926.
Dir: Theodor Komisarjevsky.
Cast: Ivor Novello, Fay Compton, Charles Laughton, William
    Kendall, Violet Farebrother.

Sirocco
by Noël Coward.
Daly's, 24 November 1927.
Cast: Ivor Novello, Frances Doble.

The Truth Game
by 'H. E. S. Davidson' (Ivor Novello).
Globe, 5 October 1928.
Dir: W. Graham Browne.
Cast: Ivor Novello, Lily Elsie, Lilian Braithwaite, Viola Tree.

Symphony In Two Flats
by Ivor Novello.
New, 14 October 1929.
Dir: Raymond Massey.
Cast: Ivor Novello, Benita Hume, George Relph, Lilian Braithwaite,
   Viola Tree, Minnie Rayner, Netta Westcott, Maidie Andrews.

I Lived With You
by Ivor Novello.
Prince of Wales, 2 March 1932.
Dir: Auriol Lee.
Cast: Ivor Novello, Ursula Jeans, Minnie Rayner, Eliot Makeham,
   Cicely Oates, Thea Holme, Robert Newton.

Party
by Ivor Novello.
Strand, 23 May 1932.
Dir: Athole Stewart.
Cast: Benita Hume, Lilian Braithwaite, Agnes Imlay, Joan
   Swinstead, Roy Findlay, Sebastian Shaw, Elizabeth Pollock,
   Douglas Byng.

Fresh Fields
by Ivor Novello.
Criterion, 5 January 1933.

Dir: Athole Stewart.
Cast: Lilian Braithwaite, Ellis Jeffreys, Robert Andrews, Minnie
     Rayner, Eileen Peel, Martita Hunt.

Flies In The Sun
by Ivor Novello.
Playhouse, 13 January 1933.
Dir: Gladys Cooper.
Cast: Ivor Novello, Gladys Cooper, Dorothy Hyson, Anthony
     Bushell, Joan Swinstead, Jevan Brandon-Thomas, Denys
     Blakelock.

Proscenium
by Ivor Novello.
Globe, 14 January 1933.
Dir: Athole Stewart.
Cast: Ivor Novello, Fay Compton, Zena Dare, Joan Barry, Keneth
     Kent.

The Sunshine Sisters
by Ivor Novello.
Queen's, 8 November 1933.
Dir: Athole Stewart.
Cast: Dorothy Dickson, Phyllis Monkman, Joan Clarkson, Irene
     Browne, Jack Hawkins, Veronica Brady, Maidie Andrews,
     Sebastian Shaw.

Murder In Mayfair
by Ivor Novello.
Globe, 5 September 1934.
Dir: Leontine Sagan.
Cast: Ivor Novello, Fay Compton, Edna Best, Zena Dare, Robert
     Andrews, Linden Travers, Jean Webster-Brough, Christopher
     Hassall.

Full House
by Ivor Novello.
Haymarket, 25 August 1935.
Dir: Leslie Henson.
Cast: Lilian Braithwaite, Isabel Jeans, Heather Thatcher, Robert
    Andrews, Maidie Andrews.

The Happy Hypocrite
by Clemence Dane and Richard Addinsell, from the story by Max
    Beerbohm.
His Majesty's Theatre, 8 April 1936.
Dir: Maurice Colbourne.
Cast: Ivor Novello, Vivien Leigh, Isabel Jeans, Marius Goring, Carl
    Harbord, Stafford Hilliard, Viola Tree, Joan Swinstead, Peter
    Graves, Charles Lefeaux, Philip Pearman.

Comédienne
by Ivor Novello.
Haymarket, 16 June 1938.
Dir: Murray MacDonald.
Cast: Lilian Braithwaite, Barry Jones, Cecily Byrne, Ralph Michael,
    Kathleen Harrison, Betty Marsden, Alan Webb, Fabia Drake.

Henry The Fifth
by William Shakespeare.
Theatre Royal, Drury Lane, 16 September 1938.
Dir: Lewis Casson.
Cast: Ivor Novello, Dorothy Dickson, Gwen Ffrangcon-Davies,
    Frederick Bennett, Lawrence Baskcomb, Sydney Bromley, Bert
    Evremonde, Peter Graves.

Ladies Into Action
by Ivor Novello.
Lyric, 10 April 1940.
Dir: Harold French.
Cast: Ivor Novello, Isabel Jeans, Lilli Palmer, Martin Walker, Finlay
    Currie, Maidie Andrews, Peter Graves.

Love From A Stranger
by Frank Vosper, from a story by Agatha Christie.
ENSA Tour, Summer 1944.
Dir: Daphne Rye.
Cast: Ivor Novello, Diana Wynyard, Margaret Rutherford, Robert
  Andrews.

We Proudly Present
by Ivor Novello.
Duke of York's, 2 May 1947.
Dir: Max Adrian.
Cast: Peter Graves, Anthony Forwood, Phyllis Monkman, Irene
  Handl, Ena Burrill, Mary Jerrold.

Musicals

Glamorous Night
Theatre Royal, Drury Lane, 2 May 1935.
Book by Ivor Novello.
Lyrics by Christopher Hassall.
Music by Ivor Novello.
Dir: Leontine Sagan.
Designed by Oliver Messel.
Dances by Ralph Reader.
Musical Director: Charles Prentice.
Cast: Ivor Novello, Mary Ellis, Barry Jones, Lyn Harding, Minnie
  Rayner, Elisabeth Welch, Olive Gilbert, Trefor Jones, Peter
  Graves, Victor Boggetti.

Careless Rapture
Theatre Royal, Drury Lane, 11 September 1936.
Book by Ivor Novello.
Lyrics by Christopher Hassall.
Music by Ivor Novello.
Dir: Leontine Sagan.
Sets by Alick Johnstone.

Costumes by René Hubert.
Dances by Joan Davis.
Temple Ballet by Antony Tudor.
Musical Director: Charles Prentice.
Cast: Ivor Novello, Dorothy Dickson, Zena Dare, Minnie Rayner,
   Ivan Samson, Olive Gilbert, Sybil Crawley, Eric Starling, Peter
   Graves, Walter Crisham.

Crest Of The Wave
Theatre Royal, Drury Lane, 1 September 1937.
Book by Ivor Novello.
Lyrics by Christopher Hassall.
Music by Ivor Novello.
Dir: Leontine Sagan.
Sets by Alick Johnstone.
Costumes by René Hubert.
Dances by Ralph Reader.
Ballets arranged by Lydia Sokolova and Antony Tudor.
Musical Director: Charles Prentice.
Cast: Ivor Novello, Dorothy Dickson, Marie Lohr, Ena Burrill,
   Minnie Rayner, Peter Graves, Walter Crisham, Finlay Currie,
   Olive Gilbert.

The Dancing Years
Theatre Royal, Drury Lane, 23 March 1939.
Book by Ivor Novello.
Lyrics by Christopher Hassall.
Music by Ivor Novello.
Dir: Leontine Sagan.
Designed by Joseph Carl.
Dances by Freddie Carpenter.
Musical Director: Charles Prentice.
Cast: Ivor Novello, Mary Ellis, Roma Beaumont, Olive Gilbert,
   Anthony Nicholls, Minnie Rayner, Dunstan Hart, Peter Graves,
   Frances Clare, Muriel Barron.

Arc De Triomphe
Phoenix, 9 November 1943.
Book by Ivor Novello.

Lyrics by Christopher Hassall.
Music by Ivor Novello.
Dir: Leontine Sagan.
Designed by Joseph Carl.
Mary Ellis's costumes by Cecil Beaton.
Dances by Keith Lester.
Paris Reminds Me Of You staged by Cyril Ritchard.
Musical Director: Harry Acres.
Cast: Mary Ellis, Peter Graves, Raymond Lovell, Elisabeth Welch,
Harcourt Williams.

Perchance To Dream
Hippodrome, 21 April 1945.
Book, Lyrics and Music by Ivor Novello.
Dir: Jack Minster.
Designed by Joseph Carl.
Dances by Frank Staff.
Musical Director: Harry Acres.
Cast: Ivor Novello, Roma Beaumont, Muriel Barron, Robert
Andrews, Margaret Rutherford, Olive Gilbert, Victor Boggetti,
Anne Pinder, Gordon Duttson.

King's Rhapsody
Palace, 15 September 1949.
Book by Ivor Novello.
Lyrics by Christopher Hassall.
Music by Ivor Novello.
Dir: Murray MacDonald.
Designed by Edward Delaney and Frederick Dawson.
Dances by Pauline Grant.
Musical Director: Harry Acres.
Cast: Ivor Novello, Vanessa Lee, Zena Dare, Phyllis Dare, Robert
Andrews, Olive Gilbert, Denis Martin, Anne Pinder, Gordon
Duttson.

Gay's The Word
Saville, 16 February 1951.
Book by Ivor Novello.

Lyrics by Alan Melville.
Music by Ivor Novello.
Dir: Jack Hulbert.
Designed by Edward Delaney and Berkeley Sutcliffe.
Dances by Irving Davies and Eunice Crowther.
Musical Director: Harry Acres.
Cast: Cicely Courtneidge, Lizbeth Webb, Thorley Walters.

Posthumous

Valley of Song
A musical romance in 3 acts.
Music by Ivor Novello.
Lyrics by Christopher Hassall.
Book by Phil Park.
Music adapted and arranged, and additional material composed by
    Ronald Hanmer.

BIBLIOGRAPHY

BIBLIOGRAPHY

Manuscript sources

THIS MATERIAL is housed by Samuel French Ltd. and was made available through the courtesy of Mr Patrick Ide and Mr J. L. Hughes, managing director of that firm. It consists of the manuscripts of numerous plays, mostly unpublished and including early work such as *The Fickle Jade* and *The Argentine Widow*. The latter seems, to judge from the neatly written emendations, to have been 'diabolised' at one time or another by Eddie Marsh. There are also manuscript scores of music by Ivor – individual songs, choral pieces, sketches – and copyists' band parts for, among others, *Crest Of The Wave* and the incidental music to *The Rat*. Other material comprises typescripts, manuscript notebooks, interleaved prompt books, copies of Ivor's plays, theatre programmes, substantial volumes of press cuttings, photographs, drawings, theatre set designs, and printed music and books, including one owned by Sir Henry Irving, from Ivor's own library together with presentation copies of work by friends and colleagues. The mementoes include a canteen set presented to Ivor by the company and staff of *Crest Of The Wave*, Drury Lane, 1936–7.

Printed sources

Agate, James. *The Contemporary Theatre, 1926*. Chapman and Hall, 1927

Agate, James. *Ego 2*. Gollancz, 1936

Agate, James. *Ego 3*. Harrap, 1938

Agate, James. *The Amazing Theatre*. Harrap, 1939

Agate, James. *Ego 6*. Harrap, 1944

Agate, James. *Immmoment Toys*. Jonathan Cape, 1945

Agate, James. *The Contemporary Theatre, 1944–1945*. Harrap, 1946

Agate, James. *Ego 8*. Harrap, 1947

Agate, James. *Ego 9*. Harrap, 1948

Balcon, Michael. *A Lifetime of Films*. Hutchinson, 1969

Black, Kitty. *Upper Circle. A Theatrical Chronicle*. Methuen, 1984

Bottome, Phyllis. *The Rat*. A Novel based on the play by Ivor Novello and Constance Collier. P. Allan and Co., 1926

Bottome, Phyllis. *From The Life*. Faber and Faber, 1945

Braun, Eric. 'Ivor Novello. The Spirit of Romanticism' in *Films*, December, 1982

Brunel, Adrian. *Nice Work*. Forbes Robertson, 1949

Cecil, Lord David. *Max. A Biography*. Constable, 1964

Chapman, Hester W. *Ivor Novello's King's Rhapsody*. Harrap, 1950

Coward, Noël, *Present Indicative*. Heinemann, 1937

Coward, Noël. *The Noël Coward Diaries*. Edited by Graham Payn and Sheridan Morley. Weidenfeld and Nicolson, 1982

Curtis, Anthony. *The Rise and Fall of The Matinée Idol*. Weidenfeld and Nicolson, 1974

Davies, Clara Novello. *The Life I Have Loved*. Heinemann, 1940

Davies, Rhys. *The Painted King*. Heinemann, 1954

Dean, Basil. *Seven Ages*. Hutchinson, 1970

Dean, Basil. *Mind's Eye*. Hutchinson, 1973

Dolin, Anton. *Last Words*. Century Publishing, 1985

Drake, Fabia. *Blind Fortune*. William Kimber, 1978

Ellis, Mary. *Those Dancing Years*. John Murray, 1982

Gregg, Hubert. *Thanks For The Memory*. Gollancz, 1983

Hassall, Christopher. *Edward Marsh. Patron of The Arts*. Longmans, 1959

Howard, Denise. *London Theatres and Music Halls, 1850–1950*. The Library Association, 1970

Ivor Novello Charities Ltd. Report and Financial Statements, 9 October, 1984

Lesley, Cole. *The Life of Noël Coward*. Jonathan Cape, 1976

Lubbock, Mark, and Ewen, David. *Light Opera*. Putnam, 1983

Mac Liammóir, Micheál. 'The Light of Many Lamps' in *The Rise and Fall of The Matinée Idol*. (See Curtis, Anthony)

Macqueen Pope, W. *Ivor. The Story of an Achievement*. W.H. Allen, 1952

Mannon, Warwick. *The Dancing Years*. The book of the film. World Film Publications, 1950

Marsh, Sir Edward. Introduction to: *I Lived With You, Party, Symphony In Two Flats*, by Ivor Novello. Methuen, 1932

Marsh, Sir Edward. *Ambrosia and Small Beer. The Record of a Correspondence Between Edward Marsh and Christopher Hassall*. Longmans, 1964

Melville, Alan. *Merely Melville*. Hodder and Stoughton, 1970

Morgan, Ted. *Somerset Maugham*. Jonathan Cape, 1980

Morley, Sheridan. *Gladys Cooper*. Heinemann, 1979

Morley, Sheridan, with Cole Lesley and Graham Payn. *Noël Coward And His Friends*. Weidenfeld and Nicolson, 1979

Morley, Sheridan. *A Talent To Amuse*. Heinemann, 1969, revised 1984

Nichols, Beverley. *The Sweet and Twenties*. Weidenfeld and Nicolson, 1958

Noble, Peter. *Ivor Novello. Man of The Theatre*. Falcon Press, 1951

Parker, Derek, and Parker, Julia. *The Story and The Song*. Chappell/Elm Tree, 1979

Peter, Margot. *Mrs Pat. The Life of Mrs Patrick Campbell*. Hamish Hamilton, 1984

Play Pictorial, The. Special issues featuring Novello plays. The Stage Pictorial Publishing Company

Robertson, Alec. *More Than Music*. Collins, 1961

Robins, Denis. *Ivor Novello's Murder in Mayfair*. Novelised by Denise Robins. Mills and Boon, 1935

Rose, Richard. *The World of Ivor Novello. Perchance To Dream*. Leslie Frewin, 1974

Sinden, Donald. *A Touch Of The Memoirs*. Hodder and Stoughton, 1982

Stage, *The. (Stage and Television Today)*. Various issues during Ivor's lifetime.

Staveacre, Tony. *The Songwriters*. British Broadcasting Corporation, 1980

Theatre World. Special supplements featuring Novello Plays. The Practical Press Ltd

Traubner, Richard. *Operetta. A Theatrical History*. Gollancz, 1984

Wilson, A. E. *Playgoer's Pilgrimage*. Stanley Paul and Co, n.d. (1948)

Wilson, Sandy. 'Jack, Bobby and Ivor' in *The Rise and Fall of The Matinée Idol*. (See Curtis, Anthony)

Wilson, Sandy. *Ivor*. Michael Joseph, 1975

INDEX